BETTER THAN GOOD

HOW TO BE YOUR BEST SELF

LOUIS A. BONEY II, MDR

ISBN-13: 9781092513449

DEDICATION

This book is dedicated to my loving sister, Taris Boney. As my older sibling, she has been both a sword and shield for me all of my life. Her wisdom and compassion are unmatched, and I am forever grateful for her love.

CONTENTS

INTRODUCTION

There are many things that separate us from one another such as geography, nationality, ethnic lines, class, gender, and race. But there is something that unites our common humanity: we all want to be better. Each of us wants to be a better friend, better spouse, better parent, better encourager, better worker, and better person. If we are honest with ourselves, we would recognize that in our marrow we have a desire to improve ourselves. God put something deep within us that evokes a longing to be more like Him. Our inner being wants better, not more. The questions is: How?

In this book, I will present the steps necessary to live your life at your full potential. Together, you and I will develop a much greater vision for your future and experience more favor in your life. Whether you are living your best life now or barely feel alive, I want to take you higher than you have ever gone before. God always wants to do more in and through us, and move us from increase to increase.

Now, I want to stretch you and push you forward into the next level. It is my hope to help you look inside of yourself and discover the precious seeds of wonder inside of you. In this book, I will reveal the keys to unlocking your potential for an exalted life lived on a higher stratosphere. These principles are not complicated and will bring forth a prosperity incursion in your life. These tools have helped shape me and continue to strengthen my relationships in both my career and my family.

All of us want to make the effort to improve these areas of our lives, but in order to witness the marked improvement we want, it demands a laser-like focus on the essential. In the pages ahead, I will explain each of the principles to becoming your best self in depth. Specifically, how they work and how you can use them to improve your life to affect generations to come. Furthermore, I will guide you where you are going, understand where you have been, and shift where you are now.

Get excited! You are going to embark on an inner journey to self-improvement, self-care, and self-awareness. Each step is about your head, your soul, and your heart. Once the inner journey is complete, prepare to watch your outer-life massively expand producing better quality relationships, productive uses of your gifts, and a better life. While I can't guarantee that you will become famous or rich, I can assure you that if you're open to the principles in this plan, you will live a more satisfying life.

1

TEMET NOSCE

"Although I search myself, it's always someone else I see."
– Elton John

KNOW YOURSELF

Socrates lived in Athens around 450 B.C. and was quoted saying, "The unexamined life is not worth living." What Socrates embodied is the fundamental spirit that underscores much of western thought that says you, *yes you*, have the responsibility for being the author of your own life. In order to do that, you must examine yourself every day. Understand yourself better, and challenge your beliefs. That requires self-assessment. Examining your life involves knowing where you're weak and surrounding yourself with people who fill in those gaps and strengthen your weakness. Examining yourself involves asking how you are different and how you are better. Where are you the same and how can you improve? More importantly, it's about being honest with yourself. These are the politics of identity.

To know who we are is a riddle. We all want to have a positive relationship with ourselves, but where do we begin? Too many of us are looking to other people to answer the questions that we need to answer for ourselves. You have to know what to do for yourself. The relationship you have with yourself needs to be a positive one. You should be self-centered, which means centered about yourself. You need to have well-defined boundaries, and know where you end and others begin. We all have a need to feel significant and unique and special. We all want to set ourselves apart. And rightly so. You weren't made to fit in; you were born to stand out. You are not everybody. You're not supposed to know how to be anybody else. All you're supposed to know is how to be you. Being who you are is the most valuable thing you have. Being "normal" is safe, familiar, and comfortable, but not special or memorable. The greatest delight comes from knowing who you are and examining it.

An essential piece of advice in life comes from William Shakespeare who wrote "to thine own self, be true." Well, it's hard to be true to yourself unless you know yourself. There's a gap between intellect and cognition. Most people aren't even aware of themselves on a cognitive level, let alone an intellectual level, and they are not aware of their purpose. They don't ask, "What are my strengths and virtues? What is my spiritual engagement and meaning?" We become the subjects and objects of other people's lives, and don't know ourselves. When you journey inward and know yourself, you don't have to apologize for who you are or for what you want; just be mindful of it. In the grand scheme, it's much more important that people know the meaning of ***their*** life, not the meaning ***of*** life. Psychologists call this "doing a life review" (asking who I am, who I have been, where I came from, et cetera). This can give life new significance, clarity, and meaning. Know your true self, not your body or your mind or any other aspect of you, because they're all changing, except for your true self. Knowing oneself leads to better decision-making. Knowing yourself is how you anchor yourself going forward. Know who you are and build on it. Many of the things about myself I didn't know innately, but I learned them through life because life has a way of teaching you about yourself. It is my hope that as we dive deeper together you will better understand who you are.

There's a difference between *"Know thyself"* and *"Be thyself."* Once you know yourself, being yourself is the easiest thing in the world. So, if you're having a hard time being yourself, it's because you don't know yourself fully yet. This is incredibly powerful and serves as rocket fuel. All of us can take time to really know ourselves, to discover our strengths, talents, abilities, and interests. Be aware of your skills and juxtapose them against opportunities. Sun Tzu wrote in *The Art of War*, "Know yourself, and know your enemies, and you will have 100 victories in 100 battles." It's important to be very self-conscious about who you are and whom you need to be; thus, you have to be self-aware. You have to be self-assured. Too many people don't know who they are, what they know, or what they believe. We have been conditioned like Pavlov's dog to accept whatever is given to us. You should have an identity and be recognized for it. This is about self-determination; knowing who you are and then fighting to get it. Once you understand who you are, put it out there and own it; people will accept it.

There are few things which can guide successful decision-making more than knowledge of who you are and what you're really good at. Self-realization is all that matters. Knowing yourself requires you to understand the factors that positively inspire you to achieve something substantive and relevant with passion every day. Whom we think we are and whom we turn out to be are often different because we usually don't always know our own hearts. Taking the dive into who we are can save us from future heartbreak.

It's important you know who you are because you can't improve what you don't know. Every day and in every way, you are showing people who you are. We teach people how to treat us, we teach people how to love us, we teach people how to respect us, and the only way we do that is to respect ourselves. Successful people are famous for respecting themselves and knowing themselves inside and out, the good, the bad, and the ugly. That’s why it’s said that ‘only the truly shallow know themselves.’ Self-understanding becomes a medium to interact with the world positively. Most of us go almost all the way through life as complete strangers to ourselves, not knowing our abilities, frailties or anything. It's an identity crisis of not knowing who you are and who you are not.

In this Social Media age, many people need to stop trying to be something they are not. Instead, it's best to stay in your lane. Stop trying to be someone you’re not; you're not going to be judged by what others have. When you do stop, you will be on the right track and moving in the right direction towards your best self. Know who you are and what you want to be. Right now you may be a little of this, and a little of that, and a lot of nothing, so be definitive and declarative. Know who you are and know where you're going and know how you're going to get there. At some point, you have to stand up to who you are and be comfortable in that position, and claim, "This is who I am and I will not be swayed." Every person has to know his or her limits. Set boundaries, run your own race, and take care of yourself. If you do, you will start to live your life deliberately. Be sure of yourself and your abilities. Don't think you are, know you are. Find out and understand who you are and stay true to who you are. Knowing yourself will help find your stride.

This is ultimately about becoming a more self-actualized person because there is no "doing" in works without "being" first. Take the time to know who you are and why you're here on this earth, then connect with yourself and that inner guiding light inside you. Every decision that has profited me has come from my listening to that inner voice first, and dovetailing that with trusting my instincts. I know you want to live a fantastic life and I know you want to live from the inside out. Well, it starts within you. It starts within me. This book is about raising the consciousness and mindfulness of you, the reader.

NO SELF OR TRUE SELF?

Spiritual teachings tell us over and over that we are not who we think we are. Christian mystics say we are filled with God, Persian mystics say we are sparks of the divine, others exclaim that we are one with all things, others assert that the world is an illusion. Hindu yogas call the world a *lila,* or a dance of the divine, similar to Dante's phrase "the divine comedy."[1] Likewise, Buddhist texts describe how consciousness by itself creates the world like a mirage or a dream. In spiritual teachings or contemporary accounts there is a common thread of golden light and luminous beings present in near-death experiences. These confirm how unaware we are of our true identity most of the time. When the Buddha confronted the question of identity on the night of his enlightenment, he came to the discovery that we do not exist as separate beings. The Buddha saw that the human tendency is to identify with a limited sense of existence and saw that this belief of a small self is a root illusion that can cause suffering, and that it removes us from the freedom and vast mystery of life.

Through his teachings, the Buddha never spoke of humans as existing in a fixed or static way. Rather, he described us as a compendium of five changing processes: the processes **of the physical body, of feelings, of perceptions, of responses**, and **of the flow of consciousness** that experiences all of them.[2] Our sense of self arises whenever we grasp at our identity with these patterns. We can identify with our body, feelings, or thoughts; we can identify with images, patterns, roles, and archetypes. Therefore, in our life, we may identify with being a parent or a child, being a woman or a man. Some of us may focus on our intellect or take astrological signs as an identity. We may choose the archetype of lover, hero, adventurer, clown, or something else. To the extent that we grasp these false identities, we continually have to protect and defend ourselves, secure our gains, and strive to fulfill what is limited or deficient in them to fear their loss. Nonetheless, these are not your true identity. We may grasp at new identities, but you are none of them, and you are all of them. You are nothing, and you are everything. Your identities contribute to all of your problems; discover what is beyond them.

Christian texts speak of losing the *self* in God, whereas Taoists and Hindus speak of merging with a *true self* beyond all identity. However, when Buddhists talk of emptiness and no self,[3] what do they mean? Emptiness does not mean things don't exist, neither does "no self" mean that we don't exist. Our world is a playground of forms and patterns. Any identity we can grasp is transient and tentative. There are many ways that we can realize the emptiness of self. When we sit silently and pay attention, we can sense directly how we can truly possess nothing in the world. Clearly, we do not possess external things; we are just in some relationship with our cars, our home, our family, our jobs, et cetera. Regardless of the relationship, it is "ours" only for a short time. In the end, things, people, or tasks die or change, or we lose them. Nothing is exempt. We are a changing process, not a fixed being. There never was a self-only; our identification makes us think so.

I believe in self-worth above all else because there's nothing to suggest otherwise. What we all want ultimately is an infinite connection to ourselves – a sense of oneness with who we are, which is our true essence. Since we live in a world of emanations, so much of success is about identity. When you look in the mirror do you see yourself or do you see a representative? The self struggles for authenticity. At its core, what has been the nature of our struggle and weakness has been our lack of self. Your 'self' has so much authority over you and my 'self' has so much authority over me. Since we're governed by such an authority, it's best we peel back the layers of ourselves to edify our true quintessence.

Over time I have tried to live for my essence and my true self. I have tried not just to live within myself and not be cognizant of the selves around me; otherwise, I start desensitizing to the world around me. So, here's a note to self (pun intended), the cracks have begun to show in you and me, and the self you feed will rule your life. If you feed your selfish self, that will rule. If you feed your generous self, that will rule. However, if you feed, encourage, and uplift your true self – who you really are – that will rule. We all would be better off acclaiming our true selves.

In order to exult your true self, the first thing you've got to do is tell yourself the truth. We tend to fancy ourselves without really knowing ourselves. Don't flatter yourself; be honest about who you are and the things important to you. Think about it, wouldn't we all be better off if we stopped lying to ourselves? Life is a journey of finding out who you are and whom you want to be, and then making sense of it. You have to make up your own mind, whatever it takes to solve the problem. Harry Truman ran his election by saying, he was going to run being himself and saying what he believed and that election became a referendum on authenticity. Truman understood that no matter what, what you have and who you are is always sufficient. Now, you're never done getting to know yourself, since it's a process. But it's a process of learning to like yourself. It's the realization that you have to say, 'This is who I am and I love it.' The thing about living is that you have to like who you are. Since the only question that matters is how do you live with yourself, we are always searching for our better selves. So begin now to do the hardest thing in the world for yourself; act for yourself and face the truth, which is your truth. Stay true to yourself always and if you believe in something, fight for yourself.

DISCOVER WHO YOU ARE

"*Man is a mystery. If you spend your entire life trying to puzzle it out, do not say that you wasted your time. I occupy myself with this mystery because I want to be a man.*"
- Fyodor Dostoevsky

Some years ago I was living in Shanghai with a number of students on a study abroad program, and I began having trouble with one of my colleagues. He just kept doing small things nearly every day to bug me. It was like Chinese water torture (one drop at a time erodes a rock over time). One day I was fortunate enough to be on tour of a local monastery. I met a monk there and I ended up going back on my own to meet with him about my situation with my colleague. After he stood silently listening, he asked me something I will never forget. He said, "What is this person teaching you about yourself?" And that has stuck with me all of my life. It was a lesson that everything around you, and everyone around you, is teaching you more about yourself. At that time I didn't know who I was because I had not taken the time to learn who I was. It is so important to understand yourself and ask, "Who am I? What am I?" I told my mother and father about this experience, and they followed up, asking what I had learned from my experience overseas. I just said, "I have a lot to learn." A spiritual guide or guru is there to introduce you to yourself. People pay over $300 per hour for a therapist, only for them to help you understand you. It's about coming to the realization that there's something to be realized about yourself. This is about learning more about who we are and the selves inside of us.

We are all born with many "selves" in us, and we select the ones who are most dominant or encouraged by our parents, peers, environmental factors, or society at large; the rest is atrophy. We hold within us various "selves" and we hear about them every day: "I can't help ***myself***," "Don't lose ***yourself***," "Pick ***yourself*** up," "You're acting ***selfishly***," "Be true to ***yourself***," "One has to do what's best for ***oneself***," "Build up ***yourself***," "He's trying to find ***himself***," "He hasn't been ***himself***," "Stop lying to ***yourself***," "Take care of ***yourself***." In the Bible, David "encouraged ***himself***." Michelangelo said, "Lord, free me of ***myself***, so I can please you." Jesus said, "Deny ***yourself***." Many people have many selves, rather than one self, and many people have conflicting selves. Deep inside us, we hold spiritual selves, lustful selves, deceitful selves, and our true selves' are kept hostage; unless we let them out on bail depending on the self we release. However, the self you feed will rule your life. In the biblical story of the prodigal son who has gone astray, we find our protagonist in the mud with pigs and the Bible notes in Luke 15:17 that "when he came to himself" he turned away from his misguided ways.

We each have a self, but are we born with one? Early on, our sense of self (who we are) is thrust upon us. Those details and opinions from the world around us become facts which go towards building ourselves our identity, and lead us to who we are. Moreover, that self is the vehicle we use to navigate the world. However, that self is often a projection based on other people's expectations. Is it who we really are or who we want to be or should be? This interaction of self and identity was tough for me growing up. The self I projected into the world was rejected, so I often became conflicted within myself. The distraction of myself was so repetitive, I saw a pattern that the self would be broken and destroyed and discouraged. However, another one would evolve, sometimes stronger, sometimes weaker than the one before. The self was not constant. I, myself, was not constant. Consequently, many selves had to die before I realized I was never alive in the first place.

Psychologists say that our sense of self develops at the age of two. For me, growing up I felt like an anomaly because although I was African-American, I found myself not fitting in with "Black" students, nor did I fit in with "White" students, but rather, I was in a purgatory of sorts, looking for where I belonged. I was looking for definition because the self wants to fit to belong, and hopefully see itself replicated in a way that confirms its existence and its importance. Without knowing yourself you can't interface with others. Eventually, you come to accept yourself. I came to realize that this is myself and I control it. I steer it and I give life to it. My own definition of self and who I am has more authority over me than anything else. How I define myself, how I see myself, how I treat myself, what I think of myself are the cornerstones of how one builds a successful life. The inherent flaw is that we make revelations about ourselves based on fear, ignorance, and information that is either outdated or misguided. We have fear of what others think of ourselves and ignorance of who we truly are. Everything around tells us who we are; war, architecture, love, anger, music, indignation, nature. Everything is just a reflection of who we are. Whenever there is a mass shooting or some tragedy, politicians tend always to say, "This isn't who we are." Yes, it is. In fact, it's exactly who we are. It's a reflection of ourselves. We just don't know ourselves.

In the 1800s Henry David Thoreau had this yearning sensation to leave the hustle and bustle of everyday life. He wanted to gain some clarity and perspective and get to the heart of what life was really about on this planet. He went away and lived a simple life alone in a cabin in the woods near Walden Pond for two years, two months, and two days. Thoreau penned *Walden*, and among his many brilliant insights he wrote, "The mass of men lead lives of quiet desperation." Even then, in far simpler times, it took extreme solitude and introspection for Thoreau to understand himself. By doing so, he uncovered a great secret of the human mind: its ability to bury critical feelings deep beneath layers of distractions and day-to-day noise of modern life. The more we distract ourselves with 24/7 communication and information, the more the compounded effects we feel from being buried in a display – tweeting, texting, posting, linking, updating, viewing, and listening, and the more challenging it is to be aware of what is happening below the threshold of our conscious minds. Self-awareness – or lack thereof – drastically affects your career, relationships, success, and happiness. So, while you may believe that you know yourself fairly well, when it comes down to what matters, chances are you don't.

Take a moment and ask yourself where you are most yourself and when you are most yourself? What happens when you interrogate yourself? When you integrate yourself? Come face to face with the question of who you are. What is it that shaped you? "Who am I?" is the only question that matters; not "What do I do?" or "Where am I?" but "Who am I?" As an English major, I was encouraged to write to question the self, because to investigate curiosity is subordination in its purest form. Take the time to self-reflect and ask yourself meaningful questions. You don't need to know the answers, but ask the questions, and life will move you into the answers. Voltaire said, "Judge a man by his questions rather than his answers." You need to understand yourself because it's your identity that is hanging in the balance.

The enigma in asking who you are is like asking a masked man who he is? The paradox is that we all wear masks and who we are depends on where we are. Who you are around your family may not be who you are around your friends. However, I want you to get to the heart of who you really are. How do you describe yourself? How do you see yourself? We spend so much of our lives trying to understand ourselves, and we act out of unconscious motives. Rembrandt is one of my favorite artists because his paintings continually show a person staring back. Rembrandt's work seems to be saying, "Now you know me; who are you? And could you explain to me?" Alternatively, in Pablo

Picasso's *Girl in the Mirror* we see who someone is, how someone sees themselves, and how we see them, reinforcing the notion that we draw our identities from everything around us. However, in Picasso's piece, none of those elements changes who the woman *actually* is. Just because we see the woman differently, or she views herself differently in the mirror doesn't change what the woman is. It doesn't matter what you call something; it matters what it is. If you call the tail of a horse a leg, it still has four legs. It doesn't matter what you call yourself; it just matters what you are. In Japan, there are words for this concept: **tattame,** 'the way things appear' and **honne,** 'the way things are.' A thing is a thing, not what is said about that thing.

Perhaps you're like me or maybe you're not, but I've been trying to fit in all my life, and every day I would like to get to know myself more and more. I don't always know who I am, what I want, or what's going on. The world can't tell you who you are; you just have to figure it out for yourself and be that. The only truth you find is the truth you bring. It's like the saying, "If you want to climb a mountain, begin at the top." You need to get quiet, and in that silence, you will find the truth. Life is an ultra-marathon, and it's a prolonged inquisition of discovering who you are in relation to everything else. In my own life, I spent so much time looking outside of myself for what I wanted, when really I carried within me all I wanted and needed all along. When I was younger, I tried so hard to make an identity and take on an identity for myself and be somebody I was not, when all along who I was, was here. I traveled the world looking for myself, and it was with me the entire time. It won't be found outside you until it's found within you. If you don’t go within, you go without. Wherever I go, I meet myself. So take inventory of yourself. Figure out who you are and who you are not. A GPS cannot function unless it knows where you are. Where you are is as important as what you are. It's not enough to know where you're going; you have to know where you're coming from. You must know yourself and know where you're going.

When I was 25, I realized the first act of my life had been completed. I took the time to think about my own character arc and to look at the internal affairs of my heart. I was conflicted within and without. What was it I wanted for my next acts? Whom did I want to be in the proceeding acts and final act? I realized I didn't know myself very well after all. Many of my memories were all about me trying to find myself. A premier piece of advice I can give you is get to know yourself as soon as possible, because this journey is for you. Life is for you. Life teaches you who you are. Every moment and experience is here to inform you more fully of who you are. Oscar Wilde said, "Most people are other people. Their thoughts are someone else’s opinions, their lives a mimicry, their passions a quotation." You have to search deep within your soul, your heart, and your spirit to find who you are. There are no one-sided coins, so figure out what's on the other side of you. It's a massive dichotomy inside us, the angelic vs. salacious, love vs. hate, light vs. dark. You have a chance to discover who you are and not just whom you want to be. To be honest, I don't know if you're special, only you will know that. However, you won't know that if you're not self-interested. Be interested in yourself and interested in learning more about yourself; be interested in discovering yourself. Every day, try to understand yourself more and better. I consider myself an artist of sorts but my goal is not to create artists; my goal is to let people discover themselves.

We're all asking the same question: "Who am I and where do I fit in this world?" Take the time to venture to find yourself. That's what therapy is, therapy is holding up a mirror to oneself. The looking glass is a guide to self-inquiry. When I work with my clients, I first encourage them to purchase a mirror, and I explain to them that it is my job to be their sounding board; more concretely, their mirror. A mirror is objective. Mirrors show you for what you truly are in an unbiased, undistorted way that reflects an accurate depiction of you. There is no person harder to face than ourselves. Now I will be honest; not every client likes this concept, since they may be afraid of what they see in themselves. There is no harder person to face than ourselves. Looking in a mirror is the best thing you can do for yourself. However, ask yourself what it will take for you to look in the mirror and say, "I like what I see?" It's tough to like yourself at all times. Sometimes you may feel in order to be loved you have to be perfect. But you need to be able to look yourself in the mirror, like what you see, and smile at yourself.

In the interest of self-awareness, it's important to learn as much as you can about who you are: What do you fear? What motivates you? For many of us, we understand our current truth too late that maybe we're not happy or we need to change. Every day we need to begin the day searching ourselves. It will order our day. We need to begin each day with a made-up mind that we are not going to be pushed left or right, and that it's better to be criticized for being who you are than someone you are not. We are constantly on a journey to find ourselves and better ourselves. Stay on that path because you can't keep going on not knowing who you are. Constantly look for your identity. Take inventory of yourself and evaluate yourself.

My feeling has always been that I've unremittingly been hard to label because I'm not just one thing. I'm many things, and you only get one life, so I live them. We all have a private life, social life, and public life, so it's important you understand how you come across to the world. People are watching you whether you know it or not. Ask yourself if people build houses or tents around you? This all adds up to you helping yourself and increasing the quality of the interior self. We spend a lot of time on the human depths but not on the human shallows. We barely know anything about ourselves, let alone other people. There is an imbalance and asymmetry in the way we treat ourselves. This is a great framework and latticework on which to hang those ideas. We artificially and assiduously find meaning in things which don't have much meaning. As Ludwig Von Mises said, "What something is becomes a function of not just its amount but also of its meaning."

WHO ARE YOU?

As discussed, we all have the same question, "Who am I?" Who is *Insert your name*? What would you say if I asked you who you are; not what you do, but really who you are? What would you say? Who you are and what you think of yourself is regularly changing; the self comes and the self goes, so it's hard to know yourself. We struggle so much with meaning in our lives and the meaning of life, and sometimes we just don't know. Who am I? Where am I going? Why do I want to go there? What do I need? What's my identity? What's my meaning? These are questions that get to the root of better understanding ourselves. Since my goal here is for you to get to know yourself, the question you have to ask yourself is who you are and what you represent.

Social psychologists argue that who we are at any one time depends mostly on the context in which we find ourselves. The Chinese proverb says, “Tension is who you think you should be; relaxation is who you are.” If you’re somebody who’s constantly tense in certain situations, perhaps that’s not who you are. When you’re relaxed and at ease, those are moments when you know you’re being yourself. Strive to be authentic because you can't hide who you are. Fame, money, hard times, and good times only magnify who you really are, so embrace who you are as soon as possible. Our sense of identity is what helps us to make all of our decisions. It helps us determine whom we will spend time with, where we'll live, what we’ll wear, et cetera. If we are attached to an externally-based identity, we lose touch with the vast possibilities within us.

I travel to Italy often and I love going to the Carrara mountains where they excavate Carrara Marble. Marble is incredible to me because it represents something with a story. I always want to understand it. It makes me want to question my own story. Everyone has at least one valuable asset and that’s your story. Your story is what separates you in a world full of clones and absent originality. When you know who you are, where you come from, and why you're doing what you're doing, you can make a dent in the universe. Once you can answer these questions for yourself, you can share your discoveries and tell your story to the world. It's kind of why I like *The Matrix* film. It's about this reluctant hero continuing to question, searching, and finding out who he is, and at every turn, realizing there are choices still to be made.

When you're searching and uncovering, think about what the real answer is, not the 'right' answer. The honest answer. Who am I r*eally*? What do I *really* want? Why do I *really* want that? As my grandma would ask me when something was wrong, "Baby, what's *really* going on?" Be honest. Honesty is the only way to know; being true to yourself is the only way to know who you are. When Faust tries to cheat the devil, he realizes that "by the power of truth, I, while living, have conquered the universe." Being honest conquers the universe. John 8:32 says, "You will know the truth and the truth will make you free." If you're not free in your life, it's because you haven't been honest with yourself.

With that being said, I encourage you to craft an honest identity statement. At the beginning of every coaching session, I tell my clients to tell me who they are. Generally, they talk about their job or their role in the family. However, towards the end, I help them have a statement that reads, "I am _______ who does ________." For instance, "I am a man of excellence, who always keeps his word." Now, some clients struggle at first, and some remain unable or unwilling because any honest exercise involves vulnerability, and not everyone is there yet. Nevertheless, remember that you are special and important; welcome the nebulous feeling.

Clients tell me they want to be more successful in certain aspects of their life, but I tell them they may think they're going to be successful because they're good looking, or because of their other attributes, but if they're going to be successful, they're going to be successful anyway. In reality, you're going to be successful because of more local reasons (who your parents are, where you were raised, et cetera). More importantly, you're going to be successful because of who you are. You're going to be successful because of what's inside you and nothing is more local than who you are.

Embrace fully who you are. You have to have the attitude that "I'm not going to let people frame my reference. I know who I am." There will be trying moments, critics will rage, and your friends will disappoint you, but trust in who you are. Don't let the critics discourage you or push you off course. Desensitize yourself to criticism and do not despair. The hate of people will pass. Dictators die; nothing lasts forever. Don't give in to people who regiment your life, who are cruel and eager to offend, or who wish to despise you. Don't listen to people who tell you what to do, what to think, or what to feel. Know who you are and have a sense of your own purpose. Remember who you are, remember that you have royalty living in you; in essence that's the lesson from *The Lion King*. Once you discover who you are, you will discover you've been given carte blanche over your life.

When I started college, my parents told me, "Don't forget who you are. Remind yourself of who you are." I didn't go to college to discover who I was, I needed to know who I was before I went because I wasn't going to "find myself" there. I had to bring it with me. So every time I encountered a trying time, remembering who I was carried me through. Put affirmations up around the house, read scripture, do whatever it takes to remind yourself of who you are and just how special you are. You are an unrepeatable miracle. Don't let the world change who you are. Understand what's a part of you and what's not. The fencer's weapon is picked up and put down again, whereas the boxer's is a part of him. Know who you are and who you are not. The worst thing you can do is be somebody you're not. Find out who you are and be that.

Separate who you are from what you do. There's a difference between what you are and who you are. We are more than we appear to be. To be is to be perceived, so to know oneself is to see oneself from others' perspectives. No one knows who you are or why you are, so know for yourself. Self-awareness is endlessly valuable. Every time people see you, they have a perception of you, and it's important you understand that perception because it doesn't have to dictate who you are. Self-awareness gives you the ability to observe the secondary effects of your actions, to mitigate your areas of weakness, and leverage your strengths appropriately. We must be the best version of ourselves. You don't have to be invisible anymore. The world makes you something that you are not, but you know inside what you are. Let your outside-self match your inner truth, your inner self. Your insides want out. Your real-self inside you wants out. Your future is not ahead of you; it is inside you. Your life is your greatest resource; don't hide it.

IDENTITY COMPLEX

I, like many others, have complicated feelings and struggled with my identity. Being Black, I learned at an early age you have to navigate both worlds, White and Black. As a result, I didn't know who I was or where I fit in many times. With ebony skin, you learn a lot about yourself when you're Black, and when you're Black in private school, you're forced to know yourself very well. My story is not uncommon, but I do have a story of being underestimated, of being stereotyped, experiencing micro and macro aggressions, and bellicose rhetoric. We live in a society in which the lighter, the brighter, the better and it's hard to embrace oneself. It took me a while to start loving myself and to understand I am special for who I am, and to realize that we negate our individuality, we negate what makes us unique when we try to fit into a world of replicas. Everyone trying to be the same denies what makes us special.

Biology tells us that your eye focuses on contrast, so be different, be unique because it makes you stand out and people will notice. I may have taken that advice to the extreme because I have friends who tell me I'm charming and complicated and like a sphinx because they can't read me. However, I can proudly say each day I'm living my truth. So always clinch what your truth is. We are in a perpetual state of identity crisis in this world. We don't know what we want, because we don't know who we are. We keep diluting ourselves since we don't know who we are anymore. The world tells us we're too this or too that, too tall or too black, et cetera. But if we are to uncover what we want, we have to figure out who we are first.

I took some acting classes at one point, and I learned quickly that as actors we couldn't hide behind an instrument or some piano or guitar or typewriter; we were our own instrument. You can't undress a naked man. All you can do is speak up, speak out, speak for who you are; stand up for who you are because for your life to work for you, you have to be you. Teach yourself to be more of who you are. You cannot make someone what they are not. All the powers of this world cannot make you what you are not. We all have different capacities, we all have different pounds per square inch (PSI) and God isn't asking you to be more than what you are. Some of us can handle more than others; some of us have higher capacities than others. What matters is that we each give our all. Everybody fails at who they are supposed to be; the measure of a person is how well they succeed at who they are. So stop being angry because people can't give you what they do not have. Stop being jealous; you're not accountable for gifts you don't have. You don't have to give an account for a somebody else's gift. God is not requiring of you what he didn't put in you. God is not asking you for more than what you are. He just wants all of what you are.

Let's journey inward now.

YOU HAVE BEEN FEARFULLY AND WONDERFULLY MADE

Every life has a story; it's a story of where you came from and how you arrived. Are you the product of nature or nurture? Contrary to popular belief you don't belong to yourself. You belong to God. I can't stand people who say, "My life is mine, and I can do what I want with it." The Bible says in 1 Corinthians 6:19-20, "You are not your own. Your bodies are temples of the Holy Spirit. You are not your own; you were bought with a price." You're not some action figure. You don't get to do whatever you want anytime you want. You belong to God and your life is not your own. You don't get to do whatever you want with it. It's not "Who are you?" It's "Whose are you?" We are not the product of mindless evolution. You're not anybody from nowhere. Who I am and where I am didn't just come out of the sky, but from a heritage. You are not your own; you are somebody's. You are under the shepherd's watch. You don't need anyone else's approval; you have already been approved. Psalm 100:3 says, "Know that the LORD is God. It is he who made us, and not we ourselves." Your life is worth something. Don't give your life away for nothing. Don't cast your pearls before swine. Don't sell your life away today for some exit down the line that may or may not ever come. Don't run after illustrations; don't give up your life for nothing. There's still more for you.

There are trees on this earth that are 1000 years old, turtles that are 500 years old. You're not a snap of the finger or just a breeze coming through; you have permanence. God doesn't sit back and wait for your approval of his works to say they are beautiful. Your opinion means little to nothing when it comes to beauty because God made it, and God makes things beautiful. We are God's most beautiful creation because we were made last. You have been fearfully and wonderfully made. Quit living like you're mediocre and ordinary. God was not having a bad day when he made you; you are perfect.

See yourself as the king or queen you're intended to be. You have been consecrated and set apart from the moment God knew you in the womb. God says in Jeremiah 1:5, "Before I formed thee, I knew thee." You are magnificently made; the world didn't give it to you, and the world can't take it away. The world didn't make you so the world can't break you. You are more than lucky; you are blessed. You are heads and tails above everyone else. You are no shrinking violet, and you are not just another cog in the wheel or just a brick in a wall. No one else can sing your song, and no one else can write your story. Your only responsibility is to be you. You are equipped with exceptional valor, pristine in condition. Everything good comes from you. I want you to declare, 'I am unique, I know what I want, and I know who I am.' This helps you to remember who you are. No matter what you do, it doesn't change your name. You may make some mistakes, have some weaknesses, but it doesn't change who you are. You have to learn to be who you really are because you are phenomenal.

I debated calling this book *Man is Myth* because I love the story of Hercules the demigod. All of us are Hercules, me and you. We are all part man and part God. There is a part of us that feels, that is flesh and blood, a part that will bleed if we cut it. However, there's also a part of us that is divine. A part of us that loves, that forgives, and that is capable of immense strength that is of godly qualities. I think it's why we consider athletes as Olympians; because they seem to be of Mount Olympus, divine in stature. We are *human*s, but we are also *beings*. You are divine and what is divine is full of providence. Our skin is full of melanin and melanin absorbs sunlight, therefore we are light filled. We all have been made with the elixirs of life. You and I have a shine about us, when the sun hits us, we both shine brightly. You are filled with infinite possibilities, infinite creativity. You are imbued with the unlimited power. Don't dim your light for anybody. Success is such an intense feeling that you may feel guilty or feel sorry for being the best you can be. But you can't feel sorry for being successful; you were designed to prosper.

God doesn't make mistakes or duplicates, so all of us are different, special, and unique. Matthew 5:14 says, "You are the light of the world. A city on a hill cannot be hidden." You're great and when you're great you cannot hide it. When you're blessed you cannot hide it. When you're good you cannot hide it. It just permeates through. Stop apologizing for who you are and what you have. Paris has Rodin's *The Thinker*. Florence has the *Statue of David*. There's the *Venus de Milo, Matisse, Cezanne, Caravaggio, Monet*; everybody has their bests, even you. We all have a design to us.

Being blessed will draw up criticism, hatred, and resentment, but the real question is can you handle being blessed? You don't need other people's approval to be who God created you to be. The kingdom of God is within you, so permeate it. Whatever the anointing is, good looks, singing, dancing, et cetera, it is to move you into a place where you can fulfill the purpose of your life. The blessing you have right now is not for you; it is for the glory of God (1 Corinthians 10:31). The reason you have that job is not to feed you; it's for the glory of God. God could feed you without the job. You know there are people taking classes, paying for classes for things that you do naturally. God has dropped so many blessings on you. It's just like in Ruth 2 where Ruth is beckoned by Boaz, but the servant drops some wheat and Ruth picks it up and moves closer to her destiny. Ruth was thankful because she was in a famine. God has done so many favors, so many blessings; he just dropped on you. That's favor and favor isn't fair. It's not fair that Ruth received what other women had to work for. God says it's just, but not fair. That's the reason so many people hate you, why they talk about you, why they look at you funny; it's because they resent the fact that God just dropped some stuff on you that they've had to work for all their life. Stop trying to figure it, stop trying to explain it to people, because favor isn't fair. It isn't fair, it's favor. You can't explain it, but you got it. You are crowned with favor, so now do your part and be proud of who you are.

When God blesses you, it will be unexpected, and others cannot explain it. Favor doesn't fit. Look at Joseph in the Bible. He is the youngest son of his father and his father's favorite who gives Joseph his technicolor coat. His brother's hated him because this little boy was running around, dragging his father's technicolor coat in the mud, because favor doesn't fit. You grow into it. So in Genesis

37, he's wearing his father's coat, but by Genesis 42 he's wearing the coat of the governor. So people's problem with you is your favor because you didn't deserve it; it's grace. I want you to know that you were born to be blessed! Don't make apologies for who you are or the blessings you've received. Celebrate yourself and celebrate your culture.

Unique You

We are born into a mystery, not knowing who we are or where we came from. We are left to our own devices to figure it out, some through religion, others through alternative means to figure out who they are and what their meaning is. Instead of stuffing people with curricula, models, and competencies, we should focus on deepening their sense of purpose, expanding their capability to navigate difficulty and complexity, and enriching their emotional resilience. What if instead of trying to fix people we assumed that they were already full of potential, and we created an environment that promoted their long-term wellbeing? Makes sense, right?

In 1872, Winwood Reade wrote in *The Martyrdom of Man*, "While the individual man is an absolute puzzle, in the aggregate he becomes a mathematical certainty. You can, for example, never foretell what anyone will do, but you can say with precision what an average number will be up to. Individuals vary, but the percentages remain constant." My favorite television show is *Sherlock,* with Benedict Cumberbatch and Martin Freedom. I also love Sir Arthur Conan Doyle's tales of Sherlock Holmes. Holmes is bored with groups of people because they are predictable, but as in *The Sign of Four* (Doyle's second novel), he is fascinated by the singularity of his cases, making the peculiar and riddling details stand out from commonplace occurrences. He is obsessed with the minutia of the individual.[4] Literature professor, Jim Barloon, notes in a paper on identity that Sherlock Holmes is an example of "radical individualism" and in Victorian England, amidst the crushing anonymity of a vast empire, he would have indeed been a radical.[5] However, the truth is that there is nothing wild or outlandish about being our specific selves. It has always been celebrated to be just that. It's no surprise then, that Sir Arthur Conan Doyle had a constant stream of callers at the private residence of 221B Baker Street. People want personal attention. The majesty of the individual and the celebrity culture we live in are illustrated in Sherlock Holmes, and yet I am always amazed at just how much we as a society thirst for the attention of others, and sacrifice who we are to be somebody we're not.

Justice Oliver Wendell Holmes said, "Too many people die with their music still in them." You are not an ordinary person or a meaningless product of creation. You carry something precious and something great in you, so don't forget that or let others steal that. Pick yourself up and remember you are somebody. Know that there are some things you shouldn't do, there are some places you shouldn't go, because you are not like everyone. You are special and priceless.

I found in my own life that imitating somebody can reveal something unique in me. Every time I fail to become more like my heroes, I become more like myself. Every time I fail to become like Nelson Mandela, I become more authentically me. This is my art, and I strive for authenticity because you can't hide what's in your heart. Work hard, stay true to yourself and don't change for anyone. No matter what happens, stay true to yourself. The more authentic you are to yourself the less you take rejection personally. Just be you, because if you try to be different, you end up being the same. Everybody's trying to be different. So just be you, and if this doesn't work, then this isn't what you should be doing. You can't be me, so be you and do you. There are duplicates everywhere, like counterfeit Louis Vuitton's, but know that you are not a copy; you are authentic and there is only one of you. Because authentic comes with a high value, be the most authentic version of yourself all the time. If you want to be an actor go to Hollywood; for everyone else be who you really are. Don't read a book about Steve Jobs and say you want to be like Steve Jobs. There's only one Steve Jobs, and there is only one you. Figure out what's important to you and whom you want to be in the world. You are the most perfect version of yourself. Acknowledge that, embody that, and let that resonate in every aspect of your life.

We're all extraordinary. Nobody is the same. There are no two people who are alike. There will never be another you. There will only be one of you – ever. In the history of the universe, you exist only once, and you are it. Therefore, there will never be another person with your unique intellect, temperament, skills, and abilities. You are the only person in the world that will ever see things the way you do. Your personality, experiences, insights, and emotions all lead you to interact with the world differently from everyone else. You may be only slightly different, but it is different.

We are continuously amazed at how far and how fast we can reach around the planet; therefore, your point of view may challenge or support another idea around the globe. You may never see it, or feel it, or know it, but it is, nonetheless there. Don't ever underestimate the value that your uniqueness has on the conversation. As people, we seek our own level. We find jobs, communities, partners, and friends that align with our personalities and our abilities. Opposites may attract, but our "ecosystem" of personalities tends to mirror ourselves. That's the beauty about America, we're all equal, but we're not the same. Know that you are unique and champion your individuality. Everybody is cut differently, and you are a cut above. Don't conflate yourself with anyone else. You are unique and different. There is no one else like you. Stop wearing sports jerseys and start wearing your own name on your back. You are different and distinct and dissimilar to others. You need to appreciate who you are. You are not common, and you are not average. You are exclusive, striking and stunning. We marginalize our individuality to fit into a dying and decaying world. Reveal the God in you. You are anointed and appointed. Every chance you get you should look in the mirror and say, 'thank you.' You are limitless and timeless.

Jean-Jacques Rosseau said, "I may not amount to much, but at least I am unique." Jean-Jacques Rosseau reminds us to always be yourself and have faith in yourself; don't try to duplicate another. You are not average; you are unique and an original. What makes you different is your strength. There is nothing ordinary about you. Nothing about you is by accident. You are an exceptional talent and can exert a strong influence. You have authority over your life.

Sadly, too many people are willing to trade their authority for acceptance. They are willing to trade their blessings for others not to reject them. Carry yourself with confidence, royalty, dignity, honor, and influence. Stand tall and speak up; it shows you are confident, determined, and well-able. Take a back seat to no one. You are terrific and great already; stop asking God for what you already have. You are already phenomenal, and you are already rich. Stop being average just because everyone else is and stop going against who you are. Perhaps that’s why it's easier to watch greatness at the basketball game or in the stadium. It's easier to pay to watch greatness than for you to be great by making the sacrifices and putting the time in. So you’re frustrated because you're not living as you should live and you're not having those things you want because somewhere deep down you know it should be you out there. That's why you're attracted to greatness. Greatness is inside you. I would hate to live and die and not know who I could have been if I had committed myself, my whole self, to my dreams. All you have to do is make a decision, and the universe will yield to you.

During the 2016 Summer Olympics, one of the Olympic body’s commercials said, “Science tells us that the same elements that existed since the beginning of time exist today in every living thing; carbon, calcium, even gold. There are trace amounts of gold in every human body, precisely 0.2mg to be exact. Gold is in our bones, and it's in our bloodstream. However, the highest concentration of gold is found in the heart. All of us are made from this ancient and rare material, gold. It's in us all. We just have to find the courage to dig it out."[6] Each of has gold already within us, but we have to unearth it because that's how God works. Everything God gives you he gives to you in a seed. He hides the orchard in a seed. If he showed you the orchard, people would steal it. What is a seed but a tree in disguise. You are an orchard in disguise. I am an orchard in disguise. The purpose of the seed is the tree. You can't see the worth of a seed. Let seeds grow. That's why you must get a hoe and a rake to clean up the weeds around, to protect the future of that seed. A seed gets choked because it can't grow. God does everything great in your life through seeds. Big things have small beginnings. Hold onto what God has planted in your life and be patient for it to grow. Remember that the kingdom of God is within man. There's a king in you. There's a queen in you.

You Beat the Odds

There are about 20 numbers that create and dictate the state of this universe, the mass of an electron, the strength of gravity, electromagnetic force, et cetera. Dr. Brian Greene is a world-renowned physicist who says these numbers have been measured with incredible precision, but no one has an explanation for why they have the particular values that they do. He says that if any of these numbers were off in even the slightest way, our universe would cease to exist.[7] Our universe has been perfectly and mathematically designed, and so have you. The number 1.618 is considered to be the golden ratio, the mathematical value that is found throughout the universe that seems to hint at a common factor amongst everything. We are going to die, and that's what makes us the lucky ones. Now, it is true that most people are never going to die because they are never going to be born. The potential people who could have been here in my place, but who will in fact never see the light of day outnumber the sand grains of the Sahara. Now those unborn individuals could have been greater poets than Keats, or greater scientists than Newton. We know this to be true because the set of possible people allowed by our DNA massively outnumbers the set of actual people. Now in the face of these odds, it is you and I, in our ordinariness, who are here. We are the privileged few who won the lottery of birth against all the odds.

My greatest hope for you is to know your worth. You are extraordinary in every way. You are proof of concept. Literally, you are phenomenal, and you have beaten the odds. I'm not talking about just one sperm and one egg. It literally is warfare, and you made it out from this complex environment in the womb. The mere act of being born means that you beat out millions of sperm to be created in the first place. That makes you in first place upon birth. You are so lucky. Think about it; you are a human! You could've been a panda bear or ladybug. Do you realize the math that your mom and dad had to have sex at the right second to have you? You've already beaten the odds.

You are a Tour de force, the Creme de la Creme. You didn't just make the cut; you set the bar. Every day and in every way you are entirely unique and exceptional. You have an incredible sense of wonder about you, embrace it. Stars wear no concealment. You have a *Je ne sais quoi* (a pleasant quality that is hard to describe). You've got something, but you don't know what you've got. Moreover, if you don't know what you've got, you won't know how to use it. There are nations inside of you. Look at Genesis 17, Abraham is 99 years old and hasn't heard from God in 13 years, and God shows up and talks to Abraham about him carrying nations and generations inside of him. God speaks to Abraham in Genesis 17 and says let me show you what is inside of you; let me tell you who you really are (Abraham). God calls this childless man, this impotent man who doesn't even have one child, the father of many nations. He is 99 years old. But that's how you know it's God when he calls you to do something that is beyond your ability, that is beyond your circumstance. You're praying to God for next week's rent, but God is speaking to you about money to lend. You're praying to God to get by, and God is showing you how to get ahead. God talks to you about plenty when you have lack.

There is a nation in you and the fight is always within you. The enemy is fighting you over what's in you and where you are going. There are nations inside of you. God says to Abraham, "I'm going to make you a father" when you don't even feel like a man. There are businesses inside of you, books inside of you, dynasties inside of you, ideas inside of you. Your life is valuable, and there is a grand plan for you. Live with confidence; you are someone to be celebrated. You are beautiful and amazing and great. You are a trendsetter, and a rule breaker. You need to celebrate yourself because every day and in every way you are exceptional.

You Are Stardust

Joni Mitchell famously sang in *Woodstock* that "We are stardust." She was right! The atoms in your body are traceable to exploded stars in the sky. You are the remnants of stardust. Not only are you in the universe, but the universe is also in you. You are literally stardust. Neil deGrasse Tyson said, "We are stardust brought to life, then empowered by the universe to figure itself out – and we have only just begun." Everything we are and everything in the universe and on Earth originated from stardust, and it continues to float through us even today. This nexus links us directly to the universe, rebuilding our bodies over and over throughout our lifetimes. Yet our bodies are in a constant state of decay and regeneration.

Astrophysicist Karel Schrijver, a senior fellow at Lockheed Martin Solar and Astrophysics Laboratory, and his wife, Iris Schrijver, a professor of pathology at Stanford University, write in their book, *Living With the Stars: How the Human Body Is Connected to the Life Cycles of the Earth, the Planets, and the Stars*, just how impermanent we are.[8] Our bodies are made of remnants of stars and massive explosions in the galaxies billions of years ago. This same material of residual stardust in our bodies finds its way into plants and from there into the nutrients that we need for everything we do – think, move, grow. Schrijver and Schrijver stated in their book that when the universe started, there was only hydrogen and helium, and very little of anything else. Now helium is not in our bodies; hydrogen is, but that is not the bulk of our weight. Stars are akin to nuclear reactors that take fuel and convert it into something else. Hydrogen is formed into helium, and helium into carbon, nitrogen, oxygen, iron, and sulfur – everything we are made of. Pretty cool, huh?

You Are the Universe

In Exodus, Moses asked God “Who are you?” God replied, "I Am that I Am." I suspect that if Moses responded, “But who am I?” God would have said, "You are who you are," in effect saying, you are the universe too. You too are light and dark, prosperity and poverty; all that I am, you are. I want to show you a world that doesn't exist outside of you, but within you. Everything is inside you. Everything you want, everything you want to be, everything you desire is inside you. You have the greatest power in the universe inside you. Jay-Z said, "I'm not a businessman; I'm a business, man.” And he’s right! You have multitudes in you. Walt Whitman wrote, “Do I contradict myself? Very well then, I contradict myself. I am vast. I contain multitudes.” Everything in the universe is within you. Businesses, enterprises, ideas, life are all inside of you. That’s why I’m always amazed; I am the product of dust and ashes, and yet the universe belongs to me. Perhaps that’s why in my own life, I have always been hard to label. I'm not just one thing. Never have been. I've always wanted to be many things. I don't want to be known for one thing I do, but for everything I do.

You will never find happiness outside of yourself because everything is inside of you. You are the controller of your own life. If you decide to live happily, you will be happy. If you decide to live unhappily, you will be unhappy. The goal is to seek the happiness inside of you; that's where the euphoria lays. You've got the whole world in you, don't throw it away. RUMI tells us, “You are not a drop in the ocean, you are the entire ocean in a drop.” Everything in the universe is made of form and matter. All form and matter are within you, it's true. Everything you want is already within you and your way of thinking. I want to be so vast within myself that there is no character I cannot play. Because it's inside me, I can't be defined, held, or stopped. I want to be so in touch with my emotions and my feelings that there's nothing I can't do. Actors are so wonderful because they can play every character. They realize that those characters are them. There’s a part of them which is a killer, which is a lover, which is confused, which is a hero, et cetera. You are your own source of light; you are everything you are searching for. Ralph Waldo Emerson said, “What lies behind us and what lies before us are tiny matters compared to what lies within us.” You are the universe in ecstatic motion.

You don't have to act so small. You don't have to feel and believe that you are no one. Believe that you are special, and you possess unique qualities that others don't have. Feel your way through life; don't overthink everything. You have to remind yourself that you’re special and you're important. All of us are special and worthy of respect, and nobody wants to be taken advantage of. Just because we're magic doesn't mean we're not real.

You have your own nature in you; trust it. Everything has a nature and a dharma. You came from a divine place of well-being. You have been given priority and first preference. Follow your own nature and not the trappings of life from nowhere to now-here. Shift from fear to curiosity; be curious about what you're afraid of. Remember that you came into this world with nothing and you'll leave the same way. Your life is a parenthesis of eternity; live in there. The point is, you’re not part of it, you're all of it. There is one ego appearing as many. We are all of one mind. When you go throughout life judging and condemning what you’re doing, you are sending a message to yourself about yourself, and it's going to yourself because there isn't anyone else out there for it to go to. Change the way you think about other people because whatever you’re thinking is just going to you.

Remember that there is something about you that is formless and timeless. It's like the Rumi quote mentioned, a drop of water is the entire ocean. The ocean is in that drop. God is in everything. God lives in you as you. You can't think of yourself as separate from everything you're looking at, but one with it. The question is who am I? I am it all. You are it all. You have to put together 'I am' and 'God is.' They are not exclusive; you are because God is. Think again about Moses when he meets God through the burning bush, and God says to Moses, “I am that I am.” In other words, when you say ‘I am,’ you are saying you are whatever you want. I am peace; I am victory. My challenge to you is just to say ‘I am that.’ Look at flowers outside and say ‘I am that.’ Alternatively, look at pain and suffering and say ‘I am that.’ In everything you see, you see yourself.

I am that person, I am that experience, I am hope, I am also sorrow, I am that. I can identify with everything and every experience. We were made in God's image, and we've been trying to return the favor ever since.

You Are Energy

In 1925 quantum physics came out which said that invisible energy is all around us. Our perception of what is physical is an illusion. There's nothing physical at all, it's all energy. If you look inside any part of your body under a microscope, take your hand for example. You will see cells, inside the cells you see your DNA at the center of the cell, inside the DNA you get atoms, inside the atoms there's nothing there. There's only protons, neutrons, and electrons. Inside an atom it's 99.9% empty space; it's all waves of energy. That means I am entirely energy. You are entirely energy. More impressively, we are the collection of atoms. In fact, there are as many atoms as there are stars in the night sky in me as in you. I am the collection of 3 billion atoms known as Louis Boney. Our bodies have 100 trillion cells; that's all we're made of. Not a single cell is conscious. Not a single cell knows who you are or cares.

In Sir Isaac Newton's *Principia*[9] we learn all of us are a little universe. There's a solar system of atoms and molecules of DNA in you. Our genetic code is encapsulated in the nucleus of each cell within our body. DNA is shaped as a double helix coded with instructions for all living things that tell them how to heal, live, and understand their environment, with an astounding 100 billion moving parts called atoms in a single molecule in your DNA. Your DNA is your barcode, and unless you have an identical twin, there is no one else out there with the same DNA as you. Through natural selection, your genes decide which ones will die and which ones will survive.[10] You have infinite potential and possibilities.

Astrologists remind us that we are stardust. We are the remains of stars. All of us are stars. Yet, transformation is the name of the game. We are constantly changing. The universe is continuously expanding, stars are dying and being born, forms and terraforms are evolving. We are constantly manifesting other dimensions because we are multi-dimensional beings. There are no one-sided coins. One moment I am happy; the next moment I am sad. Who am I? We are people of contradictions. We love, and we hate. We are admired, and we are feared. We are complex creatures beautifully made and uniquely made. There is a frequency and energy to everything, even us. We are vibrating beings. Even under a microscope, cells are moving. We are continually emitting energy. So, it's not so much about attracting what you want, but it's about radiating it outwards, and then it comes to you. The law of conservation of mass states that matter can be changed from one form into another.[11] Mixtures can be separated or made, and pure substances can be decomposed. However, the total amount of mass in the universe remains constant – it is merely changing from one form to another. It is scientific law that your body mass has been here since the beginning of the universe. You are 13 billion years old! The time you've been here on earth is just how long you've been aware of your existence. You are an infinite being in a body. Take your energy and expand it out past the seat next to you, expand it out past the walls, expand it out past your country, and continually expand it out, and in this space, you can reprogram anything. You are an infinite being, and you don't have an edge or end to you; you just keep going and keep growing. There are no limits to who you are or who you can be.

EMBRACE WHO YOU ARE

I had the opportunity a little while back to visit Independence Hall in Philadelphia, the heart of the American Revolution. In the middle of this courtyard stands an iconic bell that was hung in the Philadelphia State House in 1753 that summoned the pre-Independence Colonial Legislature into session and later on was used after the Revolution for the Pennsylvania State Legislature. The fantastic history of the Liberty Bell is that when it arrived, it cracked immediately. Not once, but twice. Numerous craftsman tried to repair the bell by filling the crack with new metal, yet it cracked again, and again. It seems the bell wanted to be broken; it had something to say.

During the 1830s the abolitionist movement was gaining immense steam and Americans were awakening to the realization that slavery was morally unacceptable and socially harmful. The abolitionists were the first to label this bell the Liberty Bell, and it soon became elevated as a symbol of American independence and personal freedom. It was in 1846 that the Liberty Bell cracked for the final time and it was at this point that people stopped trying to fix it or ring it. This cracked and silent bell has never resonated more loudly around the world than any bell ever.[12] The poet, Leonard Cohen, wrote, “Ring the bells that still can ring. Forget your perfect offering. There is a crack in everything. That’s how the light gets in.” There is a crack in everything God has made; there are fault lines in all of us. Yes, there is a crack in everything, but that’s how the light gets in.

Many people resist the wisdom of brokenness. We oppress ourselves by assuming that we alone are shattered, and everyone else is whole. We tell ourselves, "Look at how perfect their life is. Look at their home. Look how gorgeous their life is." It's sad to see and terrible to express because we assume that we are the only fractured and broken vessels struggling to make meaning out of our fragmented lives. What's worse is that not only do people impose their own sense of false wholeness, but there are external outside social forces that try to impose that same impossible perfection on us. The world tells us that if we are broken, we no longer have any utility or worth. There is an entire industry of blogs, magazines, and films that are devoted to the self-proposition that we should feel old, fat, and ugly, and we need to be something we're not; lighter, darker, shorter, taller, et cetera. In fact, certain portions of Judaism combat this ideal. There is a passage in the Torah that reflects this perfectionism. The high priest’s whole body was to be without blemish to serve in the temple. So where does that leave us?

Inscribed on that Liberty Bell is a verse from the Book of Leviticus: "Proclaim liberty throughout the land, to all the inhabitants thereof." This is not just limited to the tall, the rich, the thin, the perfect, or the flawless. This is for everyone. Liberty is for everyone. I would purport, life is for everyone. Regardless of what you look like, you are worthy of everything this life has to offer. Life belongs to us all – broken, shattered, struggling, and striving. We are beautiful because of our imperfections. The medieval author, Menachem Azariah of Fano, writes, "Just as a seed cannot grow to perfections as long as it maintains its original form – growth coming through decomposition – so these points could not become perfect configurations as long as they maintained their original form, but only by breaking." If you are like me, there are parts of you that are very good, and you may be proud of, and there are parts of you that are not so much. There are parts of you that strive and others that fall short. Those are the parts that let in the light. Don't run from your imperfections or hide from your brokenness; embrace it.

Something I've come to learn is that nothing protects the heart like patience, so don't get your hopes up too fast. More importantly, don't give your doubts too much time. You will come to learn that not everybody is built to handle the rough times. So you can't be surprised when you fall out with certain people. Not many people understand what it means to really be there for somebody. Also, that's the toughest part about being on a journey; you realize the main ones who said they would ride are the first to fall off. People make promises when the sun is shining and make excuses when the storm comes. That's why I'm always thankful for the rain, it washes away the unnecessary. Rob Hill Sr. said, "The reality is, you could be amazing, genuine, and sincere but still be overlooked. But honestly, people don't want something real anymore; they just want reasons to complain and excuses to avoid. Having a good thing is so hard because meeting a strong person is so rare. So I've learned to respect when people run from me. I realize my kind of love isn't for everybody. I'm at peace with that."

As I got older, I learned to be comfortable enough to act like myself. I don't have to be someone I'm not. It took me a while to be very proud of my accomplishments and to relish them. I'm easy to look at, but hard to see. However, I want to thank my family for loving me exactly the way I am and giving me the luxury of being myself. Now it's my time to return the favor to myself and embrace myself. Wishing to be something you're not is an insult to God. Because you're saying, God, you didn't make me the way you wanted. We always want the talents of others, but find what makes you special and embrace it. My favorite scene in the 1995 classic *Mr. Holland's Opus* is when Mr. Holland asks his red-haired student named Gertrude, "What do you like most about yourself?" She replies, "I like my hair." Mr. Holland responds, "Why?" She answers, "Because my mom says it reminds her of the sunset." Mr. Holland tells her, "Then play the sunset." In effect, telling her you have to embrace that thing you love most about yourself and let it out.

Too many of us are afraid of being ourselves because we don't know ourselves. Change that today. I know it's a difficult thing to accept oneself because the most terrifying thing is to accept oneself completely, but that's what it's about. It's about embracing who you really are. Embrace who you are and use it as an opportunity. D. H. Lawrence wrote, "I have never seen a wild thing, sorry for itself." When it comes to being confident, own who you are and keep going with hope and optimism. The imperfections of man and the limits of reason all should be embraced. You don't need everyone to like you; you just need to like you. It took me a while to be somebody who is at home with himself. Whoever you are, I want you to know that you have earned the right to be just whomever you are. Resistance is futile. You have to move back inside yourself and own who you are.

The hardest person to be is yourself. Stop being evasive. Everyone is striving for authenticity. As mentioned before, everyone is trying to be different, but when you try to be different, you end up being the same. So be you and when you're you, people think that's different. You can say she's beautiful, he's so smart, et cetera, but God didn't leave anybody out. What's inside you has been there all the time. You will find that everything you needed was already inside of you. You’re not average, you’re not ordinary, you're exceptional, you’re one of a kind. Confidence doesn't come from what you have or how much of it you have, but who you are. You are who you are so all you can do is learn to play who you are well. It's better to own who you are because it's a good thing to be oneself. I can tell you right now that the only way things are going to work for you is if you are yourself.

It took me a while to realize that you can't beat me being myself. No one can beat you if you're being yourself. That's why it's so important to be comfortable with who you are and embrace who you are and not make apologies for who you are. Do you; it'll work for you. Be you; it'll work for you. Louise Hay suggests in *Life Loves*

You that you look in the mirror and into your eyes every day and say, 'I love you. I really, really love you.' You do not need to do, have, or be anything different to be worthy of love. You are worthy of love simply because you exist. That's it. Just by your being, you qualify. When you truly love yourself, you allow yourself to be the *real* you. You begin to vibrate at a frequency that deflects fear and inspires others to be themselves too. It's alluring. It allows you to reject self-sabotaging behaviors in favor of more normative ones. You cease busying yourself doing what other people are doing because you understand that your needs matter. Embrace the good, the bad, and the imperfect parts of you.

Paul wrote in Romans 7:15, "I don't really understand myself, for I want to what is right, but I don't do it. Instead, I do what I hate." We all are fighting internal struggles. Part of us wants to do right, and another part wants to do what's wrong. Theology would say that we all have a little 'Jacob' and 'Israel' in us. However, that's where the magic is. Water that is too pure has no fish in it. We need some imperfections to keep us alive, so embrace your imperfections, live free and confident. Too many people will cut off their nose to spite their face. You need to know that you're enough. You can't be hesitant about who you are. If you're hesitant, you can fall into a bad habit of continually checking yourself. We have a tendency to edit ourselves, to be unsure of ourselves around others, and to pretend that we don't know who we are or what we want. You need to know who you are and what you want. You need a sincere belief in your own worth and your dignity. Don't allow anybody to make you feel that you are nobody. Always remember that you count, always remember you have worth, and always remember that your life has significance. Still, know that your value is absolute. Stop doing things that make you feel bad about yourself. Honor yourself, love yourself. This is foundational. Always know that you are the best thing. You are original and spectacular.

I've always prided myself on being different because when you're different people respond to you differently. One thing I hate are apologies, especially for the truth. Whomever you are, embrace that and stop lying to yourself. Be true to yourself despite what others think. Do whatever it takes to protect your individuality. Everyone can't be president or the quarterback. You are who you are, and you can't make someone something they're not. People are frustrated because they are trying to be something they are not. Know what you're not; that's how you know what you are. With that said, don't try to be more than you are, just be the best of what you are. It's like making gumbo. There's the rue, and then there are the ingredients. We're the rue; we're not the ingredients. We are all different. Some of us walk on water; others can barely swim. But that's ok. Being different, being unique are the key components to being successful. If I strived to be normal, how could I be different?

Understand what makes you different. What makes you unique and embrace that. Dr. Seuss wrote, "You have to be odd to be number one." What makes you different must be difficult to replicate. Distinguish yourself from others. Cascade who you are to everyone; let them know it. In my own career I didn't set out to be different, I just set out to be myself, and people thought that was different. So own what makes you unique. Nothing's more important than your authenticity. The only way you fail is if you try to be someone else. Don't steal someone else's thunder. Have the courage to be yourself. Be your own work of art. Don't replicate or try to be like everyone else. Most people are stupid anyway and not worth replicating. A top lesson sports coaches will tell you is to allow people to be themselves, so that when they're comfortable being themselves, 'YOU' show up.

I have found that shame is another form of self-hatred. I live in Los Angeles and Hollywood is big on Award season, especially the Academy Awards. I love seeing "perfection" and adore it when things are at their best. Yet, I'm imperfect myself in every way, and we all are imperfect. Perfection is only for God, so that in itself is a huge relief. That need to please, that disease to please, demands that we usher perfection to the door. God is perfect. We're mortal, and our job is completion, not perfection. Perfection is toxic.

Don't be afraid of who you are. Don't be scared of your own light. When we cannot find tranquility in us, it is useless to find it elsewhere. Only by being at peace with yourself and with others is it possible. Find the courage to be yourself. Be more of who you are. Be honest about your weaknesses and capitalize on your strengths. John Lancaster Spalding said, "If I am not pleased with myself, but should wish to be other than what I am, why should I think highly of the influences which have made me what I am?" You can't guess, you can't hope, you have to know and be sure; otherwise, equivocation is defeat. You've got to be who you are in this world and be sure of it. Life is about becoming who you really are. You don't have to play up to people; they don't have a hell or heaven to put you in. It's one thing to listen and respond to critics; it's another to answer them before they've done anything. Don't sacrifice who you are just to fit in or be accepted by people who don't matter. Don't trade your authenticity for approval. Your need for acceptance can make you invisible in this world. Stand out and be you. The issue with many people is they are so busy trying to get away from where they came from or be someone they're not, that they don't know who they are. Whatever the narrative is about you, you have to just embrace it and not fight it. Otherwise you're just creating another opponent. People will talk about you no matter what, and you can't please everyone. It's better to be hated for who you are than to be loved for who you are not. So, stay true to who you are. Don't change yourself for other people. Don't try to change others, and don't allow others to change you. You control your own life. You make the decisions.

Ralph Waldo Emerson said, “There is a time in every man’s education when he arrives at the conviction that envy is ignorance, that imitation is suicide, that he must take himself for better, for worse as his portion." It's better to accept who you are than to fight it. We spend our lives running from or running towards an identity (ours or other people’s). The privilege of a lifetime is genuinely being who you are. So many people spend way too much time apologizing for their age, their color, their lack of classical beauty. Be proud of who you are, for whatever it's worth. Be truly comfortable in your own skin. Say a mantra every day if you have to. I like to say, "I am conscious of who I am, I am thankful for what I have, I am my mother's child and father's child, I am a towering figure." What you have, everyone else can have. However, who you are, nobody else can be. How can you shine sitting on someone else's sun? Let your own light shine. You have to realize that everything about you is beautiful. I have spent most of my life trying to figure out what the difference is between good and great. Good is fitting in. Great is fitting out. Great is being your own person. The world is filled with rules; be the exception.

If you're not comfortable with yourself, who are you comfortable with? You are all you have. If you don't love you, who will? It's exhausting trying to be perfect or somebody who you're not. Why are you fighting so hard not to be yourself? I think it's time to do something different and be you. I was called different and a lot of other words I can't say here, but I knew it was a good thing to be different because it means you can make a difference. That's living favor minded. So don't listen to your critics; their words will fade, but you won't. Thank God for your life and for your family, and don't wish to change a thing about your life. As a Minnesota native, Prince taught me it's ok to be different, and being different makes all the difference. My voice is my voice, and it's different from my colleagues'; that's why it's so special. Don't be afraid to be different. You don't have to be somebody different to be important. You don't have to be a CEO or a celebrity to be important. You bring you and that's what makes you special.

Your mission, should you choose to accept it, is to be authentic to yourself. Many of us need to stop running away from ourselves, because who else is there better to be? It's hard being told who you are is not ok. Sometimes that's a positive because rejection makes you stop running from yourself. Sometimes rejection is the best gift God can give us. Someone or something not wanting you may be the beginning of you wanting yourself. It teaches you to love yourself and not rely on anything external. You realize that you are enough. It's ok if people don't like you; most people don't like themselves. What matters most is how you see yourself. Be comfortable and have complete confidence in who you are. Love and respect yourself first.

Most importantly, have an unapologetic approach to your life. Don't apologize for who you are. You don't need to agree with the majority to look cool. Being cool is being different. Have something to say. Have an opinion even if no one agrees with you. Be interested; that's more important than being interesting. Always stand up for yourself. No one in this world will have your back better than you. Stand up for yourself and guard yourself. Allow yourself to be who you are, and don't peg yourself in. The world doesn't need you to be a hero; it needs you to be you. Stay true to yourself and remember that you are forever becoming who you are. The older people get, the more they become like themselves. So my message is don't defend yourself if you're not being attacked. Apologize for your mistakes, but don't apologize for who you are. I hope by speaking my truth, it inspires you to live yours.

YOU HAVE EVERYTHING YOU NEED

In Exodus 4:1-17 God tells Moses, “I want you to speak for me.” Moses tells God essentially, I would do it, but they will not believe me. However, was it really that they wouldn't believe him, or that they wouldn't believe something that's he's imposing on them? God doesn't even respond to Moses' saying they won't believe him. Subsequently, God asks Moses, "What's in your hand?" God tells Moses to do an inventory of what he has. Before you assign your destiny to something external, ask yourself what's in your hand. God does not need anything that is not in your hand to bless you. You have everything you need to be blessed. The problem is that Moses thinks his rod is just a stick. God is saying I want to show you the potential of what it could be. You're looking at your situation, thinking it's just a stick, but what is the potential of it? Now if Moses had not learned this in private, it would have messed him up in public, because when Moses got to the Red Sea, he had to use that same rod/stick to part the water. If Moses had not had any confidence in private, he wouldn't have had any power in public. I want you to know that you have more than you think you have, you can do more than you think you can do, and you can have more than you think you can. The problem is not coming from what THEY believe; the problem is coming from what YOU believe. Moses threw the rod on the ground, and it became a serpent; he snatched it, and it became a rod. Sometimes you won't see it until you seize it. Most people want to see their way clear before they proceed, but God said you have to pick it up when you're scared, nervous, unsure, then you will watch it change. You don't even know what you have until you pick it up. Things change from your hand, not from your eyes. When you touch it, it will change; when you grab it, it will change because you will be grabbing it by faith. God's calling you to snatch what you've been running from. You cannot overcome what you will not confront.

Your miracle is not in what you lost, but in what you have left. You may only have two fish and five loaves of bread, but that's all you need. In 2 Kings 4:2 Elisha asks the woman, “What do you have left?” The woman had only a jar of oil, but as she poured it, it increased. You have to pour yourself entirely into something and stop playing it safe and watch yourself increase. In Luke 9:16 it was two fish and five loaves of bread, but as he broke it, it multiplied. When God doesn't give you more, it's because you have enough for what he created you to do. Don't be more than what you are. You fit. You don't have to be taller than you are or shorter than you are. God gave you what you need for the role you need to play. So many people live their lives trying to fit into places they don't fit. God has had a place for you all the time. Find where you fit. Just because your not the general doesn't mean the army doesn't need you. John the Baptist said, “I am not the light. Jesus is.” He said in John 1:29, “Behold the Lamb of God, who takes away the sins of the world.” John’s job was to point out Jesus, not be Jesus. When you know what you are and what you’re not, you can do what you were created to do. What is real and what is lasting is who you are and what you were meant to bring. What is the gift you were meant to give?

You are equipped, empowered, and well able to do what you are called to do. I thought I had to have all the bells and whistles that someone else had, but I needed to be myself. You don't need to have gone to a blue-chip college to make it. You have what you need to succeed. Use it. There is no excuse for not being prosperous. You have everything you need. Even if you start with what you consider to be little, you have everything you need to make it. Every provision for your success has been made for you.

I was watching the Animal channel, and one thing I realized is that we all have what we need to survive. Certain frogs can camouflage, giraffes have long necks to get food, cheetahs run fast, elephants have intelligence, and you have everything you need to be victorious. We all have the tools we need already to be successful. All that you are is enough. You don't need to be like anyone else to be successful or look a certain way or anything else. Just go with what you have because you are sufficient. There is no secret ingredient; it's just you. In a world where you can be anything, be yourself. Stop being envious, jealous, and wanting what others have. It's not what you have; it's the anointing on it. I have the gifts necessary for my assignment. You have the gifts necessary for your assignment. We each have things we can offer the world. People go to great lengths to find what has been inside of them all along. You alone are enough. You are a sufficient condition.

There were many times when I was younger that I kept coming to the world with my hand out. But as long as I was coming to the world with my hand out, I was at the mercy of other people. So if I was going to get control of my life, I needed to gain control of the resources. I kept asking myself, “What do I have? What’s in my hand?” I realized I had more than I needed. I think that's the most important question you'll ever be asked. What's in your hand? What are you going to do with what you've been given? You want more, but you're doing less with what you already have? If I take a skinny person and a buff person and place them side by side, the skinny person has the same number of muscles as the buff person. The difference is one of them has worked what they have. Your life is a direct reflection of what you exercise. My message to you is this: you have it; you just haven't worked it yet. There is nothing that a successful/rich/athletic person has that you don't. You have it; you're just not using it. You don't need anything you don't have to bless you, all you need you already have. Your life is a direct reflection of what you choose to exercise.

I like to think about nature sometimes, and notice how everything of God lives and grows. More importantly, God doesn't have to create again. Everything of God can reproduce itself on its own. It's a self-sustaining process in nature. We are the same way. We have seeds in us and our job is to procreate. Look at the beginning of Genesis. God makes everything in the world and the universe, and it lives and grows. However, each thing has a seed in it to reproduce itself. We have it in us to do, have, or be whatever we want. Our destiny is within us. Our seed is already within us.

There are 3 stories of loss in the book of Luke in the Bible; A lost coin, a lost sheep, and the prodigal son. But the lost coin is most telling. The woman swept her house and found her lost coin. The message is that if you sweep inside of yourself, you will find what you're looking for. That thing you're looking for is already in you. John 4:14-15 says, "The water is in me." We search outside to get our thirst quenched. We go to Las Vegas to quench our thirst. But what you're thirsty for is already down inside of you. We ask God for something that we already have. We're just not adept at tapping into it. It's an art, not a science; it fails when it's supposed to work, and it works when it's supposed to fail. But its there.

You don't have to be first, fastest, or best to make it. Napoleon was a big power in a little body. You don't have to be big and brash; dynamite is small and compact. The only thing you need to be is the best version of yourself. Larry Ellison said, “I have had all the disadvantages required for success." You have everything you need to make it. If you didn't, you would have had it. You are precisely the way God made you, and you have everything you need. If God had wanted you otherwise, he would have created you otherwise. So figure out what you have. You have whatever it takes. If it takes hard work to be successful, you've got that. If it takes good looks to make it, you’ve got that too. If it takes smarts to get ahead, you’ve got that too. You lack nothing. You've got everything you need to make it in this world. Everything you need is already in you and in your hand.

EMBRACE YOUR GIFTS

Deepak Chopra writes in *The Seven Spiritual Laws of Success*, "Inherent in every desire are the mechanics for its fulfillment." So it's no accident that if you love to dance/sing/paint/<u>fill-in-the-blank</u>, you were given talent in this area. You were meant to be doing it. The extent to which you use your gifts and capabilities is entirely up to you, but it is there to be shared and experienced with others. Whatever your talent, use it, don't lose it. Wherever, whenever, always do what you do, and don't stop. If you sing, sing. Sing whether you get paid or not. Your genuine talent will find its way to success. The Bible says in Proverbs 18:16, “your gift will make room for you.” If you follow your talents, focus on your quest, then you will achieve meaningful goals.

I saw an old interview with Whitney Houston and Oprah Winfrey in which she talked about her desire just to go away and sell smoothies on a beach, but then she remembered her God-given gifts, and that would have been selfish of her. The message I gleaned is that gifts are meant to be shared. The only question that matters is what have I done with what I've been given? How will you use your gifts? What choices will you make? We are our choices, so build yourself a great story You have limitless, but not indefinite, potential. You can be whatever you want to be, and the extent to which you use your gifts and capabilities is up to you. The goal of life is to become the highest expression of yourself. I believe and declare that you will go out in this world and take your gifts, talents, and skills and pursue the highest, most valid expression of yourself.

We all want the same thing: to express ourselves fully and be validated in the process. You can't wait for others’ approval before you use your gifts. You're gifted, and when you’re gifted you’re not going to understand. It's been given to you. Your job is to nurture it and grow that gift. The Bible shares a story of talents in Matthew 25:14-24 in which a rich man gave to each ACCORDING TO THEIR ABILITY. The gifts you have were given to you according to your ability and God is looking for a return on his investment in you. God is saying you're wasting what he entrusted into you. Too many of us bury our talents. That's why the cemetery is the wealthiest place in the world. People die with their dreams with them. It starts from within, including being happy. Wanting to be happy has to begin with contentment and joy with yourself first. The lion share of people who are miserable are miserable and unhappy with themselves first, and then that portrays out. Les Brown provides an illustration of imagining laying on your deathbed and around you are your dreams, ideas, talents, and abilities that you never acted on. Visualize that they're looking at you with large angry eyes, and they say we came to you! Only you could have given us life, and now we have to die with you! So the question is if you die at this very moment, what will die with you? What dreams? What ideas? Don't let fear and the seduction of playing it safe draw you in.

The first thing God said to man after he made him was to be fruitful. I didn't save you so you could quit, I didn't keep you so you could die, I didn’t love you to lose you, I didn’t pull you in to let you go. You are to be fruitful. John 15:16 shows us that it is an ordinance, an order, a commandment to be fruitful. Your purpose is to be fruitful. Fruit is produce. If you’re productive with what is inside of you, you don't have to find joy. Yours is the earth and all that's in it. You don't have to be rich or famous, but you need to be productive in some way in some place. Don't let a day go by without producing something for that day. This is a day you will never see again. I'm not saying not to rest; everybody needs a sabbath. But that's one out of seven. For abundant life and maximum capacity, it's one out of seven, not six out of seven. At every age, at every stage, be productive. God says to be fruitful and multiply. However, you can only multiply what's fruitful, what's working, your strength. But you can't have fruit without a seed, and the seeds are inside of you. This is a time of self-discovery. What can you be? What can you do? Who are you? What's in you? Life is a fleeting vapor; you are here today and gone tomorrow. Don't come short of your destiny and not know what's in you. Find your highest use, your ultimate destiny. Find what your seed is; discover your talents. When you combine your talents with your skills, knowledge, and experience, they serve as multipliers. Identifying your specific innate abilities will set you apart. Now put your talents to work. The gift is already inside you. People often say, "Do what makes you happy," but a lot of what's gotten me here is hard work. And I'm not always happy. So, I don't think you should do what makes you happy; I think you should do what makes you great.

I was thinking during last Christmas about the birth of Jesus, this prince of peace and king of kings born in a manager by a virgin mother, wrapped in swaddling clothes. So I thought, what Mary is about to birth will redeem her. What she delivered will deliver her. Whatever your prayer is, the answer is in your promise. Whatever is in you, whatever gift is in you, that's what's going to answer your prayers if you release it. The answer is in what you birth and what's inside you. Everything good in my life has come from what I've given birth to. My question to you is what are you carrying? Whatever you're carrying inside of you, that's been the answer to your prayers all along. You are pregnant with possibilities. I want you to know that God has a baby for you. Something that's yours and yours alone. God will cause you to be noticed. Let me ask you, what gift is inside of you? All of us have desires inside of us that itch. All you have to do is let it out. That itch, whatever it is, is already yours. You just have to claim it. We all have a gift. The Bible says in James 1:17, "Every good and perfect gift is from above." 2 Corinthians 4:7 says, "We have this treasure in jars of clay to show that this all-surpassing power is from God and not from us."

Have a dream for your life. Ask for it, reach for it, and march towards it. Figure out where your power base is inside you. Then align your gifts and talents with your purpose for being here. As mentioned earlier, we all have talents and gifts, but we're so busy wishing for the talents of others. Use what you have, don't try to be someone you're not – people can tell. Every one of us is born with unique qualities, and it takes our whole life to understand our purpose and to explore our true potential. Many of us understand it at the end of our life, but by then we are only left with regrets. Find it now and join your true journey for life. Use what's been given to you. Don't hide your talents, multiply them. Whatever your gift, athlete-body, singer-voice, et cetera, that is your instrument, and you need to be a steward of it, and take care of it. Use your life. God gets pleasure watching you be you. Why? Because he made you and when you do what you were made to do he goes, "That's my boy. That's my girl. You're using my talent and ability that I gave you." So look at what's in your hand: your identity, your influence, and say, "It's not about me," and make the world a better place. If you use what you have, you'll be just fine. You are God's gift to you and what you make of yourself is your gift to God. Don't let someone else's judgment stand in the way of that. That's why judgment is the biggest obstacle to peace. So embrace your gifts and share your gifts.

Hidden talent counts for nothing. Whatever is in you, use. Whatever song is in you, sing. Whatever story you wish to tell, tell it. Whomever you need to make amends with, do it. Use everything you have. Romans 11:29 says, "For the gifts and the callings of God are irrevocable." That means that the gifts, talents, and calling on your life can't be taken away; they're yours. Use them.

FIND YOUR GREATNESS

To be unique in this world is almost impossible. All art and everybody is either taken or borrowed, but you stand alone and are completely original. So when asked what makes you different, answer that you're not everybody. You should be interesting, not perfect. You can't lead from the crowd. You need to stand out and be yourself. Be sure of yourself and benefit society. Don't be afraid of the reflection in the mirror because on the other side is greatness. Greatness isn't being an Olympic athlete, running 300 miles, or getting a promotion; greatness is whatever you see in your mind. However, you have to see the vision first. You have to first create this vision in your mind, and once you create this vision, the next question is how you are going to get there. We are all great, no matter if you're dumb or think you're dumb, you're fat or think you're fat, or you've been bullied. We all have greatness; you just have to find the courage to put your headphones on, silence the noise of this world, and find it.

True greatness is about transcendence; it's about being great in any generation and in any context. Greatness is not this unusual elusive feature that only the special among us have. It truly exists in all of us. This is what I believe, and what I'm willing to die for. This is who I am, and I do what I need to do. We live in an external world; everything needs to be touched or seen. However, I'm challenging you to live the rest of your life inside of yourself. Stop listening to the people who are calling you ugly, fat, stupid, and everything that's useless. The world is full of insecure people placing their insecurities on you. You have to flush it out. You just have to be whomever God created you to be and take everything else and throw it away. You have to believe in one thing, and that's yourself. I'm not saying not to believe in God, but what I'm saying is you're not going to find greatness in yourself looking out there in the world; you're not going to find it in a book or by reading my words, or listening to me. I may give you the spark, but you've got to go inside yourself to find it. Greatness exists inside of you – tap into your future.

2

WHOM DO YOU WANT TO BE?

"Be your note."
– Rumi

NAME YOUR FUTURE

Take time to think about the direction of your life and ask yourself what you want. Everybody wants something. So what do you want? What do you want to be known for? What do you want to do? How do you want to live? A good man? A good woman? A loving mother? A hard worker? Think about whom you want to be. Go ahead [Insert *Noun* + *Adjective*]. If you don't know, in law there is something called a counter-factual that may help you decide. What wouldn't you do? What should you not do? Knowing what you don't want to do is the best possible place to be if you don't know what you do want to do. So think about it, what is it that you want for and from your life? What is going to be the most self-edifying experience for you? What characteristic do you most admire in others? What kind of impact do you believe you have on other people? Fast forward your life 15 or 20 years down and see if that's where you want to be. If it's not, change it. The future influences the present just as much as the past. Your job is to think independently during this exercise. Whom do YOU want to be? What's important to YOU? These are questions only you can answer. In our hearts, we all know what we want to be. The task of life is not what you do but whom you become. You need to decide what's more important – what you want for your life and your future or what other people have to say about it.

If you're feeling stuck or unsure of your future, turn off Facebook and stop worrying about what others think. Start re-discovering yourself just like a company does research and development for a new product or service. It's time to do research and development on yourself. What do you care about? What do you value? What are you good at? What do you want to be good at? What makes you come alive? Don't be scared if you don't know who you are or what you want. Instead, find out. Ask the right questions, and experiment with opportunities that align with your interests. Take internships, try other jobs, challenge your assumptions, and try something you have never done before. The best way to discover your highest true passion is to try different things. This is how you can build a meaningful career/life you can believe in. In order to follow your bliss, you need to find it.

Elizabeth Gilbert writes in *Eat, Pray, Love,* the importance of pursuing curiosity, not passion. Gilbert writes, "Passion is rare, passion is a one-night-stand. Passion is hot, it burns. Every day, you can't access that; but every single day in my life there's something that I'm curious about – follow, it's a clue, and it might lead you to your passion." I have found that a lot of what I stumbled into by following my intuition turned out to be priceless later on. Curiosity is the vehicle that leads us from finding to living our passion. It builds the bridge.

Most people have typical goals: I want to be successful by 30, retire by 40, et cetera. However, the eternal question remains: "What should I do?" Well, it depends on what you want. Most people just want success and power. However, what do you really want? See through your heart. You can't be confused about where to go as if you were in a labyrinth. You have to know what you want because only you know where you're going. Think carefully about what you want. Plan it, calculate it, and discuss it. Success defines the right thing to do and the correct path to take. Make a commitment to a great endeavor. Don't just be interested in it; be committed to it, and sacrifice and be dedicated for it. The pace of life goes by so fast, but you have to slow down and evaluate what you have and where you want to go with that. Make a mind map of where you want to go, whom you want to be, what you're going to do, and how you're going to do it. Make up your mind. Ralph Waldo Emerson said, "The only person you are destined to be is the person you decide to be." The key is to sacrifice who you are for what you might become, and if you think about it that way, you won't stand still. It's not who you are that holds you back; it's who you think you're not. The most important thing is to keep searching. Look at the Jewish faith, which is a reminder to keep looking for that jar of oil even in the night. Keep seeking; keep asking for what you really want. If you don't know what to do, think about whom you want to be. And if you don't know whom you want to be, think about what you want to do. Look at it from the point of dynamic analysis rather than static analysis. If you could do anything, what would you really do? This is your life. You have to ask yourself what you want to accomplish with your life. Everyone has the same amount of time, and the difference is what you're willing to do with your time. So decide, because nothing is stopping you from being whom you want to be. You can live your life on your own terms.

I acknowledge that my suggestions may not be the right suggestions for you, so I implore you to explore, experience, learn, and most importantly, enjoy life yourself. My prayer for you is the same as 2 Corinthians 9:8, "that you may abound in everything you do and that you are richly blessed more and more in every area of your life." It's about having more and more, moving from increase to increase, and always going higher. The end goal is ultimately prosperity.

Inquire of Yourself

A prevailing belief that we can be whomever we want to be and achieve all of our dreams emerges again and again in our novels, films, and news. Inside all of us, there is a primal desire to do something meaningful with our lives. It's a concept I believe in wholeheartedly. You can do anything you want; you are bound to nothing. We control our own destiny. The only two questions which matter are "What do you want to do?" and "Whom do you want to be?" More specifically, what do you want to do with the time you have left? Even something as low as a brick wants to be something better than what it is, such as a coliseum or pyramid. You must have some vision for your life. Even if you don't have a plan, you need to have a direction in which you wish to go. I say that because you want to be in the driver's seat of your life; otherwise, life will drive you.

I'm always amazed at how many people don't have any belief system. A part of being successful is having a belief system. Apple languished for 10 to 15 years until Steve Jobs came in with a point of view. He had a belief system; he had a core and a vision for where he wanted the company to go, and he eventually led Apple to be the most valuable company in the world. It's about having a belief system and knowing what's driving you and why you do what you do and having complete conviction in that vision. However, it starts by integrating what you want to do. Have a belief system and follow that compass. In my own life, I wanted to do public speaking, but I was terrified to speak publicly. However, I did it anyway, and I learned to just go with my gut because it's what I wanted to do. There's a reason you think the way you do and want to do the things you do. You can't let anyone stop you or tell you don't do it, especially yourself. Too many people do what's expected of them as opposed to what they want to do.

Life's toughest question is what kind of person do you want to be? In this world, you're either nobody or somebody. We all want to be somebody. We all want to win, be special, and be historic. We all have a desire to make something of ourselves for ourselves. Think about what you would want to be said about you at your eulogy. Make decisions about how you want to be remembered yourself. In my eulogy, I want them to describe Louis in three words: **practices then preaches**. In my own life, I want to live and work around the world. I want to experience culture, I want to be a local, and I want to be global. It's no longer just about money anymore to me. It's about life and challenges and doing things I never thought were possible for me. I want to be the best of me, and I want to be as good as I can be. Most people are vague in their dreams and desires. Stop. Drill down on your heart's desire. Lily Tomlin wrote, "I always knew I wanted to be someone, I guess I should've been more specific." Think about it and know you're allowed to have second thoughts and change your mind.

There's always a part of us that wants to be special and needs to be accommodated. Truly, I don't believe that God would place us on this earth only to be "ordinary." People sit around not knowing what they want to do or be and they hang around low-level jobs or until the spirit moves them. No wonder why 75% of Americans are disengaged at work. You are capable of much more than you think. You have to dig down deep and ask yourself whom you want to be. Not what but whom. It starts from within. You have to know what you want before anyone else can. You have to figure out for yourself what makes you happy if you're going to be engaged. Always trust yourself and listen to yourself no matter what anyone else thinks. Explore where you are today and where you want to go. It's a brave new world, and the world is changing every day; make sure your future is clear. Life is brief and we only get a few opportunities to actualize ourselves. Don't be like crows on a wire, where everyone is doing the same thing. You're better off standing out, being different.

Questions to ask yourself: What more are you wanting in your career or life right now? Why don't you have it? Look in the mirror and be real with yourself and say, 'What do I want for me?' We wrestle with these kinds of questions: Can we change our lives? Can we change the world? How do we find our moral center? What's the process for growing up? What do I want to do with the life I lead? Consider this question: What do I desire? Have an ideal to strive towards. You have to figure out what kind of person you want to be. Whomever that person is, s/he will change the world. The time is now to determine whom you're going to be.

You have been elected and selected to lead your own life. We're all hungry for self-discovery. So explore what you want to do before committing. Keep yourself flexible. Inquire of God. What does God want from me? What does God have in me? Whom does he want me to be? These are the questions that plague us. What is that you want? What do you want to do? Make it a choice, not a challenge. These are the questions you need to ask yourself. Not everyone is ready yet for the answers to them. You need to think long and hard about whom you want to be because a little decisiveness goes a long way in this life.

In this ever-waging war inside of us, it can feel like your heart is suspended between your left and right hemispheres inside your brain. To help with that, using a process of elimination is the fastest way to finding whom you want to be and what you want to do (i.e., listing this is who I'm not or this is what I don't want). So determine what the highest expression of yourself is. It can't be touched tasted or felt; it has to be experienced. The magic is inside of you. Take hold of your future. Look at what energizes you, what makes you feel fulfilled. This is an existential moment for you. What is your future going to be? Ask yourself what you want and why you want it because the purpose gives you the energy to see it through. You have to get serious and ask, "What do I want to do with the rest of my life?" You have an obligation to be who your heart knows you can be. In this life there are no accidents or unreachable goals that exist within your desires. You can't deny human aspirations, especially your own. You owe it to yourself to find out who you can be.

Construct a life that has meaning and satisfaction in it. Figure out how you can be a world-changer and difference maker. Steve Harvey tells a story about his mother asking him, "Do you know your great-grandfather's name?" Steve replied, "No." She said, "That's because he didn't leave you anything." We all want to leave something behind and leave a legacy. It's time you started fighting for your last name rather than your first name. We each have two names: the one we are born with and the one we make for ourselves. At some point, you have to decide for yourself whom you're going to be. You can't let someone else make that decision for you. Stop worrying about what people think, say, or feel about you. We cannot become who we want to be by remaining who we are. You have to say 'this is who I am,' and 'this is what I'm working towards.' Implicit in 'whom do I want to be' are the instructions on what you need to do to get there. Epictetus says, "First say to yourself what you would be, then do what you have to do." That's the cornerstone of self-efficacy and self-realization.

Be True to Yourself

The biggest mistake in this life is hoping who we are instead of auditing who we are. I mean everybody wants to be something. For example, I want to be point guard for the Los Angeles Lakers, but the truth is it's not me. I don't have the pieces. People are chasing a narrative rather than pursuing what they're good at. Self-awareness is not being deployed enough. Look, I suck at 99% of stuff, but I figured out the 1% of things I am amazing at. Success is about self-awareness and being true to yourself about your abilities. The only success is your inner journey; everything else is material. My first jobs were a broken exercise in figuring out what I'm not good at. You have to find what you do well to satisfy your overall goal of whom you want to be. Working in a corporate job confirmed what I already knew: I wasn't made to work for someone else. I came to a crossroads in my life, and I realized I had to get out of there. I felt I was too smart for this because either I'm going to hurt someone or someone's going to hurt me. While working in corporate America, if I were true to myself, I would know this wasn't for me. Maybe it's just who I am, or I suppose it's the card I drew. Either way, I was done being someone I'm not and decided to pave my own way.

The focus can't always be on whom you should be. Instead, make decisions around who you are and not around what you think is externally valued. We must be honest with ourselves. If something isn't you, say it. Only trust your own palette because history is made from the inside out. That itch that you have, that desire inside of you is God's promise to you. It's already yours; all you have to do is claim it. You have to stop pretending to yourself that you are something other than what you are. You can teach what you know, but you can only reproduce what you are. Be confident in yourself, in who you are, and love who you are. Be you, with no gimmicks. Don't betray yourself. The quest for authenticity and meaning is a constant process of being true to yourself. Your heart is your authority within you. Tap into yourself and know your truth and affirm who you are, especially in an intolerant world. I wish I had been myself earlier in life, but I guess better late than never. Nothing's more important than your authenticity. Don't sacrifice your individuality for security.

The most important thing I have learned is to be yourself. For too long people try to please others, do what others want them to do, and as a result, they are unhappy. Be honest with yourself and others about who you are and what you want. That means you have to live the life you have, the life you've been given. Be true to yourself. Sunlight is the best disinfectant. You need to answer to your own truth. Live your life from truth, and you will survive anything. There's a story of God and Satan walking together, and God bends over and picks up something shiny and glowing and translucent. Satan asks, "What is that?" God says, "It's truth," and Satan says, *"Let me have it and organize it for you."* And I believe that truth is very personal, and we don't need organizations to manage it for us. My own truth and only my own truth could set me free. Ultimately, it's not the truth that sets you free; it's the truth you know that sets you free. That's the truth about dishonesty.

Brand Yourself

Think about how you want to be seen professionally. You are a brand. Think of yourself as a company. Your personal brand needs to be consistent in every touch point you have with any potential client or employer. Branding yourself can be seen as a foreign objective, depending on your cultural background. In Australia, it's tall poppies – and the tallest poppies get their heads knocked off. In India, it's crabs in a bucket – their compatriots drag down the one who seeks to escape. In Japan, the nail that sticks out gets hammered down. Nearly every culture has its own metaphor for what happens to the people judged by their peers to be overreaching. However, in the United States, it's a different story. Personal branding is viewed positively as a way to differentiate oneself. Various research has indicated that personal branding or self-promotion can cause discomfort for people around the world.[13]

In countries like China or India or Korea, characteristics such as composure, modesty, and self-control are more valued than tooting your own horn. However, branding yourself is incredibly important, and the benefits are wide-ranging – including taking control of how others perceive you. The best definition of a brand is ‘the promise of an experience.’ Consider the experiences you can offer people. Any experience consists of both ‘what’ (the identifiable results and events), and ‘how’ (the feeling it gives you). So when you consider your brand, don't forget that the most important part of the experience is how your promise will feel when people deal with you. How do you want people to feel in dealing with you? You're responsible for your own branding from the beginning. Personally, I am not the first person to swing and miss on this issue, but now is the time to take ownership of your brand.

Own yourself, own your brand, own your image, own your joy, own your happiness, own your truth, own who you are, own your rights, own your masters. Control your image, and be protective of that. Own everything you do; you are the CEO of your life and your brand. It's You, Inc. We all have a **PERSON**ALITY. **LOUIS**ALITY. ***INSERT YOUR NAME***ALITY. Whatever you do, own it. Be serious about who you are and whom you want to be. Consider the branding of successful people. Successful people have a certain look. They wear certain clothes, walk a certain way, carry themselves in a certain way. Ask yourself, what's your look? How do people perceive you? How do you come across? Figuring out your personal brand is challenging because it requires the capacity to look at yourself and your skills objectively. Here are some tips:

- **Be yourself** (Your personal brand is just that - you. Focus on your unique talent or passion).
- **Know your why** (Ask yourself why you are doing what you do. What is your purpose and mission?).
- **Get some support, not advice** (The challenge is knowing the difference. Support is when someone helps you understand what is right for you).

Make decisions for your brand that are in line with your strengths, goals, and talents. Your brand is as important as your resume, but it's tough to define and communicate your brand. Constantly be in the business of personal brand building. Build your own brand instead of relying on others to do it for you. Let excellence be your brand. When you are excellent, you become unforgettable. Live your brand, then define your brand, then communicate carefully, but often. Present yourself in a way that you're proud of. Value your own self-worth. Stand out from the crowd; develop your brand. You are your brand, and you must protect it mercilessly. In *The Crucible*, John Proctor says to Hale, Parris, and Danforth when they try to convince him to impugn his integrity and confess to conspiring with the devil, “[I won’t] Because it is my name! Because I cannot have another in my life!” Your name is your reputation. Don't let anything spoil your good name.

When it comes to branding yourself, how soon is now? Everyone needs a compelling brand because how you live is sending out a message. Furthermore, you have to rebuild and rebrand yourself. Carry yourself like a prospect, not a suspect. Dress how you want to be addressed; represent yourself well. Be a good custodian of your brand. An image is everything. Never do anything to hurt your image. If you're not selling it, people aren't buying it; so sell yourself. You can't outproduce your own self-image. Get your name out there; be relevant. I've played sports all my life, and I've realized that it's your name on the back of that jersey. It's not your coach’s name; it's your name. You need to step up and protect your name and protect your brand. Take control of your career and your work brand. It's about curating your image and being selective about what you align that with. We all need makeovers from time to time, but ultimately, stay true to your brand's essence. So take control of your brand by deciding the environment that will suit you best. Especially since we live in a Social Media age, you don't want to be overexposed. You want people to say, "Oh, I can't wait to see him!" not "I see him everywhere." You want to keep some mystery about yourself, so that it keeps building up suspense, and people are looking out for you. Think about being an actor for a moment. Branding for an actor is being good, not being known. It's about whether what they did was any good, not how many movies they've done. So don't overexpose yourself; be selective.

Simply What's Best For You

When you get a chance, look up the story of David and Goliath in the Bible. The king told David, "I want you to fight Goliath using this armor," and David said something very important. David said, I can't fight your fight; I can't use your armor. I have to fight my fight. I have to use my armor. The point is you have to do what works for you and fight your battles, the ones that matter to you, not other people's battles. Make sure that you're fighting the battle in front of you, not behind you. Ask yourself what you need for your life so that you will experience more joy and less sorrow. The story of David and Goliath shows us that no one knows what's best for you because it's unknowable. Only you can know. In effect, David tells us I need to serve my needs and do what's best for me. It's a question of what's right for you, not necessarily what's right or what to do. You know what you're capable of, and it's more than what you're doing now. Remember, you don't owe your parents or anybody else any explanations. You’ve got to do what's best for you. Teams, organizations, and companies do what’s best for themselves all the time; don’t be afraid to look after your own interests too.

I fly often and the safety protocol is the same: “in case of emergency, secure your own mask before assisting others.” In effect, take care of yourself first because you are of no use to anyone if your incapacitated. You have to do what's right for yourself. This is your life, and if you don't take care of yourself, who will? I learned the hard way that if I'm down and out, everyone else's life goes on. Your first job is to yourself because if you're not satisfied, the first collateral damage is with yourself. They teach in sports, first and foremost you play for yourself. Life is a big game. There are fans, and there are fanatics, and there is no greater satisfaction than the adulation of other people, but live for yourself. Play for yourself. Get better for yourself. Don’t live trying to be a *soup de jour,* or trying to please everyone. You are magnetic. Magnets repel and attract. Not everyone is going to like who you are or care for you, and that’s ok. You can't please everyone, so you've got to please yourself. There are many paths to becoming a success, but trying to please everybody is a sure way to failure.

Success is about having your own truth. Sometimes you have to realize this isn't what you want or need to do. Do what's in your own best interest. Stay in your own lane. Stay true to yourself. Be true to your nature, true to form, trust that inner voice, know what you're good at and what you're not good at. Ask yourself a battery of self-awareness questions: What am I pretending not to know? Why don't I do the things I know I should be doing? Stop deceiving yourself. Don't become like a magician who starts believing his own tricks. Life is about figuring out what to do. Have enough self-respect and confidence to live life on your terms. If something isn't right in your life, change it. When people ask, "What do you do?" or "What's your profession?" answer the question in terms of what you want to do or whom you want to be. Uncover your greatest hope. Be sincere and honest with yourself, then work hard to deliver on your words. When it comes to interacting with other people, we have to be careful what we say. But when it comes to interacting with ourselves, we have to be careful what we think. Remember, what we think, we become.

Focus on Your Joy

You will find that at different times in your life a call will be different. Some people know what they want to do from an early age; I didn't. I spent a lot of time feeling my way around for what seemed like the right thing. However, I knew that whatever that right thing was I wasn't going to be what everyone else told me it was. After college I was at the tipping point. I needed to decide whom I was going to be. Once college ended, I didn't know who I wanted to be. So, I had to learn to be myself. School teaches you what to do; it doesn't teach you who to be. After college, I asked, What do I have left to say? What do I do now? I felt screwed and lost. Perhaps many other graduates feel that same way. People and family were saying, "You spent how much on college and didn't know what you wanted to do?" "You're competing with 5 million other graduates for jobs." However, the truth is that you are not screwed. No one ever says this at graduation, but it's okay not to know exactly what you want to do with your life. There is not only one answer or only one career ladder. Most likely, you do not have one calling or one life purpose. Over the course of my life, I have had numerous "callings," from being president to being a sportswriter to making movies – and I'm currently doing none of these things. I've lived in five cities in three countries, held numerous jobs, and gone down six different career paths. What matters ultimately is not whether you feel lost, because we all feel lost. What matters is what you do when you feel lost. When most people feel lost they spend lots of time on Facebook, comparing themselves to others, and overdose on FOMO (fear of missing out), or end up taking a job that makes them miserable or go to business school because they don't know what else to do. For me, I found myself saying, "Maybe I should move to London? Maybe I should go to grad school? Maybe I should work for a nonprofit?" The choices besieged me. I felt alone and depressed. However, only when I looked at myself instead of my newsfeed did I gain some clarity. The reality is all of us are figuring it out, even our Facebook and Instagram friends, whose grass looks really green. It seems that everyone else is in the best position. If you're driving a sedan, you want an SUV, and if you're driving an SUV, you want a sedan. I have so many friends who are self-employed artists who speak in awe and intrigue about working for Google and getting free kale smoothies all day, and I know just as many Googlers who hate their jobs and want to be artists. The grass isn't always greener, but few people take the time to figure out who they are and why they're here. If you do, you will find that the grass is green wherever you water it.

CREATE YOUR LIFE

The most significant lesson life taught me after academia and living in the “real world” was that no one is going to tell you what to do. It's up to you to chart your own course and determine your path. Life is nothing more than a blank canvas, and you are the paintbrush. It becomes what you want it to be. Destiny is not the path given to us, but rather the path we choose for ourselves. No matter how bad it is, you always have a choice about how to handle it and what do next. You get to decide whom you want to become. There are so many people who live their lives on the default setting, not realizing they can customize everything. Don't settle for the default settings in your life. Find your talents, your loves, your passions, and embrace them.

Design your journey every step of the way and don't let others tell you what you want. Make your own path. If the world places you on a road you do not like or if you look ahead and do not want that destination being offered and you look behind, and you don't want to return to your place of departure, then step off the road. That’s the time to pave yourself a new path. No matter where you are, you can start right now. Everybody starts somewhere. Nobody is born successful; we all start somewhere, and usually from the bottom. You have to fight for the life you want; no one is going to hand it to you. Claim your life. Create the life you want to lead. You are the author of your own life. If you don't like the story you're living, it's up to you to change the plot. Life is full of destinations, choose yours.

Have you ever gotten a suit from the store? Alternatively, have you ever gotten a suit tailored to you? A tailored suit is different from a one-size-fits-all. The way you feel in it is different. The way you walk in it is different. Why? Because it's tailored to you. You need to have a tailor-made life. You were created with a specific purpose, a particular design. You are special. You were created to do what only you can do. When you become the right person, you begin to separate yourself from other people. Do not live someone else's life or someone else's idea of womanhood or manhood. It's everything that's inside of you. Tailor your life to you. Forge your own path. It's not about history; it's about being a pioneer. If you don't like something, change it. If you don't like your job, quit. Forge your own path. Be your own man. Be your own woman. If you want something, go for it. Have a bias for action. Don't wait for mine or anyone else's approval. If it matters to you that's all you need. That's all that's required. Go for it.

Don't think about it; commit to action. You need to live more and think less. The distinctive life is an achievement, not something that falls in your lap. Successful people understand that the world is pliable, and most rules are not set in stone. You can choose your facts and bias and create your own story. Create your own opportunities. Don't wait around for someone to recognize your talent and offer you a break. The world rarely works that way. If you want something, *you* have to figure out a way to make it happen. Virgil wrote, "*Flectere si nequeo superos, Acheronta movebo (if I cannot move heaven, I will raise hell).*" Do whatever it takes to create the life you want. Life is about creating yourself, it's not about finding yourself. Stop trying to find yourself and create yourself. You are your greatest masterpiece, your most challenging and important work of art. Build your own life don't just live one. Choose your own autobiography; this is the life you author.

Nothing is stopping you from being whom you want to be. If you're in a dead-end job doing something you don't want to do, I don't care if you're 21 or 40, you can get off that road at any time, pave your own path, and go after the life you want. At the end of the day, it comes down to a choice. It's a binary choice. Either you move forward or stay where you are. Do you stay or do you go? Period. It's always a choice, whether it's apparent or not. If you can't map your future success to your current responsibilities, it's time to find a new opportunity. Know when it's time to move on. You are always one decision away from the life you want. Your next decision could be the most important in your life. Make a choice for the life you want, because if you want an abundant life, those choices are necessary. It all comes down to choices, and not making a choice is a choice. It's not chance. It's your choices that make you successful. The journey you take will be led by you alone.

Erich Fromm said, "man's main task in life is to give birth to himself." Fromm reminds us that you are destined to become the person you decide to be. Each person invents himself, and we are each a figment of our imagination. So, pursue the concept of your life and create the grandest life vision for yourself. Declare that this is the life you choose to live and you will hold yourself to a higher standard. I believe you're on the right path; now you just have to go the distance. Don't just be successful or make a mark or legacy, fulfill the highest sense of yourself. Have a vision for your life. Don't give up on the person you're becoming. Create the kind of self that you will be happy to live with all your life. Your fantastic life is waiting for you, so go make it happen. Be serious about what you decide to do, but don't take yourself too seriously.

Define Yourself

I was always told to go to school, do this, get a job, do that, et cetera, but what does that really mean? What does it mean to be normal? What does it mean to conform to society's expectations? When life points you in a particular direction, ask if it's possible that the arrows for you don't point in that direction. Is it possible that all the "supposed to's" in life aren't really what you should be doing? You can either follow your peers and follow what everyone else is doing, or you can lead your own life. When opportunity knocks, sometimes it's better not to answer. Having too many opportunities can be destabilizing and can cause inertia.

Now, I will admit that I used to be a people pleaser and cared what other people thought. However, over time I began to measure my worth in terms of my standard and personal achievement. I defined myself. Don't let people define you; define yourself and stay true to yourself. It is incredibly important not to let others define you, pigeonhole you, or whittle you down to their preconceived notions. Don't let others judge you. You are not someone else’s opinion of you. Create your own set of standards. Having your own standards will help you weather moments when others doubt you or say your work is no good. Moreover, having your own personal standards allows you to perceive success where others may see failure. Only by being authentic to who you are can you keep your head on straight and your feet planted firmly. Don't strive to be someone else's notion of perfection. It's nothing more than an unattainable and ultimately ridiculous goal. Strive for authenticity and uniquely yourself. When you're in doubt, listen to your gut because somehow it already knows what you want to become. You still have time to define yourself and control your brand.

We have a society and a generation of people who don't know who they are. However, when you do know who you are, you don't need other people in order to feel good about yourself. You don't need to be like other people. We live in a world that will try and tell you who you are, but you need to know for yourself. Define yourself before the world does, or before the world works to put you in a box. If you don't know who you are and where you want to go, the world will tell you. Since humans are built to be part of communities, don't let other people or ideologies tell you who you are. You don’t get to define me, and I don’t get to define you. You define who you are. The first rule of politics is to define yourself before the other side does. The first lesson in crisis management or public relations is to control the narrative. Never let others define you or define your narrative. Don't abdicate that authority. If you don't know who you are and where you want to go, the world will tell you. Don't let anyone ever tell you what to do; how to do it is ok, but not what to do. Know what to do for yourself. If you don't control who you are or what your message is or what your brand is, other people will. Take control of your brand. This is your time to take back the narrative over your life. Take back control of the conversation, take back the discussion around you.

Stereotypes can be devastating, especially when you apply them to yourself. In fact, one of the most persistent is that you have to be a certain way to be successful or to have peace. The critical thing is to understand how to make your psychology work for what you want. The goal is to work with what you are. People envelop themselves with certain definitions. You get to decide what kind of person you're going to be. You are not your father or your mother, you are not your circumstances, you are not what was done to you; you are whom you say you are. Ask yourself what restrictions you're imposing on yourself. What's possible for you? Do you believe that things can be different and can get better? Do you think you can be successful? The people around you don't make you who you are. You determine who you are. You are not what people say about you. Your self-worth must come from within. When your sense of satisfaction and pleasure are a consequence of comparing yourself with others, you are no longer the master of your own destiny. While it is impossible to turn off your reactions to what others think of you, remember that your self-worth comes from within. You are never as good or as bad as they say you are. We are put into boxes by our family, our moment, our history, even by our own bodies. However, don't be limited by the beliefs of those around you. Make this declaration: 'I am not who you think I am. I am not who you say I am. I define myself.' The only thing limiting you is your definition of *who I am*. No one can tell you who you are; only you can. Don't ever let the world determine who you will be. That right is yours and yours alone. All of us must determine our individual path. You carry yourself the way you see yourself and people will see you the way you see yourself. Perception is reality; how people view you will play into how people experience you.

Don't let anyone place labels or limitations on you. Don't let your age, color, race, or anything define you. Define who you are and own who you are. Be you; everyone else is taken. Be you; the world will adjust. No matter where you go in this world you take yourself with you and remember that self-esteem comes from being able to define the world on your own terms.

Follow Your Own Path

People often ask me what the greatest metaphor for life is, and since I live in Los Angeles, I say a freeway. Everyone is going to a different destination, everyone is going different speeds, and everyone looks different (each car looks different). What's important is that your hands are on the wheel and you are headed in the direction you want to go. It doesn't matter how fast or slow you're going, but that you're on the right road. No matter what, someone will always be ahead of you, and you will always be ahead of someone else. Just stay in control of your vehicle (your life). Moreover, don't be concerned with everything going on around you. Just pay attention to the road ahead. Know where you're going and keep moving in that direction. Your success is in your hands. That's why you don't blindly follow others, because other people may not be going where you are headed. Question everything, otherwise it's just the blind leading the naked. Successful people think on their own. Make your way through life, no one's master and no one's slave. Following someone else's path limits your own growth. If you're on a paved path, it's not your path. Rumi said, "Your heart knows the way. Run in that direction." Find your own opportunities and chart your own course.

True success is charting your own path, following your own course, marching to your own beat. Rumi continued saying, "My soul is my guide." Success is no longer an ascension of steps. You need to climb sideways, and sometimes down, and sometimes swing from the jungle gym and establish your own turf somewhere else on the playground. There's no set path for success. Success is just about going off a gut feeling and being in tune with what's going on around you. Realize there is no straight path to where you are going. William Shakespeare tells us in *Hamlet* to "hold a mirror up to nature." Let nature be our guide. Look, I love nature, but nowhere in nature will you find straight lines; there's always curvature. So, follow the curves of your heart. March to your own drummer, listen to your own beat. Follow your dreams and do what's in your heart. You're the only one who knows you, so follow your inner voice. Rather than following a written path, follow your instincts, and bet on yourself. Most of the time you will prove yourself right. Things started changing for me when I started listening to what felt like the truth for me. Get busy unlearning and forgetting what other people and society want and expect from you. The sooner you stop listening to others the sooner you can hear your inner voice.

You get to decide what kind of person you're going to be. You have to make your own decisions about what you're going do in your life. You have to make a personal decision for yourself and then stick with it. You have to make a decision for your life. Are you going to do what everybody wants you to do or will you be led by who you truly are. Listen to opinions of other people you respect, but in the end, it has to come from you. You can't look to the left or the right, worrying about what the competition is doing, or what other people are doing. It has to be you and your vision. Always ask yourself what the choice is. I can be like everyone else, dress in a suit, and go to work, or I can swim upstream and pave my own path. Then whatever I achieve is mine and not like what everyone else has. Choose to be a contrarian. When everyone else zigs, you should zag. When everyone else is selling, you should buy; when everyone else is buying, you should sell. Do the opposite in most cases, and you'll be successful.

My hope for you is that you will make up your mind. From this day forward, nothing will seem familiar to you. The next phase of your life is unstructured, and your success will be determined by the choices you make. Let me tell you as someone who was not popular in high school: It's better to be cooler later in life than earlier. Don't be concerned about what anyone thinks of you. It's your own view of yourself that matters. You can only live your life and lead your own course. Don't fight to become what you were not meant to be; just be whom you want to be. You don't owe the previous generation anything. How you live your life is up to you. You are not obligated to follow in the footsteps of either parent. Do what's right for you. You don't owe anybody anything. You owe it to yourself. Understand your own value. Know that you have something to offer both essential and valuable in any situation. Forge meaning and build your identity.

Pave your own path. You can't live for your dad or mom; you got to live for yourself. Skip the queue and be you. Blaze your own path and play the hand you were dealt. Your path to success is custom made. The path you take to whatever you're trying to accomplish will not look like anyone else's. Life is a marathon, and it requires nothing less than all of you. Life will throw you many twists and turns, but as long as you're trying, you're not failing. You must find your own path. Learn now the hard truth that you must always make the path for yourself. Every generation must define itself, and you are no different. There is no straight path to where you're going. You don't have to have it all figured out. It doesn't matter the road, what matters is that it's your road.

That's part of why I'm proud to be American. America saw itself as exceptional because it said we would not move by horses, but instead by train and automobile. Exceptional America broke the trends of the time and was not limited by the thinking of other people. So what is ordinary today (driving cars, flying, et cetera) was at a time, exceptional. America was founded by people tired of oppression who wanted to be the architects of their own destiny. So declare that you will break out of the box; you will go further than your father and mother because you will not be limited. You are exceptional. The question is will you run with the pack and fit in, or will you stand out and pave your own path?

People want to know what the ports of entry for success are? What leads to success? What's the key for considerable success? Is it just hard work or smart choices? What does it take to be successful in life? There's no simple answer because your path in life will rarely be a straight line. Everybody has their own formula. Every journey is different. You have to follow your dreams and work hard, and you will create your own beautiful path. Just don't worry about fitting into the mold; do what you do best and break the mold. Before the beginning of each school year, my mother always said to me "I hope you like them," not 'I hope they like you.' She knew that I had value to contribute as well to my classmates. Too often we're concerned about the opinions of others and we discount our own contributions. She never made me feel any different or think I was any different.

You can't swim without getting wet, and you can't be different without getting some backlash. So if you don't want to be criticized, do nothing. Whenever you gain success in anything, people will want to tear you down. However, it's essential to get to the point in your life where you stop listening to the noise, and you begin to be honest with yourself about the work you're doing. Always ask yourself if you are doing the best *you* can do. Know what you want, know what your end goals are, and visualize them. Most importantly, don't give a rat's ass about what anyone thinks of you. I used to care what others thought until one day I tried to pay my bills with their opinions. I couldn't do it. People don't have a hell or heaven to put you in. Don't worry about what people think, they don't do it very often. Real success is about freedom and the ability to live life on your terms.

Trust Yourself

It took me a while to trust myself and trust the voice inside of me and follow my intuition because, in order to trust yourself, you have to have a relationship with yourself. Always stay true to the most genuine, most real, most authentic parts of yourself. Ask yourself the basic questions of whom do I want to be? What inspires me? How do I want to give back? Then take a deep breath and trust yourself to know the answers for yourself and chart your own course and make your mark on the world. Don't shrink from risk and tune out the critics and cynics. History rarely ever yields to one person, but think, and never forget, what happens when it does. That can be you, and it should be you. It must be you.

Everything you need to know is already within you. All you need to do is trust yourself and act. Some of the best advice I ever received was "You already know the answer." Don't second guess yourself; You know more than you think you do. Do not overestimate the competition and underestimate yourself. There is so much creativity and genius inside you that will surface if you just slow down, get off the autopilot, be still, and listen to the voice inside you. You get so much advice from parents, teachers, the world, but you need to dig deep and figure out whom do you want to be. Not what but who. Be determined to be unique, to think big, and to dream big. Listen to yourself and write it down. Sometimes, to find the answers to questions you have to look within yourself. You will have questions about your path. You will have doubts about yourself, but if you listen to that small voice within you and are willing to be guided by it, you will be just fine, and life won't seem so unceremonious. Learn to trust that you know what you want for your life. Trust yourself to know and do what's best for you. Don't trust anyone over your own judgment. Trust your eyes when making decisions.

People will always expect you to fail first, but trust yourself anyway. Go all in and let your intuition guide you. Don't listen to what anyone says because things are changing all the time. Remember the intoxication is that you're breaking new ground. It takes courage to think for yourself. Maybe that's why so many of us fail to think for ourselves. It takes courage to have a dream for our lives that's our own, not our friends, or someone else's. Whatever you do, there will always be naysayers and people who want to silence you. But don't let them silence you or your intuition. Trust your gut and believe in yourself. More importantly, take a chance on your heart. I think it's a slippery slope to weigh too much of the good things or bad things people say about you; take it in stride and trust your inner voice. Value other people's opinions, just not over your own. If you want to be successful, be prepared to be doubted and tested. So learn to trust yourself when it comes to making decisions. Follow your heart, not your fear. You are stronger than your fear.

There are so many conflicting messages and information. You have to do what feels right and safeguard your gains.

Dream On

Let me ask you, where is the wealthiest place in the world? Rome? New York City? London? The most affluent area in the world is in the cemetery. It's the only place in the world that is full of unrealized dreams. People who wanted to become painters but were too afraid to. Musicians who kept their music inside them and didn't dare to venture forth. Politicians who never ran for office. The goal of our lives is to live a full life and pursue our dreams. This belief is so prevalent in our time that even the final book of the Bible, Revelations, consists of primarily dreams (albeit, both dreams and nightmares). Authored by John after he was exiled to Patmos, the Book of Revelations doesn't have any ethics or messages. It just consists of dreams and nightmares. So what are the dreams you have for yourself? What do you want for your life? I'm surprised at how often people don't even know what they want because they're so concerned with what others will think. I'm always amazed at how much people care about other people's approval over their own satisfaction. I want to encourage you not to live anyone else's dream. Inside all of us, there is something ours and ours alone, protect it.

During his commencement address to Stanford University in 2005, Steve Jobs was quoted saying, "Your time is limited so don't live it living someone else's life." Have a dream that's yours and yours alone. Oprah Winfrey mentioned a moment she had with

Sidney Poitier: “I was crying just weeping, and he told me you have to remember that you are carrying people’s dreams, and when you are carrying people's dreams, often they put burdens on you that are not yours to bear. You have to decide what your dream is for yourself.”[14] There are people who have dreams and hopes for us, but what are the dreams you have for your own life?

One of the problems with some people is that they want others to support their dream. They don't realize that no one owes them anything. It's their dream. They have to fight for it and fight to defend it. Don't ever depend on someone else to support your dream. Chase your dreams and be self-reliant. If you can dream it, you can achieve it. Don't expect anyone else to support you, it's your dream that you have to fight for, and your dreams are worth fighting for. Not everyone will respond or be receptive, and that's ok. If you have a dream, you need to protect it. Bet on yourself and bet on your dream. Dream a dream that is authentic to yourself. But the question is always the same: how do you take the invisible and make it visible? How do you turn your dreams into a reality? Parents do what they do because they believe a cruel world still has a place for their child’s dreams. My parents risked so much to keep my hopes alive. They used to tell my sister and me to “turn your dreams into a lifestyle. You can make your dreams a living reality." The older I became, the more I came to the realization it's time to live my dream. With all the sacrifices my parents made for me, the least I could do was achieve my dreams.

The Bible says in Proverbs 29:18, “Where there is no vision people perish.” Another way of reading that is dreams keep you alive. Purpose keeps you alive. Vision keeps you alive. So, the unintentional way you're holding yourself back is because you're not dreaming big enough. Dream big and bigger. Don't limit yourself. Have a long-term dream in mind; it doesn't have to realistic or specific. Just have some ideas about the general sense of direction in which you want to go. Take your dreams and connect them to your reality, and eventually a larger shared reality.

Some say, well there's a gap between my hopes for myself and the realities of my life. But one of these things is not like the other. Let your vision, not your circumstances, guide you. Don't be led by obstruction and setbacks, but be led by your dreams. Don't let anyone or anything stop you from reaching your dreams. This is why it's so important not to be afraid to dream big. Your dreams will feed you, clothe you, protect you, and direct you. Don't let anyone, not your family, not your loved ones, not your friends, tell you that the dream you have for yourself is impossible. It is possible. People don't determine your future; God does. You are who God says you are, and you can do what he says you can do, so just do your part. When a seed is planted in the ground, all you can do is water it. You can't control what the sun does, what the wind does, or what the locusts might do. All you can do is water it. Water your seed. Protect your dream and water your dream. The question is asked when to follow your dreams. I say when you can afford to fail, which is always. Always follow your dreams.

Dreams can come true, and dreams do come true. With hard work, sacrifices, and perseverance, you can turn your dreams into reality. People with imagination is what this world needs. Dare to dream big. If you put your mind to it and your heart to it, there's nothing you cannot achieve. If you can dream it, you can do it. Martin Luther King Jr. didn't say “I have a plan;” he said, “I have a dream.” That’s why it's important that you know what your purpose is and what direction you want to go is. It takes hard work, dedication, and tremendous sacrifice. So you have to love it because it's not going to be easy. However, if you work hard, dreams do come true.

I am where I am because I had a dream and it was made of everything that's made me. Don't follow your dream, lead it. Don't always chase the dream, catch the dream because sometimes when you chase something, you don't always get it. Whatever your dream, tell yourself you will catch it. Dreams without goals remain dreams and ultimately fuel disappointment. It's ok to dream big, and it's ok to realize those dreams. Whatever your dream, whatever your vision, take the steps towards it, trust yourself, believe in yourself, and don't give a damn about what anyone else thinks. If you can achieve your dreams on your own, your dreams are too low. You need something so big that only God can provide. When you step out on faith, that's when you see God's favor. Faith doesn’t make it easy, faith makes it possible. As you extend your reach towards your dreams, you will see that what once seemed unattainable is now within your grasp. You'll never get further than you can dream, so dream big. Increase your imagination and watch the flurry of activity.

Tackle big dreams; there's no competition. Make a list of every dream you have. These are not goals; they are themes. Have a dream and then communicate it and do it. Follow your dreams – say, "I'm going to live my dreams and fantasies." You need to have both dreams and the ability to imagine a better future. So be clear about your desires, dream big, and reach higher. Make it specific and big. Narrow your focus and get clear about what you want. Go after it as if your life depends on it. Why? Because it does. Ask big. Ask for your dreams and ask for dreams that seem impossible. James 4:3 in the Bible says, "You ask and do not receive because you ask amiss." In other words, you don't ask large enough. People just ask, Lord let me make rent this month, let me pay my bills. No, don't ask amiss; ask to set a new standard, ask for more. That's what releases your faith. This is the year for God to show out in your life. Look at 1 Chronicles 4:10. 'Jabez' means trouble, so whenever someone said his name, Jabez, they were saying hello trouble. However, the prayer of Jabez says, "Enlarge my territory; bless me indeed," and God granted the request of Jabez. You may have many reasons for where you are, but God is for you. God can thrust you further than you ever imagined. Ask in spite of what others tell you or what your circumstances are. Psalm 2:7-9 says that God will give us nations and continents. Stop having low expectations and ask for more. God is saying don't hold back; tell me your dreams; come boldly to the throne. Expect big. This is your moment.

Define your dream, put a reasonable timeline on it, and go for it. Put a bounty on your dreams. Your dreams cannot start without you. Go for it; if you don't somebody else will. The choice is clear, work on your dreams or you will work on someone else's. I want you to live your imagination, not your history. Dream your reality. I want you to know, from me to you, that your dreams matter. Your dreams matter because you matter. I want you to know that you belong, so don't be afraid. Be focused, be empowered, be hopeful. Every life is extraordinary, and it's up to you to take action in the direction of your dreams. Once you do, you'll be met halfway, I promise. A person without a vision for their future always returns to their past.

Take time for dream-setting. Dream-setting is the process of writing out a script of your ideal perfect life. It is this script that becomes the blueprint for your life. Don't be discouraged when things don't go the way you think. How many of us turned out the way we thought we would when we were kids? How many of us grow up to become astronauts or pilots or firefighters? We all do the best we can. So if I could I speak to Louis at 16, I would tell myself to be more kind to myself because there's already so much against me. Don't be so hard on yourself. I wish I had followed my dreams and not my fears earlier on. If there's a pressing on your heart, go for it and don't let anyone stop you. Dream big, set high goals, and work tirelessly towards them. Nothing is impossible.

Consider that I'm only writing this right now because someone thought that the personal computer was possible. I mean, who believed we could fly in 1900? No one cared or believed, but the Wright brothers did it. Without them, there would be no planes today. They knew that nothing is as real as a dream. Your dreams are a glimpse of reality. The world has been created by the ideas of unrealistic people. Those people have believed in possibilities, while most people believed it's impossible. I'm glad impossible is just an opinion. It's an opinion until it's done. Pablo Picasso said,

"Everything you can imagine is real." Where there's a will, there's a way. Just start small. Dream big but start small. Mighty oaks from little acorns grow. Ideas are the beginning of all achievement; they shape the course of history.

Don't be afraid of your dreams, of your ambitions, or even your ire. Those are incredibly powerful forces, but harness them and use them as a form of offense. Whatever your dreams are, I want to challenge you to dream even bigger. Wherever you have set your sights, set them higher; don't limit yourself. If it's worth doing, it’s worth doing big. Go hard or go home. Pursue big dreams. Those dreams will fuel your energy and passions. When you tackle big dreams, you will find there's no competition. You need to dream a bigger dream for yourself. Dream big, live bigger.

Are you ready to level up your life and dreams? The dream you have for you is nothing compared to the dream life has for you. Every success I have I attribute to leaning into the flow life has for me, and being open to it. So yes, dare to dream and pursue your goals, but stay available to the flow of the universe. Your goals and dreams will change in life; if they didn't, we all would be cowboys and princesses. Be open to where your dreams take you**.** Dreams don't show up between your eyes; they come from behind you. They sneak up on you. When you have a dream, it doesn't come screaming in your face saying 'this is who you are or this is what you should do.' Sometimes dreams whisper. What's more, sometimes the hardest thing to do is listen to your instincts, your human intuition. So every day be ready to listen to what whispers in your ear.

Life is short; live your dream and share your passion. I don't know if it's going to work out or how it's going to work out, but I believe it will. Protect your dream and keep going for your dream. Never give up on a dream because of the time it will take to achieve it. The time will pass anyway. Take the time to follow your dreams because your dreams are waiting for you. Pursuing your dreams will help you avoid distracting temptations. Be obsessed with your dream and pursue it relentlessly. Start living your dream out. Don't ever ask for permission to follow your dreams. All dreams are within reach; you just have to keep moving towards them. You can be everything you want to be, still. It's not too late. No matter if you have the wisdom of age or the energy of youth, regardless of your circumstance, you can make your success happen. The time to get started is now. There is no such thing as being too young or too old to do something. It's merely a matter of deciding what you want to do and taking the steps necessary to get there. The time to get started is now.

IT'S NEVER TOO LATE

- At 5, Mozart was already competent on keyboard and violin.
- At 6, Shirley Temple starred in "Bright Eyes." (After her career as a child star ended, she became a diplomat).
- At 12, Anne Frank wrote her wartime diary.
- At 13, Magnus Carlsen became the second-youngest grandmaster in the history of chess.

- At 14, Nadia Comăneci became the first female gymnast to be awarded a perfect score of 10 in an Olympic event.
- At 15, Tenzin Gyatso was recognized as the 14th Dalai Lama.
- At 17, Pele led Brazil to a World Cup victory.
- At 17, Alexander Hamilton was George Washington's right-hand man.
- At 19, Elvis Presley became a superstar and was later known as "The King."
- At 20, John Lennon performed at his first concert as a Beatle.
- At 22, Jesse Owens won four gold medals in the Berlin Olympics.
- At 23, Beethoven was already known as a piano virtuoso.
- At 24, Isaac Newton wrote *Philosophiæ Naturalis Principia Mathematica*, setting the foundations for classical mechanics.
- At 25, Roger Bannister broke the four-minute mile.
- At 26, Albert Einstein wrote the theory of relativity.
- At 28, Michelangelo created his sculptures *David* and *The Pietà.*
- At 29, Alexander the Great had created one of the largest empires of the ancient world.
- At 30, J. K. Rowling finished the manuscript of *Harry Potter and the Philosopher's Stone.*
- At 31, Amelia Earhart became the first woman to fly solo across the Atlantic.
- At 32, Oprah Winfrey launched her first talk show.

- At 33, Edmund Hillary became one of the first two people confirmed to have reached the summit of Mount Everest.

- At 34, Martin Luther King Jr. wrote his iconic "I Have a Dream" speech.

- At 35, Marie Curie (along with her husband, Pierre Curie) was awarded Nobel Prize in Physics.

- At 36, Wilbur Wright, together with his brother Orville, built the world's first successful airplane.

- At 37, Vincent Van Gogh died virtually unknown after creating the paintings that would later establish him as a major artist.

- At 38, Neil Armstrong walked on the moon.

- At 40, Mark Twain wrote *The Adventures of Tom Sawyer.*

- At 41, Christopher Columbus made landfall in the Americas.

- At 42, Rosa Parks refused to obey a bus driver's order to give up her seat.

- At 43, John F. Kennedy became the 35th president of the United States.

- At 45, Henry Ford manufactured the first Model T automobile.

- At 46, Suzanne Collins wrote *The Hunger Games*.

- At 50, Charles Darwin published *The Origin of Species*.

- At 51, Leonardo da Vinci painted the *Mona Lisa*.

- At 52, Abraham Lincoln became the 16th president of the United States.

- At 53, Ray Kroc bought the McDonalds franchise, which then comprised eight restaurants.

- At 54, Theodore Geisel wrote *The Cat in the Hat* under the pen name Dr. Seuss.

- At 57, Chesley "Sully" Sullenberger III successfully crash-landed US Airways Flight 1549 in the Hudson River with no fatalities.

- At 61, Colonel Harland Sanders granted the first Kentucky Fried Chicken franchise.

- At 62, J. R. R. Tolkien published *The Lord of the Rings*.

- At 69, Ronald Reagan became the 40th president of the United States (and the oldest to date).

- At 70, Jack LaLanne--handcuffed and shackled--towed 70 rowboats for a mile against strong winds and currents.

- At 75, Nelson Mandela became president of South Africa.[15]

KNOW WHAT YOU WANT

Be honest; you already know what you want. You already know what to do. You're just stuck on THINKING about doing it. Why? Because you keep building up in your head what it means to take action. You're focused on writing the entire screenplay instead of a single sentence. If you want to make any permanent and lasting change in your life, willpower won't get you there. If you're going to get healthier, improve your relationships, or whatever; willpower won't help you achieve any of those things. Making personal progress and achieving success is best approached like you are overcoming addiction – because that's what you're doing. Helia said, "Willpower is for people who are still uncertain about what they want to do." So if you have to exert willpower to do something, then there is obviously an internal conflict. You want to eat the cake, but you also want to be healthy. That's the tension between your environment versus your goal. I believe that once you make a decision, the universe conspires to make it happen. If your life requires willpower, you haven't fully determined what you want. After you make a decision, the internal debate is over. After you decide what you want, the decision is made; thus, all future decisions regarding that matter have also been made. Period.

The truth is if you don't know what you want in and from life, you will be passive and dysfunctional. What's more, you will resent people who aren't this way. The best thing you can do to improve the world is not to "help others," but to have passion for a goal. To be successful, you must decide exactly what you want to accomplish. You can't equivocate. Cato said, "He who hesitates is lost." You need to have a clear picture of whom you want to be and how you're going to get there. Life needs to be lived by design, not default. In *Alice in Wonderland*, Alice asked the Cheshire cat, who was sitting in a tree, "What road do I take?" The cat asked, "Where do you want to go? "I don't know," Alice answered. "Then," said the cat, "it really doesn't matter, does it?" You can't get lost if you don't know where you're going. You can do or be anything you want to do or be; all you have to do is make up your mind.

Too many people are playing fast and loose without a sense of direction. You need structure, you need direction; otherwise, it's wasted talent. The worst thing you can do is not have structure, because then you wake up without a sense of purpose or sense of direction. The most important principle in life is to know where you are going. Make sure you're sure. Map out a timeline for yourself. Plan out the next 12 to 18 to 24 months of your career. Make it a continuum, like Isaac Newton's spectrum of light, of who you are today. It is not who you will be in the future. Don't float aimlessly on a sea of possibility; know what you want and whom you want to be. Have a clear vision of what you want your life to look like and whom you want to be. You can't confuse the universe. You have to have a plan for your life, a strategy, because no one else is going to do it for you. What do you want to do? You can do anything, but you can't do everything. Make it clear and specific. You need a detailed understanding of what you want and where you want to go. Some people don't know if they're coming or going. While most people aren't a one-pitch pitcher, throwing the fastball, they do many things well, like throwing the curve or the change. You can't have a hero complex or be a jack-of-all-trades being everything to everyone. Be focused and get clear on where you're going and how you're getting there. Ask yourself, "What is the aim of the pursuit? What do I want? What is my supreme desire? What are my expectations? Which of the things I desire are within reach? If not now, when? Will there be any left for me? What am I following? What am I after?" We're all running to something, and we're all running from something. Just know in which direction you're going. People respond well to people who know what they want.

If you know what you want and you have a sense of direction with your life, and desire to progress, it will happen to you. It will happen for you. The gravity of life doesn't always go against you. Ralph Waldo Emerson writes, “The world makes way for a man who knows where he is going.” When you know what you want, you know what to ignore. If you don't know where you're going, you'll end up somewhere else. You have to know what you want and go after it and demand nothing less than that. That way you can bend time and bend the universe and command your reality to be what you decide it to be. Frankly, sometimes it can be smart to be shallow; to know what you want and go after it relentlessly. Mike McLaren said, "If you want to be something, be conceited about it.”

Know what your end goals are and visualize them. Don't apologize for who you are, or what you want. Choose what's best for you and follow your own rules. I was in Hong Kong a couple of years ago and didn't want to go out to a night club a particular night, and my friend told me, "You don't like clubbing, that's fine, but play by your own rules when you do. Say, ‘when I do go clubbing, we'll only stay for an hour, I'll only drink what I want, et cetera.’" That was incredibly useful for me. Even though you may not like something, you can still make choices that put you in control. I am now living fully on my own terms and absolutely loving it. Unfortunately, most successful people have fluid career paths. You do not need to have your career or life all mapped out. However, what is essential is that you keep your eyes open for new opportunities, stay open to change, but play by your terms.

Sadly, so many people get pushed along in the “system” of life because they don’t know what they want to do, so they pretty much let their careers be chosen for them. Most people only half-heartedly decide what they want. You have to get really clear about what it is you want. It’s always a question of how badly you want it. Figure out what you want, get rid of poverty thinking, then ask for it. Let the world know you’re there and let them know why you’re there and what you want. Determine what you want and then burn your vision into your mind on a daily basis. As a caveat, be careful what you ask for. The things that are hurting you the most are often the things you wanted. People tell me all the time, they want that Lamborghini or that mansion or they want fame, but **How much do you know about what you want?** If you ask God for more, you get more of everything. More money, more problems, more enemies. So be careful what you ask for. A new level comes with a new devil. The more blessings, the more burdens. It's just my hope that you know who you are, know what you want, and know where you are going.

ESSE QUAM VIDERI

(BE REAL)

We live in a world where lust is mistaken for love and chaos is misconstrued for order; where nothing is sacred anymore, and clothes wear people and not the other way around. Our world values appearance over substance, celebrity over character, short term gains over lasting achievements. What's new today is obsolete tomorrow.

You can look vogue on the outside and vague on the inside. Everybody is dressed up and going nowhere. People look good but have no direction, no sense of purpose for their lives, nor do they know what they're doing. Sometimes people hook their self-worth on their appearance, tying beauty to their perception of themselves. We compare how we look to how other people look and we make a decision about whether we are much better or much worse. Those comparisons can have negative or positive emotional and psychological consequences. We tend to think of ourselves in terms of appearance or abilities. It's still socially acceptable to say things to others that we wouldn't say to ourselves. We don't filter our judgments of ourselves in the same way that we filter judgments of others, and we're in desperate need of kindness to one another. So the question is how do you stay relevant in an ever-changing world? Do you lose or keep your identity in doing so, especially when nothing is meaningful? Real success is not what you have; it's who you are. You don't have to be born on third base to be a success in your career. All you have to do is care, be committed to the work, and be honest about it. Be authentic to who you are and authentic about what you care about it. Success is about being real. Find the value within yourself.

The best advice I ever got was to be me. So here I am. This is me, all of me. Moreover, for the first time in my life, it's honest and real. No charity no pity, just me, and it's pure. It took me a while to accept myself and that's freedom. Cars, homes, and money are not freedom. To be, rather than to seem, is freedom. Happiness and success come in greater abundance when you start loving who you are and accepting yourself entirely. From that arena of acceptance, you can more readily achieve a deeper connection to the world around you and move towards your highest potential. You don't need a new personality; you only need to open your eyes to who you really are, which is someone amazing, talented, and important to the world. A healthy dose of self-love and self-care is critical to happiness. You can't experience a happy life and reject yourself continually. Success is about discovering – usually through trial and error – ways to integrate different aspects of your life so that success is not achievable at the expense of the rest of your life, but because of commitments to your interior life, home, and in your community. Success is achievable to you when you can be real, be whole, and be innovative. Being real is about acting with authenticity in order to clarify what's important to you. To be whole is acting with integrity, witnessing how the various aspects of your life (community, work, home, self) all influence one another. This allows you to be innovative; you can act with creativity to experiment ways for things to get done that are good for you and those around you.

When asked which is more important to you, to be admired or loved, what should be most important is to be real. Nothing is perfect, not even me, and you don't have to be. You just have to be real. From *The Velveteen Rabbit* he says, "You become. It takes a long time. That's why it doesn't happen often to people who break easily or have sharp edges, or who have to be carefully kept. Generally, by the time you are Real, most of your hair has been loved off, and your eyes drop out, and you get loose in the joints and very shabby. However, these things don't matter at all, because once you are Real, you can't be ugly, except to people who don't understand."[16] Many of us, if we were to be honest, before we die want to be completely ourselves. Nothing lasts forever, not sorrows, not beauty. Everyone gets older, eyes bag, you age, flowers bloom and die, everything passes, and it's just a matter of time. However, what truly lasts is your authentic power of being yourself and at peace with the flow inside you. What is real and what is lasting is who you are and what you were meant to bring.

The greatest privilege in our lifetime is to be who we are. Run your race and be comfortable with whom God made you to be. Learn to be comfortable with who you are so that wherever you go, you will know that you belong. No apologies or excuses. Be nobody but yourself. You can't be anyone or anything other than who you are anyway. We are who we are. Consider that sharks are born swimming. Nobody can be more than they are. Be secure in who you are forever and always. You have to accept the fact that not everyone will like you; you're not going to win everyone over. Not everyone is going to celebrate your existence, nevertheless, own who you are. You know yourself best. In a world where people have many choices, your individual story may be the deciding factor. You can have anything you want in this world, just make sure it's your own.

Emotionally intelligent people don't set perfection as their objective or prioritize perfection. They understand that perfection doesn't exist. Human beings are fallible by nature, and when perfection becomes your goal, there's always a nagging sense of failure. Rather than lamenting everything you failed to accomplish or what you should have done differently, you should be enjoying what you were able to achieve. We are not meant to be perfect, we are meant to be whole. We're supposed to be complete and whole, and you can't be whole if you're trying to be perfect. Salvador Dali said, "Have no fear of perfection. You 'II never reach it." I'm not perfect, and I never will be, and I can't tell you enough how much of weight that's been lifted. What I can be though is whole and complete, fulfilling my purpose. John Steinbeck said, "And now that you don't have to be perfect, you can be good." The secret is that there is no secret. Just be yourself. You can't make the public like you. Love what you do and live to make yourself proud. Truth > Trend. You don't need to be like me; you only need to be like you. Authenticity wins every day. Know how you contribute uniquely and the value you bring to the table. Realize that people don't care as much as you think they might, so be who you are. Go back to the natural order of things. To express yourself as you are is the most important thing. What people want is to be able to express themselves.

Ultimately, we're all just looking for a way to express ourselves. That's why I like martial arts. It's a way to express yourself. So be authentic, be real, and be honest. Just be yourself, and everyone will adjust to that. Stay centered in who you are and stand for what you know to be true, and everything will fall into place. You need to be at peace with yourself whether times are good or bad, things go your way or don't. It's character assassination when you're trying to be someone you're not. When all you do is try to fit in, all you do is negate the difference our differences make. Every time I try to be someone I'm not, it blows up in my face. I've realized if you're not who you are, it doesn't come across well. You can be the fastest, you can be the strongest, you can be the smartest, or you can be yourself.

Towards the end of our lives we can feel unfinished in a way. Our lives are about completion. I want to feel at the end of my life, a sense of completion, that I did what I wanted to do. I loved, I lived, I fought, I won, I lost, I overcame. But the only way to accomplish that is to be real. I enjoy watching *American Idol.* A core lesson from that show is that everybody wants to be somebody and everybody wants to be validated, whether it's the audience clapping or the judge saying their performance was terrific. Everybody is looking for a new life, a better life. We all have a desire to be noticed. To be "somebody." The best thing you can do to achieve that is to be real and be authentic. That's how you get noticed, being different is what makes you stand out. Sooner or later your truth will be acknowledged. Now, fame is fleeting, and it's hollow, and life is full of short stories and tall tales. Only what is real will last, and you will last. Power is not revealed by striking hard or often, but by striking true. Being real is true power. If you're real, fame, money, and power comes.

The singers on *American Idol* should know that a singer is nothing more than an artist. As an artist, you can't live in a revisionist place. All you can do as an artist is talk about humanity. Humanity is messy. People are messy. It's more important to be concerned with image and message than with execution. As artists, we want people to see us for what we really are: complicated. The human condition is complicated, but authenticity works. So you have to find what works for you. Decide to be your best, and whatever happens,

happens; at least it's authentic. No matter what happens to you in life, stay true to yourself. When you acknowledge all aspects of your authentic self, including shortcomings and counterproductive tendencies, it gives you license to do your best work.

I can't stress how important it is to be comfortable being authentic. In my adult life I've realized I can have money, cars, and clothes but it means nothing if I can't be who I am. True freedom is about being able to be yourself. My hope is to give you the gift of going second. If I show you who I am first, then hopefully you'll join me and be yourself, and watching me be myself will make you want to be more of yourself. I believe if you let people be themselves when they perform, it's *them* that shows up. You can't outproduce your own self-image. You don't have to be anybody for anybody; all you have to do is be you for you, and all I have to do is be me for me. Don't be anyone else or like anyone else. You just need to be more of who you are.

3

DISCOVER YOUR GENIUS

"Where your treasure is, there your heart will be also."
– Matthew 6:21

WHAT IS PASSION?

How did you start your day today? Did you wake up thinking, "wow, I get to run my own enterprise today!" and jump out of bed capped full of energy and expectation? No? Don't worry, many people didn't. So many of us have been told to "follow your passion," but you've also seen enough of the ruins of people who have failed at their passion to know that being passionate alone is not enough to create success. Any success is built on action and hard work, and passion helps aid that effort. I'm here to tell you the truth about passion.

Passion can either be a thing that you love to do or can be the feeling you get from doing something. Do a thought experiment with me. Imagine it's Friday and you've worked your ass off all week doing things you don't enjoy and producing results that you don't really care about. The only thing good about this week, in fact, is that you made a decent amount of income. However, it's the weekend and yet you're too tired to do your regular TGIF happy dance because when Monday comes, you have to go back and do it all over again. Ok, now compare that feeling to how you feel when you performed the same tasks and pulled in the same income, but your week was spent producing results that make you proud and brings you joy and positively impacts the lives of people you care about. That's the *energy* of passion. That energy keeps you going when tasks are unpleasant, money isn't coming in, and your physical energy is all but gone. Passion is the energy that pushes you over the finish line, that keeps artists chiseling or painting. Passion is your inner fire. It's not complicated, and you should promise yourself to choose work that fires you up inside. Moreover, if the work doesn't fire you up, connect with something in the work (the outcomes, your abilities) to get fired up about. Wherever your fire is, whatever your heart's desire, wherever you find oxygen, go do that.

WHY PASSION IS IMPORTANT

As a parent, you want your kids to be passionate and care deeply because you know how invaluable having that level of passion is. You know that the world can be cruel, and the only way to make it through a cruel world is by having love. You want them to make a choice based on their passions and interests, not on what others are telling them to do. It doesn't work that way. You wind up living a life for all the wrong reasons, and you never get the most out of it. Always think about why you are doing what you're doing. It's not about the money, it's about the joy of the journey. The most successful people don't have jobs; they have passions. So if you wake up in the morning saying I'm going to work, then you're doing it wrong, and I will submit to you that you need to reinvent yourself and find your passion. Any list of traits of "successful" people almost always has passion at the top of the list, and the reason is simple; if you love what you're doing, it will be much easier to push through nearly every setback.

There are two types of people in this world: strivers and seekers. Strivers innately know what they want to do and whom they want to be from an early age, like Michael Jackson. On the other hand, the majority of people are seekers. Seekers discover what they love. The key is to do what successful people do and follow your heart, not your wallet. When I worked in the Parliament of the United Kingdom, my Member of Parliament told me, “If you can imagine doing anything else, you should be doing anything else because this job takes a lot out of you.” If you’re not passionate about what you do, you might want to consider doing something else. Steve Jobs elaborated on this point saying, “They say passion is important and it’s so true because it's so hard, and if you’re not passionate you're going to give up because you're sane. Who would keep working hard at something they don't care about."[17] It took me a while to figure it out, but it’s all about passion. If you’re not passionate, you're compromising yourself every day.

You have to really love what you do. You have to have such a strong passion for it that you will break through any barrier and jump over any hurdle to see your vision through. Passion is the fuel that will give you the energy to run through every blockade placed in your path. Unless you are prepared to be obsessed, you probably won't be that successful. It takes a fire in your belly to make it. When you don't have genuine passion, everything else suffers. It becomes not an economic crisis, but a crisis of the heart. If you're passionate about something, go for it because people are great at what they love and when they are the happiest. It's essential you don't see work as work. It has to be something you enjoy. So have a passion for your life. Successful people realize that any goal isn't worth arriving at if they don't appreciate the journey. They love what they do. If you don't love what you do you won't succeed. It's as simple as that. However, you also have to work hard at your passion. Stay as late as you can and always be the first person to work in the morning. This becomes a lot easier if you love your job. Understand that putting in the extra time will move you a lot closer to what you want to do.

You have to enjoy what you're doing. You won't be very good if you don't and you will feel like you're contributing something worthwhile if you do. Living through life without passion is the cardinal sin. Passion is required. You have to love what you do because it's tough, and the only thing that's going to get you through is love. Love what you do or don't do it. The passion has to be real where nothing will stop you. You have to have the perseverance to stick with it. Don't just have passion, also have tenacity. Doing something you love will make you work harder at it because it needs to be a labor of love. Your passion-work will be the hardest thing you will ever love. Successful people know it's easier if you do something you love. Find something you're good at and love to do, and be great at it; work hard at it for the sake of its own pleasure, and contribute your gifts generously and sincerely.

When it comes to being successful or taking your business to the next level, you have to be very passionate about what you're doing. It's not just about selling products or services; it's about empowering your customers and giving them something that makes their lives easier. The passion for inspiring others has to get you excited, and if you don't love what you're doing, you're not going to work as hard as someone who does. You’ve got to have energy, a spark, a vibration about you that's magnetic, that gets others excited. The key to success is enthusiasm because enthusiasm creates action; you don't get enthusiasm if you're not passionate. Enthusiasm is infectious. More importantly, passion keeps you honest. It makes sure that what you’re doing is for the right reasons. Moreover, without passion, you don't have energy, and without energy, you don't have anything. Follow your passion. Passion fuels your mission. Skills can be taught, but passion cannot. Empowered people pursue their passion relentlessly. Now there will always be someone who is more naturally talented than you, but whatever you lack in talent you can make up for in passion.

Finally, passion makes work fun. Fun is one of the most important components of pursuing success. If you're not enjoying yourself, it might be time to stop doing what you're doing and call it quits. If you’re engaged and having fun, you will enjoy your work and do a better job. When you're surrounded by people you love, and you're doing what you love, it doesn't matter how much money you make or where you live. So have fun with everything you do and be confident in all you do. Inspire others with your passion, and have fun. There's so much fun to be had so if you're having fun, you're winning. The world's a playground, living your passions makes it fun, and play is the business of adults. Fun is the destination. The oldest struggle of our time is that between reason and passion, and right now passion is winning out.

HOW TO FIND YOUR PASSION

Your life is about being in "flow" or being in the zone. "Where people are utterly absorbed in what they are doing, their awareness is merged with their actions," according to Dr. Daniel Goleman.[18] Things we love doing get us in 'flow.' The things we do in our free time get us in flow. It may be a sport, a hobby, or being with your kids. The goal is alignment, to get in alignment with your life's purpose. Mihaly Csikszentmihalyi, a psychologist and author of *Flow: The Psychology of Optimal Experience*, notes that as human beings we are happiest when we are operating in a "state of flow."[19] This state of flow is where our work is so enjoyable and absorbing that we lose track of time. This state of finding our genius and creating flow comes from having a clear goal, feedback on that goal, and the ability for us to find that sweet spot of challenge. This kind of thinking comes naturally to you and is essential for a specific kind of problem-solving. Begin to start thinking about those moments in your life where you feel "in the zone" or "in flow." Ask yourself what thinking got you here. When you identify that, and you have your genius, this is where your best work manifests itself, and your passions make room for you. First, find your area of specialty and become really good in this area. Each one of us is excellent at something. The hard part is figuring out what that is; you have to try and experience many things. Secondly, push yourself every day to become the best in that area. Next, make sure people know you are an expert in that field. Irreversibly, take the initiative.

Focus on discovering your passion rather than obsessing over the correct path, or following what others tell you. This and only this will take you where you want to go. Take an opportunity from time to time to imagine yourself at the end of your life. Take stock and then recommit on the here and now to the things you value most. This will ensure you have a life you respect. Find something you love to do so much that you can't wait for the sun to rise to do it all over again. Find that thing that gives you joy. Figure out your passion. It's possible to do what you love and also get paid for it, but first, you need to nail down just what that is.

I had a friend who wanted to be a sous chef. I asked her if she ever considered volunteering for a local bakery over the summer. She didn't believe it would be possible, but it was, and she ended up being paid for it. Begin to pursue the career of your dreams. Remember that you own your career. In this world, nobody else is going to make career decisions for you or live your life for you. Only you know precisely what motivates you or makes you happy. Make it a point to know yourself more deeply, and what will and what won't work for you in a career. Success is never easy, but your odds go way up if you enjoy what you're doing. In fact, the people I know who do the best do work related to their experience, not their education. Find something that is interesting to you because you tend to excel at the things you're interested in – and do that. You have nothing to lose. Prioritize passion. If you do what you love, everything else takes care of itself. When I was playing basketball, I wasn't really thinking about wins and losses, I just wanted to play free and stay in the moment, and the wins took care of themselves.

Ask Yourself

I have realized that just telling people to follow their passions, without guidance or any other advice, only sends them on a dream chase that can often become harmful in the long-term. Usually it's more prudent to think about what excites you and follow that. Ask what makes your heart skip a beat. The saddest thing is wasted potential. Any employer wants to see if there is any fire present when they are hiring. They need passion from you. So figure out what gives you life. Boredom is an offshoot of melancholy. Ask yourself what makes your heart beat like a drum? What represents the best of what you do? You must gravitate naturally to what your heart yearns for. Ask yourself what makes you excited. What turns you on? Where is your strike zone? What subjects are you literate in? What moves you? What gets you out the bed each morning? Where does your passion lay? What gives you life? What's your passion? It's not about choosing the 'right' path; it's about knowing what ignites your passion. What are you passionate about, and what are you willing to do to go after that? It has to be something you're passionate about because otherwise, you won't have the perseverance to see it through. It's easier if you do something you love.

Continue asking yourself: How do you find your happiness? What do you wake up wanting to accomplish every day? What drives you? What are you excited by? What do you care about? What are you working towards? Why do you do the work you do? If life could be perfect, what would it look like? How do you recharge? When are you the happiest? What are you passionate about? Are you any good at your passion? Are you constantly falling in and out of love with your work? It cannot be the passions and joys of others, but rather your own. What's your first love? Go back to that and do it for yourself. Trust yourself to know what 'you' needs. You have to ask yourself if it's what you're passionate about or if it's what you're gifted at. You can be as passionate as you want, but if you're not gifted at it, you won't be as successful as you otherwise might be. For example, some keys for success include loving what you do and being great at it. The second part is important: being great at it. There are some things I love to do, but I am not great at. I'm not great at interior design, so that's not the best use of my time. So be true to yourself when uncovering what you should be doing. Your calling is where your joy meets the world's need. You've got to love it because it's a challenge; the challenge is what you have to love. What's the intersection of your strengths, aspirations, and market realities? Whatever it is you want, it's out there. However, it's not going to fall into your lap; you have to go get it.

Drill Down

Some athletes say passion is being "in the zone." Psychologists call it a state of "flow." Musicians describe it as being "in the pocket." It's that transcendent experience when time slows down for a performer or artist and everything clicks. Passion can sometimes be very nebulous and tangential. What's important is to get very concrete regarding your future. From personal experience, I know that not everything I am passionate about are things that I should devote my energy to or pursue as a career. You can be passionate about many things, but it doesn't mean that's where you should be putting your efforts. It may be exciting and something you want, but it may not be for you now. Instead, it's more important to carefully research professions you may seem passionate about before an all-out commitment to that role because some work only appears to be glamorous or appealing until you are doing it day in and day out. Passion is lovely to have, but talent, strategy, and determination also must accompany it.

Keep Searching

One of the big mistakes people make is trying to force an interest on themselves. You don't choose your passions; your passions choose you. Maybe you can caress a note like Whitney Houston, or perhaps you can inspire like Nelson Mandela. Whatever your gift is, whatever your passion is, whatever your love is, follow it. Find your field of play. You have to be lucky to find passion, but even more fortunate to find passion at an early age. For many people, it takes time to find their passion. Don't wait for passion or purpose to find you. Get up, get out, explore. Find it yourself and then hold onto it with both hands. Scratch that itch. Find whatever interests, because whatever interests is interesting. You have to use a lot of intuition and do what feels natural to you. Rumi said, "Respond to every call that excites your spirit." Whatever you respond to is perfect.

We are born pleasure seekers. Babies love the taste of sweet and hate the taste of bitter, and they like smooth surfaces rather than rough ones. Within us are impulses, appetites, and drives. Follow them. If you haven't found what you're looking for, don't settle. If you haven't found what you want or what your passion is, keep looking. Go back to your instincts, pay attention to persistent and constant hunches. Trusting your gut makes all the difference. Your passion is there; it's alive, well, and kicking. You just have to work for it. If something isn't up to your standards, don't settle. Keep taking risks until you find your passion. Be mobile. If it isn't working, try something different. If you're miserable and would rather be anywhere doing anything else then what you are doing, it's safe to say it's time for a change. Don't even wait. Regret is the most tragic aspect in life; the best way to avoid it is to know yourself, face your fear, and follow your heart. Always. Keep trying new things until you find something that sparks an interest, then do that. Passion is something that's hard to discover purely through introspection. You also have to have experiences. You have to learn in real time and through experiences, what makes you tick.

Let Love Guide You

People generally do well with things they enjoy doing, and they generally do poorly with things they don't enjoy doing. Love will make it easy, and a lack of love will make it hard. That's why it's so important to love your work. Work is supposed to be enjoyable. If you do something you love, then it's not work. It's only work if it's something you don't love. If you love what you do, then you will thrive when the inevitable challenges arise. If you're not passionate about what you're doing, it's hard to be successful at it. Always be in love. Always have a passion for life, a love for something. Focus on what you love, not on other people's opinions. That's why the Bible says in Philippians 4:8, "whatsoever things are true and pure, think on these things." Focus on the love, not the loss. As long as you find something you love to do, it doesn't matter where it takes you because you're in love. So your passion cannot be wrong, because you're in love. Few people are actually passionate about their life or their work. We live for the weekend, and we live for the holidays. Why not do something you love every day of the week. We all want to be someone who does what they love and knows what they want. Once you have what you need, more money doesn't make it better. Love is the only consequential element.

It's your right to listen to your gut, and it's your right to follow your passions. Everyone has to get through life following their own path and doing what's best for them. Everything isn't for everybody. Everyone isn't meant to be a musician or an office manager or an entrepreneur. You have to have that itch in your blood. People have to make up their own mind on what's best for them. Find what you love, have a passion for it, and go after it relentlessly. It's love. It's not rocket science. It's not the championship, it's not the money, it's not the fame. It's the sheer love of it. The rewards, the money, the fame just come. Success is not the key to happiness; happiness is the key to success. When you love what you're doing, you will be successful. Follow your bliss. Your success is built on fire not flash. Your emotions are vital to success. Passion is a beautiful thing. When you're working it's not a question of whether you would do this for a living, but whether you would do it for not a living. Would you do it for free? What's worth doing even if you fail? Don't let your head attack your heart; follow your passion and your instinct.

Follow your passion and do what you love. Just know that passion and persistence will get you through anything. There are so many paths to success, but at the end of the day, all that matters is what makes your heart sing. The key is to believe in what you're doing and have a passion for it and get a team to carry out that vision. Don't chase the money; chase your passion. If we don't enjoy each day, then our performance eventually will suffer. Dr. Robert Holden, a British positive psychology expert, emphasizes that enjoyment is mostly a choice not purely determined by our circumstance.[20] The best performers and most successful people choose to enjoy every day. Don't waste time on work that you don't enjoy. It's an evident axiom that you cannot and will not succeed in something that you don't like. Patience, dedication, and drive come easily when you love what you do. Don’t procrastinate on this; follow your love(s) today. Whatever you love, you are.

Follow Your Heart

Follow your heart for success. Always follow your heart. Don't do anything your heart says no to. Our soul never lies to us; it's the brain that's the real culprit, it's our thoughts. True grief comes when we override our soul's decisions. Feel your heart, then build your life. If you follow your heart, do things out of love, and don't do it for money or any other motivation, then everything else will take care of itself. Do things because it's what you want to do. What I realized was that when I follow my heart, if I follow my feelings, everything turns out ok and I'm able to live with myself. We try to control everything in our lives, but sometimes you have to let go and go with what's inside you.

During his commencement address to Stanford University in 2005, Steve Jobs said, "Remembering that you are going to die is the best way to avoid the trap of thinking you have something to lose. You are already naked, so there's no reason not to follow your heart. Your time is limited so don't waste it living someone else's life. Don't be trapped by dogma, which is living with results of other people's thinking. Don't let the noise of others’ opinions drown out your own inner voice. Most important, have the courage to follow your heart and intuition. They somehow already know what you truly want to become.” Only do what your heart tells you; everything else is commentary. Most feedback isn't constructive, whether it's positive or negative. Listen to your heart: it won't ever lead you astray. When conflicted, go with your heart. Whatever you do, go with your heart. Wherever you go, go with your heart. Take your heart's advice because it's wisdom to believe the heart. Let your heart be the compass. Genghis Khan said, "No friend is better than your own wise heart. Although there are many things you can rely on, no one is more reliable than yourself. Although many people can be your helper, no one should be closer to you than your own conscious." The best path we can choose for ourselves follows our hearts more than our heads.

In *The Little Prince*, we see that "Growing up is not the problem, forgetting is;" forgetting that you were once a child, forgetting what brought you pleasure. *The Little Prince* tells us that "only with the heart can one see rightly; what is essential is invisible to the eye." Find a way to do what you find exciting. If it sounds exciting to you, that's your heart telling you something, so listen and find a way to do it. Do what's in your heart. Pursue your passions. You know what's best for you, just follow your heart. Listen to the gut and not the mind. Your gut is a second mind. Follow your heart and intuition. Not your mind, ego, or wallet. Your heart knows things your head can't explain. Follow your own heart and don't listen to the naysayers.

Fyodor Dostoyevsky wrote in *Crime and Punishment*, "To go wrong in one's own way is better than to go right in someone else's." So do it now. That podcast? Launch it. That blog? Start it. That book? Write it. That idea? Flesh it out. That app? Develop it. That gift? Put it to use. That life? Live it. Joseph Campbell said, "Follow your bliss. If you do follow your bliss, you put yourself on a kind of track that has been there all the while waiting for you, and the life you ought to be living is the one you are living. When you can see that, you begin to meet people who are in the field of your bliss, and they open the doors to you. I say, follow your bliss and don't be afraid, and doors will open where you didn't know they were going to be. If you follow your bliss doors will open for you that wouldn't have opened for anyone else." I think that's why the most intelligent kids, the most brilliant kids, do the worst in schools. They are busy pursuing their passions and not falling into a strident academic structure. Do what you feel obliged to do; follow your intuition and instinct. If your first thought in the morning is "ugh," it may be time for a change. Sometimes following your heart means losing your mind. Control your mind to listen to your heart. Trust your instincts and do what needs to be done. Trust your gut, and your heart will tell you what to do. Listen to your heart because that's the voice of God and your voice is God's ear. So, if you do what's in your heart, you'll be just fine.

YOUR PASSIONS WILL CHANGE

Some of the time, you're not going to like your passion. In general "liking what you do" doesn't mean enjoying yourself and having a pleasant time all of the time. You will find that your passions will change and evolve over time. I like going to Disneyland, but I don't like riding Space Mountain the whole time. It's not that I'm not having fun, but I want to ride something else.

Moreover, that's the way life is. Maybe we're having fun in one regard, but we want to change things up. Your passions will change, and it's ok to change your dreams. Your passions at 16 won’t be your passions at 30. You need to be agile by pursuing your passion but maintaining perspective along the way. Remember that you won't end up where you start. Nobody ends up in the first job they chose out of college, so find something that is interesting to you, because you will tend to excel at things you're interested in. You have nothing to lose, so don't wait. Our lives are constantly in flux. Events change our perception, and our perspectives change with experience. It's only natural that our professional and personal goals and interests will evolve over time. So don't feel pressured to find that "one thing" that you love to do, or to do it until the end of time. Life is long, and your career is a marathon, not a sprint, so don't hesitate to pivot or change direction when needed. The older you get, the more you realize attraction comes in different forms. I'm not attracted to the same things at 30 that I was at 18. I'm 30 now, and I'm no longer trying to attract pretty faces. I'm attracted to intelligence, I'm attracted to clarity, I’m attracted to passion.

DO WHAT YOU LOVE

In life, fear is as powerful a motivator as love. We might do things out of fear the same as if we did things out of love. Regardless, just make sure you are doing things out of love. People will fight much harder for their interests than their fears. Do things out of love rather than fear. Only do the things that you love, and believe in their importance. Do more of what you love and less of what you don't love. Start with the love. You have to love what you do, and it should hurt. Artists will tell you they do better work when it hurts. You have to risk, and it has to hurt a little for you to fully grasp all this will entail.

Do what you love and put one foot in front of the other. After enough steps, something good will happen. Work what you're passionate about because then you can control your own destiny. Don't live a wasted life, love every second, and love what you do. If you're doing something you don't love, do something else. Don't waste a second. Above all else, live and live more abundantly. Choose your own path to travel. Always. Do what makes your heart beat fastest. Exude passion; do what satisfies you. Declare that you will not live by what you see alone, or what you feel, but will live by choice. Choose to live with intention. Find your passion, harness your passion, live your passion, and live your purpose. Unfortunately, we don't have forever. This is your life; do what you love and do it often.

The best advice I can give you is to assume that whatever career you're in is going to be a massive failure. This way, you're not making decisions based on money or superficiality. You're only making it based on doing what you love. I have a friend who is a police officer. Being a cop is such a thankless job, but he loves it and it's who he always wanted to be. Whatever you do, don't let money be the deciding factor. Arranging your life around money will not make you happy. Focus on your passion, not your paycheck. Be obsessed with what you love but make your work purpose-centered.

Do things that are purposeful and lasting. In ancient times when someone died, the Greeks had only one question: did they have passion? Make sure you're passionate about what you do because that's the measure of your life.

The people who are the most successful have the most fun with what they're doing. Everyone wants the opportunity to showcase themselves and their talents, and you are no different. So let your light shine. Take what you absolutely love and turn it into a decorated career. Get in your wheelhouse. You can't go into something half-heartedly and expect to be successful. You don't want to make it through your life, and get to the end of your life and say 'I made it through my life!' There's more to life than just surviving. You want to enjoy your life, and you want to celebrate your life. Whatever you do, it has to be a decision you make in your heart.

It's better to be a failure at something you love than a success at something you don't. Listen, you're going to fail. Whether today, whether tomorrow, it doesn't matter when, but you're going to fail. So at least fail at what you love to do and don't play it safe doing something you don't like. You can also fail at something you don't love, so you might as well do something you love. Trust your instincts and follow your heart. Spend your time working on whatever you're passionate about in life. Enjoy what you do, because the only way to do great work is to love what you do. Be passionate, not strident. Do the things that only you can do. Have something about you, something about your business, that's proprietary. Focus on finding a unique benefit, setting goals, and being conscious of your perspectives; this is critical to walking out your passion. Then, with each successful milestone accomplished, it's easy to feel passionate about every day. When you love what you do, it is its own kind of trophy, and it is not only an acceptable reason, but it is the best reason. Finding success is just about being happy. No matter what you're doing in your career or life, the first thing to always go back to is whether or not you're in love with it. If the answer is yes, you're headed in the right direction. There are no guarantees in life, so you just have to do whatever makes you come alive. Do what makes you happy, and you are in control of that.

There's nothing more important than your own happiness. Do what's right for you. Stop doing mindless repetitive and unfulfilling work. Do what makes you happy and make no apologies for it. Watch for signs of resentment. Burnout is about resentment. The question is whether you can replenish your energy when you get tired. Do things that replenish you. You want to design a life for yourself in which you can engage in the activities that you're passionate about. Some studies show if you enjoy life you are more likely to live longer. There's a correlation between people who report lower life enjoyment and those with chronically illness or mobility issues.[21] Real success is about doing what makes you happy. No matter what I do, I don't consider my audience; I do it for myself. I do it because it's important to me and it matters to me. That's how I know my success is my own. The secret to success is that there is no secret. It's just about enjoying what you're doing and putting in the work. People can tell when it's real, and they can tell when you're faking it. You will live a much better life if you decide to pursue your passions. When people work on things that they usually love doing, they tend to enjoy life more than everyone else because they're chasing their dreams. It's important to do something that makes you happy and is for you. Live your passion and then thicken your skin.

DIVE IN

Dante's *Divine Comedy (Inferno)* said, "The hottest places in hell are reserved for those who in time of great crisis, maintain neutrality." In Revelations 3:16, God says he spews out lukewarm people because they are neither hot nor cold. God is saying he wants you to be on fire. He wants you to love what you do. He wants you to be hot or cold. Don't live your life in neutral and remain ambivalent. Some people live their lives indifferent, cold, and aloof. Everyone in the Bible who got their prayers answered was passionate. Consider Hannah in 1 Samuel 1:13 wanting her baby so badly that she laid prostrate at the altar. That's why the Bible says in Mark 11:24 "whatsoever you ask in prayer believe you have received." If you don't want it bad enough, don't pray about it. People think if I don't have passion, I can't be disappointed when it doesn't happen. That's the wrong attitude. Have the courage to want something bad enough. Your power is in your passion. People try to discourage you. It takes courage to follow your passion. Think about it: whatsoever YOU desire, believe it's yours; have courage for it. Have a burning desire to live. The world will push you around if you let it; you have to push back and fight for your passion.

God wants our love to grow stronger and stronger. We don't need embers, we need the fire. Frederick Douglas said, “It is not light that we need, but fire. It is not the gentle shower, but thunder. We need the storm, the whirlwind, and the earthquake.” We need to move people to action. Whatever you do, do with all your heart. Give things your all, but not your best; that’s for God. Colossians 3:23 says, “Whatever you do, work at it with all your heart.” Ecclesiastes 9:10 says, “Whatever your hand finds to do, do it with all your might because there is neither work nor planning nor knowledge nor wisdom in the grave, the place where you will eventually go.” Shunryu Suzuki said, "When you do something, you should burn yourself completely, like a good bonfire, leaving no trace of yourself." So, find something you’re good at and stick with it. Be all in or get all out. Find what you are passionate about and pursue it with your full heart.

4

SUCCESS VS. SIGNIFICANCE

"A life is not important except in the impact it has on other lives."
– Jackie Robinson

GIVE BACK

There is something strange about the geography of Israel, where there are two seas present: the Dead Sea and the Sea of Galilee. The Sea of Galilee is filled with life; it contains 27 species of fish. Some aren't even found in other parts of the world. The shores of the Sea of Galilee are full of birds and lush with vegetation. Whereas, the Dead Sea contains no life at all, and is bitter and toxic. Both seas are fed by the same river, the Jordan River. So how are two seas fed by a single source so different? Well, the answer is the Sea of Galilee receives water at one end and gives out water at the other. The Dead Sea receives water but has no outlet; it keeps it all within itself. Similarly with life, if you only receive but do not give, you do not fully live. So give and live. Maya Angelou said, "You shouldn't go through life with a catcher's mitt in both hands, you need to be able to throw back." I love playing Chess. In

Chess, you can be the king or queen, but you still have to move the other pieces on the board. You have to help others. It's a reminder that the best way to enhance your life is to contribute to someone else's life. In fact, the most selfish thing you can do is something for someone else because it makes you feel good. The goodness you do comes right back to you. What goes around comes around. If you know something, teach. That's why the only thing to do with knowledge is to spread it; it's of no use to you. If you have something, give because it will come back to you in a very profound way. Recognize that you get what you give; your outer life is a reflection of your inner life. So I want to encourage you to move from success to significance. Successful people know that if you're going to be successful or wealthy, you need to solve problems. Provide clean energy, provide fresh water, find renewable sources of energy, et cetera. Don't think of these as problems; think of them as opportunities. Success is about solving problems.

In my life, I have seen how some people are so heavenly that they are no earthly good. They are so spiritual and righteous that they never get practical or put their faith into action. No. Get involved. You don't have to do everything, but God deserves some of your time. Dedicate part of your time to giving. No matter how busy your daily schedule is, allocate some time to committing good deeds. Positively minded people know that their good deeds tend to eventually 'return to sender.' By doing nice things for others, we enrich our own lives as well. Whether it is voluntary work or a simple act of kindness, such activity benefits one's physical and mental condition. Furthermore, it acts as a good defense against depression. Psychologists have coined this term ‘giver's high,' likening the joy of helping others to a drug-induced state of bliss.[22] In some ways this is a perfect comparison: charitable behavior triggers the secretion of dopamine, which gives us that feeling of elation and euphoria.[23]

Successful people understand that giving is the lifeblood of their success. All of us have had an experience in which we have seen a great movie, and the first thing we want to do is call our friends to share with them how great it is. The best thing about an experience is not the experience itself; it's the opportunity to share it with our friends. This is part and parcel of why social media has exploded. It's based on a simple idea of giving. The traditional philosophy of giving is that giving is all about charity to large, not-for-profit organizations. Giving is not about donations at all. Giving is what makes the world go ‘round. Giving involves using the gifts you have to make people’s lives better. There are unlimited ways for you to give back without necessarily going down the path of charity.

Here's my advice: Don't wait to make a million dollars before you do something special for others; do it now. Don't wait until everything is perfect before you give; do it now. Some people don't share their success; they just keep it in the family. Every day offers us the opportunity to affect and touch others’ lives. No matter who you are, you have been blessed too much to let indolence be your advocate. If you have been blessed, you have an obligation to do more for the lost, the least, and the leftover. Time is the greatest donation you can give. Read a book to, or spend time with someone. You don't have to give back; just give. Help the poor, the sick, and the dying. If you've been given a platform, you have an obligation to give back and to do more. If you can do more and help others, you must do so. You have a responsibility to be a generous person. There is a difference between responsibility and choice. You don't have a choice to give, you have a responsibility to give. Don't hold so tightly to what you have. The tighter you squeeze, the less you have. You have two hands for a reason, one is for you, and the other is for others. Give back; pay it forward. Always give more than you can take. Give now, get more later. You have to give to get. Moreover, you get what you give because you receive in direct proportion to what you give. So live by giving. Live by the 80-20 rule, which says of all that you have, you only use 20% of it (i.e., you only wear 20% of your clothes). Lao Tzu said, "When your cup is full, stop pouring. If you realize that you have enough, you are rich." The goal is to be in balance. Whatever we put into the universe will come back to us.

The law of giving states you are to feed what is feeding you. Everything God created is in a system of cycles. God doesn't have to intervene. The cycle always reproduces itself. It's a system of sowing and reaping. A cloud bursts into rain because humidity turns into the cloud again. It's feeding itself. The grass feeds the soil, and the soil is feeding the grass. Everything in life is in cycles. You have to give what's giving to you. Don't muzzle the mouth of an ox; you can't keep working the ox. You have to feed it too. You have to feed what's feeding you. You bless what's blessing you. You pour into what's pouring into you. You have to pay your employees, reinvest in your business, et cetera. Everything is a system of reciprocity. Reach back for the left out and left behind. Ask yourself, "How can I cultivate success and inspire inspiration in others?" Farah Griffin said, "Take it, hold it, my brothers, make it, my brothers, shake it, squeeze it, turn it, twist it, beat it, kick it, kiss it, whip it, stomp it, dig it, plow it, seed it, reap it, rent it, buy it, sell it, own it, build it, multiply it, and pass it on - can you hear me? Pass it on! – 'who set you flowin'?"

It's not about what we give others but what others have given us. What have they taught us? What are the gifts they've given us? Help others, reach back for someone, leave a path for others to follow. Everything we do should be for the next generation to come. You have to give something back and leave something behind. I know that I've received so much more than my share of good fortune in this lifetime. I've been blessed to have witnessed grandiose displays of love and smaller personal acts of kindness and love, and what I've learned is they all matter. Corporations have even realized that you can do well by doing good. In business it's a concept affectionately known as **first do well, then do good.** Yes, companies should make money and do well, but then do good and be charitable.

Even in relationships, being smart, thoughtful, and generous is attractive. Nobody wants to be in a relationship with someone who is not giving. In politics it's a benefit as well. You win elections by lifting peoples' sights and contributing positively to the discourse. Help people expand their horizons or what they might be instead of what is. Ralph Waldo Emerson said, "Treat a man as he is, and he will remain as he is. Treat a man as he could be, and he will become what he should be." The point is you will get all you want in life if you help others get what they want. Reciprocity is the name of any relationship game and always will be. To move forward, you have to move something back. In essence, you're not successful until you can help someone else be successful. Helping others is how we help ourselves. Pay it forward. The good you do comes back to you. So find a way to serve. Reach back and give back. Do what you can, give what you can. We move together or not at all.

CORE VALUES

If I told you right now God doesn't exist, would you go murder and pillage? No, of course not. So there's something deeper guiding our choices, and I'm talking about morality. There is an internal compass guiding our decisions and choices, and we should not shy away from those things we feel strongly about. Truth in principles is more important than popularity. In Hinduism, there is a concept called "dharma," which means one's "duty." Your dharma is always to do "the next right thing," without attachment to the consequences which is karma. So when you follow your dharma, good karma naturally flows from it. Consequently, when you don't, it doesn't. In the novel *Huckleberry Finn*, when it comes to advocating for the slave Jim, it's all about having "the courage to go to hell but to do the right thing."[24]

Having a core foundation of values is like a compass. You always know who you are and in which direction home is. The overriding issue is whether doing the right thing conflicts with one's goals; this is part of squaring the circle. Consider the events of 9/11 in which terrorism kept people so afraid that violence could come anytime, or anywhere. The first response was to hunt terrorists down, not bring them to court and make their case. You always need the rule of law, a trial, and a verdict. Even in the midst of pain, have the courage to maintain your ethics and values no matter what happens to you. Anchoring your values in integrity is about doing the right thing in all circumstances, whether or not anyone is watching.

Our values are instilled in us from an early age, but as any parent knows, no matter how much you do for your kids, you are not their only influence. We adopt values from the media or from our environment as well. This world is morally bankrupt and there are few profiles in courage. That's why I'm so thankful for my parents who provided me with correct guidance and values. And sadly, in today's world, parents need to better parent. Parents need to teach what Henry Ward Beecher said, that it's so important to "hold yourself to a higher standard than anybody else expects of you." They are values that how you do anything is how you do everything; so live and work with honor. You have to ask what you have to do for yourself to sleep on the pillow at night, and then do that. It requires an insurrection from within rather than a revolt from the outside. Let your values vault you forward. You have to define what's important to you. What is a value for you? We're myopically focused on the wrong things. What matters to you? What do you focus on? Abraham Maslow said, "If the only tool you have is a hammer, everything starts to look like a nail." What are you measuring in your life? Count the intangibles in your life, not just the tangibles. Johann Wolfgang von Goethe wrote, "Things that matter most must never be at the mercy of things that matter least." Measure what makes life worthwhile. Establish what your core values are. These intrinsic values are non-negotiable, and they are the traits you want to be known and remembered for. Establishing your values pulls your real self out.

Real success is about knowing your personality, skills, and interests, and making sure they align with your current occupation. This process allows you to shine in areas for which you are best suited. So let's take a moment and think about your character and pinpoint what your values are, or what you espouse them to be. Let's try the legacy test: Imagine you are attending your own funeral. What do people say about you? How do you want to be remembered? What memories would you want to be passed on? The works of some famous philosophers can help us here. David Brendel of the Harvard Business Review suggests the "**SANE**" mnemonic, drawn from some critical questions posed by prominent Western philosophers: Socrates, Aristotle, Nietzsche, and the existentialists.

- **Socrates:** What is the most challenging question someone could ask me about my current approach?
- **Aristotle:** What character virtues are most important to me and how will I express them?
- **Nietzsche:** How will I direct my "will to power," manage my self-interest, and act in accordance with my chosen values?
- **Existentialists (e.g., Sartre):** How will I take full responsibility for my choices and the

> outcomes to which they lead? I can be anything I want to be. I'm free to be a father, and I'm free to be a businessman, but how do I reconcile both (What's important to me? What are my values? Et cetera.).[25]

Define what your core values are and don't concede their power. Your core values are there to guide your behavior and choice. Get them right, and you will be swift and focused in your decision making with clear direction. Get them wrong or leave them ambiguous and you'll always wonder how you got into this mess. Use your core values to consciously and unconsciously select friendships, relationships, and business partnerships.

The older you get, the more you realize that when push comes to shove, some people are gutless and spineless. They seemingly have no values; there's no 'there' there. There's no soul to sell if they wanted to. They will believe the answer is always yes unless no is required. They will sell their own family to make it to the top. Some people don't know what ground to stand on. They will lie, and if they will lie, they will steal; and if they steal they will cheat. Most people don't know what's important anymore. So figure out what's important to you and what you value – not the values of the world or those that other people place on you, but your own. You can fake your way to the top, but it's always real coming down. Maintain perspective and humility.

The intersection between drive and respect is an important one because there are people who are highly driven but don't think twice about running someone over, and there are others who are respected but stagnant. The atmosphere is so decadent; we live in a world of celebrity and excess. What we need is people with substance and depth. We need people who live from the inside out. That's why I live from the walls in and not the walls out. I live in Los Angeles, and I can tell you, life isn't Hollywood, its Halloween; every day it's trick or treat. The only values you find in this town are the values you bring, so make sure your work is grounded. I don't do the work I do for external glory; I do it because it's important to me. That's why it's so important to keep the spotlight on your work, not on you. Keep your head in the clouds but feet on the ground. I take Yoga weekly, and they say "Namaste," which translates to "The divine in me recognizes and bows to the divine in you." People want integrity from you, and you owe it to them. That's what people expect and respect. We lose ourselves when we compromise the very ideals we fight to defend. Life is about God, family, and love. Those are values we can all rally around.

We are a lost and broken generation. Few of us know what we care about or what we stand for, or fight for our principles. The Bible says in John 3:19, "Men loved darkness rather than light." We live in a world where people trade relationships for resources; people would trade their family for money, or loved ones for cars or things. We live in a world of uncertainty and change, so your values and core need to be constant. If you don't stand up, you get run over. There are times in life when you have to stand your ground, plant your feet and make your point. We need to focus on and enrich our values. Psalm 119:9 says, "How can a young person keep his way pure? By guarding it according to your word." It's about our values, beliefs, and attitudes. It's not so much about priorities because priorities change depending on circumstance, but values don't. Challenge assumptions that are an affront to your values and an insult your beliefs.

You have to have certainties; some things in your life have to be absolute. You always need values because you need some foundation to stand on. Have some depth to you and don't be swayed by how others "appear." Some people look like Tarzan but run like Jane. My grandfather used to say, "You have to have some rock in you." What he was saying was that you need to have some core in you, a strong foundation like the Rock of Gibraltar. You need some principle to stand on because there comes a time when silence becomes betrayal. You have to stand up for what you believe in, for what's right. It's time to get less flexibility and more backbone. You need to be able to stand up to pressure and not buckle under it. Sometimes you need the brass to say things just because they need to be said.

We have to ask ourselves what the right thing to do is, and then do that thing — always doing the right thing. There should be an element of anxiety in each ethical decision we make. The absence of anxiety is immorality. Test what you see against your values. Test what you hear, what you feel, what you see against your values. I was interviewing for a job once, and they wanted me to do some things against my values. I know my truth and what's right for me. If you can't get a job on merit, why have it? I'm not going to play politics. There are two things that are important to me: my family and my integrity. So you need to know when to walk away. It's easy to say you wouldn't cross the line, especially when the line is presented to very few people. But a situation will arise, and you're going to have to decide who you are and what you stand for in that moment.

The defining moments in our lives don't come with canaries in the coal mine. You have to have moral courage, and you have to be constructively subversive. More importantly, you have to be willing to go against the flow if the flow is not appropriate. There is no point to only challenging the status quo, challenging the flow, without having opinions yourself. Don’t horse trade your values. If something is close to the lines, it’s out. Don’t let anything impugn your integrity. Stay true to who you are and do the things that are important to you, and you will be like a tree bearing fruit.

Advocate and negotiate actively for yourself and what you care about. Have something to look up to and something to look forward to. Personally, what motivates me is taking care of my priorities: family, love, purpose, et cetera. I find that by doing so, I make myself truly valuable professionally. Focus on what matters. Developing character, having a value system, and having grit are far more important than how well you do in math and science. Just keep living right, just keep doing good, and in the end, truth will win out. In the end, things will work out. People ask, “What's the use in doing right?” “What's the use in pursuing virtue?” “What's the use in doing good?” But let me tell you: Be a good person anyway. One of my favorite commercials is an old Fiat commercial with Charlie Sheen driving in circles inside his house party in a Fiat. He steps out with an ankle monitor on and asks, "What do I get for good behavior?"

It's a silly commercial, but instructive nonetheless. In this world, it may seem like good behavior accounts for nothing, but let me tell you it does. Do right anyway.

Everyone has a different moral compass. Most people don't know their values and don't know their value. Know yours and trust your intuition. After I graduated from university and law school, I realized that I would no longer have to rely on grades or guidance from professors to tell me how I'm doing or where I stand. I have to rely instead on my inner compass. Only if that compass is true will it determine whether you become a drifter blown about by every breeze, or a doer, an active citizen of the world who is determined to chart your own course and question your assumptions.

Having a diploma isn't the only thing that matters. Don't forget what doesn't come from a diploma: a heart to know what's meaningful and what's ephemeral and a head to know the difference between knowledge and judgment. People have a right to do a lot of things, but it doesn't make those things right. We talk so much about rights but not so much about responsibilities in this world. It's up to you to right wrongs; it's up to you to stand up and be heard. Starting today, take time to identify the core values you have and develop an actionable plan to bring them into your everyday life to bring purpose and meaning to your career. What are your values, and are you being true to them? In what ways are you being perceived that maybe you're not aware of? Keep your integrity intact and have a strong constitution. Be outspoken and stand by your convictions. Remain true to your values and remember that just because you're lost, it doesn't mean your compass is broken. Let your values guide your career decisions. People who have values and act on them can change the world. That can be you. That must be you. Your values matter. They are your North Star. Take the time to figure out what you value, and lean on that when it comes to decisions in your life, especially career ones.

There is a story of a man's wife who was bleeding, and he sees a shack nearby with a sign that says 'Doctor' on it. He goes and brings his wife in and begs for help. The old man comes to the door and says, "I haven't practiced for years." The husband replies, "Well, if you're not going to practice, please take down your sign." The point is, there are people out there in this world hurting and needing help, and someone might be looking to you. And if all you do is practice and never compete, what good are you? If you're not going to practice your values, take your sign down. So the next time you feel a little lost, consider what your values are and watch what happens when you let them make decisions for you. Live your values; don't intellectualize them. You have to live by a higher standard. It's about knowing what you stand for and what you stand against. Do what's right even if no one follows you. You have an obligation to do the right thing. Even with the randomness of the winning and losing in life, justice is impossible, but we should always pursue it. We should attempt to still do right and still be right. Nothing is more powerful than someone who lives out their convictions.

I've learned that everybody treasures something in the end. What do you cherish? What is important to you? Where do you place value? Know what matters to you. Know what you care about and what you stand for, and fight for your principles. Our values cannot be multiple choice. The ten commandments are not multiple choice. Our values and things that we cherish are not inevitable; they are fragile. There is a thin veneer, and we have to fight for them. There's an old Irish story that tells of a man who arrives at the gates of heaven and asks to be let in. Saint Peter says, “Of course, just show me your scars.” The man replies, “Scars, I have no scars.” Saint Peter says “Pity, was there nothing worth fighting for?” To me, there's plenty worth fighting for. Turn back the tide of indifference and take a stand. It's never wrong to do the right thing. At the end of the day, all you can do is what you think is right. If you do the right things for the right reasons, good things will happen.

If you're going to build a house, you need a strong foundation. I briefly worked in construction with my grandfather when I was younger, and part of the job in construction was having to dig massive foundations. It sucked. You have to dig holes and then lay steel, and eventually pour in concrete. And you do all that work, and nobody ever sees it. No one. The only time people talk about the foundation is when the house is falling apart. Yet when it's done right, nobody talks about it. But if it's done right at the beginning, it can hold the weight of anything it's designed to hold. So, whatever you’re building towards, make sure your foundation can support the weight of whatever you can dream. I was a personal trainer in college, and I can't tell you enough how important proper technique is. Most people in the gym want to show off how much weight they can push, and they add weight to bad technique. We are no different; we constantly load on dysfunction. We need a strong foundation.

You can't just be against something; you have to be for something. Be for love, be for second chances, be for joy. Your values cannot just be about resistance, it should be about building towards something. It is much more powerful to be for something than to be against something. My personal values have meant everything to me. So wherever your life takes you, I hope that your values are that kind of touchstone for you. Know what you stand for. Think about what's most essential and who's most important, and pursue that; forget the rest.

YOUR VALUE

IF

If you can keep your head when all about you
Are losing theirs and blaming it on you,
If you can trust yourself when all men doubt you,
But make allowance for their doubting too;
If you can wait and not be tired by waiting,
Or being lied about, don't deal in lies,
Or being hated, don't give way to hating,
And yet don't look too good, nor talk too wise:

If you can dream—and not make dreams your master;
If you can think—and not make thoughts your aim;
If you can meet with Triumph and Disaster
And treat those two impostors just the same;
If you can bear to hear the truth you've spoken

Twisted by knaves to make a trap for fools,
Or watch the things you gave your life to, broken,
And stoop and build 'em up with worn-out tools:

If you can make one heap of all your winnings
And risk it on one turn of pitch-and-toss,
And lose, and start again at your beginnings
And never breathe a word about your loss;
If you can force your heart and nerve and sinew
To serve your turn long after they are gone,
And so hold on when there is nothing in you
Except the Will which says to them: 'Hold on!'

If you can talk with crowds and keep your virtue,
Or walk with Kings—nor lose the common touch,
If neither foes nor loving friends can hurt you,
If all men count with you, but none too much;
If you can fill the unforgiving minute
With sixty seconds' worth of distance run,
Yours is the Earth and everything that's in it,
And—which is more—you'll be a Man, my son!

- *Rudyard Kipling*

I have inserted my favorite poem here because I believe that Rudyard Kipling gets to the heart of the matter in this chapter, which is to always be a steady person because that's how you sustain excellence. Kipling's burgeoning case study at personal reinvention is incredible. It's about how to live your life better than expected. It's about how to be the best version of yourself that you can be and how to be somebody for yourself. Life has taught me just to try and be the best that I can be, to reach for the best of me, to exercise excellence in all walks of life, and to cultivate excellence in others. Internalize excellence and let your work be your signature.

Sadly, schools today don't measure if students learn relevant skills and behaviors. A single number like a GPA doesn't say nearly enough about what students have learned. In school there isn't enough emphasis on these critical skills and abilities: self-awareness of strengths and weaknesses, integrity, understanding of cross-cultural reality, team skills, critical thinking, communication, comfort with inevitable ambiguity and uncertainty, creativity, the ability to persuade and influence others. Moreover, schools overemphasize theory, which means less time for students to apply what they've learned. Formulas can't factor in intangibles. So that's why you need to be careful of people only caring about numbers and statistics or analytics in this data-driven world, especially when it comes to admissions, hiring, or quantitative measures. Consequently, I use the eye test more than analytics: What do I see? What are my eyes telling me? You don't know someone's true value. Tom Brady was drafted late in the NFL Draft; Aaron Rodgers was drafted late in the NFL Draft. Many successful people were overlooked. Never underestimate anyone because you don't know someone's worth. That's why St. Augustine said, “You couldn't judge someone by their post.”

The importance of the individual should be christened, and the emphasis should be put on someone's value system because sometimes people surprise us even when we've given up on them. So don't throw anyone away; people can surprise you. We live in a throwaway society – throwaway paper plates, throwaway cups, et cetera. But people are like fine china, and they should be washed and not tossed away. People don't mind being used; they mind being discarded. Your value is on the inside. You are a vessel; God made you a container. A container's value is what's inside of it. If you steal my money, you have stolen the cheapest part of me. I made my money; my money didn't make me. I made my degree; my degree didn't make me. Real value is internal and cannot be overlooked. Make sure the main thing stays the main thing.

BE GOOD

I'm always curious as to what it takes to be good. It's not enough to just drive Italian sports cars or wear expensive clothes. In my own life I don't want just to look good; I want to be good. I don't want only to do good; I want to be good. We cannot only be good; we must be good for something. It is a poverty of ambition to think only of what goods you can buy and not what goods you can do. Most people don't want to do anything; they just want to be something. They say I want to be CEO, I want to be a celebrity, I want to be famous, et cetera. But in 1 Samuel 16:7 God shows us why he chose David to be King: "Man looks on the outward appearance, but the Lord looks on the heart." David was kind; he was humble, he was a shepherd boy, and was a giver. Look at the lion; why is the lion the king of the jungle? He's not the fastest (cheetah), or the tallest (giraffe), but its because of his heart, he is the king. That's why people say have 'a lion's heart.' It doesn't matter to me how long I live; it matters how I live. It matters what I do with the time I've been given. So my question to you is how are you living? Every day ask yourself that question. I had a friend who went to a Division 3 school. He asked, "Will I get drafted?" I said, "Just be good." If you're good at what you do, the right people will find you. If you're good you don't have to kiss up, suck up, or play *Game of Thrones*. Don't worry about what you look like or sound like or what others might think of you. If you're good it will all take care of itself. The truth is, you can be amazing, genuine, sincere, and talented but still be overlooked. It's how you live that matters. I want you to know your life matters if you live with integrity. If you lead your life the right way, good things will come to you. How you do things matters much more than what you do. If you live your life with the right attitude, your dreams will come to you, karma will work on your side.

BE IMPACTFUL

Martin Luther King Jr. said, "The arc of history is long but it bends towards justice." But the arc doesn't bend on its own; it bends because we bend it. We have to reach out, put our hand on that arc and move it in the direction of justice, freedom, equality, kindness, and generosity. It doesn't happen on its own. It happens because we make it happen. So we continuously have to make a choice as to what kind of world we want to live in and what kind of people we want to be. The best way to change the world is to change yourself. It starts right here, right now. Do it in your community and in your arena. **That's how you change the world: <u>you change your world</u>**.

It starts at a local level. You can have an impact. You may not touch the world directly, but your influence does. You may think making lunch for your sister is pointless, but this could be a future chancellor. Never underestimate the power of your example. Somebody may have been a jerk since high school, and maybe it's been a reflex ever since, but even they can change. We have to search ourselves as a society for the type of impact we want to have and the legacy we want to leave.

The most important things in life aren't things; they're people. We're so used to using people and loving things, rather than loving people and using things. Success is a value. Success is about the difference you make in people's lives. It's about adding value to the lives of people. It's not so much what you can't do, but rather what you can do and what you can help us with. Give what you can: your time, your talents, and your money. Always ask what you are doing for others. Success is one thing; impact is another.

Anyone can find success. It's not based on your wealth or education; it's based on who you are and what you do with who you are. If you aren't making a difference in the lives of other people, you shouldn't be in business – it's that simple. You have a responsibility to make a difference in this world, to your community, to your family. This is about translating values into governance. Count on being the difference. Every coach in every sport is looking for impact players and force multipliers. Focus on being a difference-maker. When I ran for Student Government Association president in college I said, "I'm not running to make history, I'm running to make a difference." If there are things we can and should do, then we must.

Even if you're scared, let's move forward and let's make clear that fear won't stop us. Fear cannot be an option.

Success isn't just about what you decide to accomplish in your life, but what you inspire others to do. Try not to become someone of success, but a person of value. If you're going to be here on this earth, there's a necessity to make a difference. You don't have to redeem the world; that's already been done (Jesus). You don't have to be captain of industry to make a difference; you just have to care. The more we deny ourselves, the better we become. The most important thing in life is how you live your life and how your life moves and touches lives. That's true success. The goal has to be transformation. That's why the Bible says in 1 Corinthians 15:53, "This mortal body shall put on immortality." The purpose of our life is transformation.

We all have a pulpit. It may not be like mine, but people are watching how you live. Always act as if someone is watching you because someone always is. Wherever you are, that is your platform, that is your stage, that's where your influence lies, and your power is what I know for sure. Speak with your life, not your lips. Lead by influence, not authority. We don't know what impact we have; just keep planting seeds even if you don't see the harvest. Every day we are impacting eternity. Focus on the impact you want to have. Jane Goodall said, "What you do makes a difference, and you have to decide what kind of difference you want to make."

Growing up I always wanted to make a difference, but I finally realized *I was the difference.* Each of us can make a difference, and all of us ought to try. If you care and you act on it, you make a difference. Simple as that. Let your impact be immediate and intimate. Know that the world needs you to change it. Even with all the progress that has been made, we still have a long way to go. The world is turning to you to change it and fix its challenges. One person can make a difference. The world is filled with trials and obstacles, but find ways around them. Turn fear into hope. Your life's journey is not going to be determined by doing the things you are certain you can do. It will be determined by whether you try the things that are hard. Don't let yourself believe that something is out of your reach. You are a part of a generation that knows no boundaries, fears no fears, and changes our world. Figure out where you want to go, aim high, then march in that direction.

BE VALUE ADDED

I once had a profound exchange with my former supervisor and mentor regarding my work duties. He said, "Don't wait to be told what to do. Look around and see what needs to be done, and do that. No one is going to tell you what to do. You have to figure out what needs to be done, and do it. You need to be able to look around and see what's missing, and then fulfill that need. Where there are problems, you need to see opportunities. You can't have a sense of entitlement without a sense of responsibility. You'll never get ahead by waiting for someone to tell you what to do. Err on the side of doing too much rather than too little. If I say 'here are ten things I need done,' and you do them, that's support. But when you say 'I've done those ten things you asked and I noticed these five things which could change/need attention, and I did them,' that's leadership; that's being value added." It was a wonderful lesson or me early in my career. So my message to you is to pick a problem, any problem, and do something about it because to someone who is hurting, something is everything. Your job is to do the best you can with this life you have been given. Do something with yourself that is eternal. My parents always taught me to make sure your life adds value and make sure your life is consequential. They taught me to matter – not to necessarily be successful or the best, but the most impactful. They taught me to give up selfishness. Successful people put their vision, family, and goals before everything else. Be incredibly focused on giving and serving others. Life is not all about you. It's not all about me. It's about us. So do the best you can with this life, to be of use.

My message is simple: Be useful and be kind. If you are useful, you will always have a voice. No matter what room you go into, you will have a voice. And if you're kind, you will always be welcome. If you're both, you will be a welcome voice. Be a voice, not an echo. There is a concept taught in business school that you are always interviewing. People are always asking if you fit or if you don't fit, in their life, in their family, in their future, et cetera. So always ask yourself, "How can I be used?" "How can I be of service?"

Richard St. John writes in his book *The 8 Traits Successful People Have in Common* that "it's important to ask yourself who you serve because most people only care about how you can fix their problems." It's essential that once you have determined who you serve that you then figure out what unique value you can offer. For example, Martha Stewart learned how to be a master homemaker, and her expertise netted high value for millions of women looking for tips to make a better home. When you shift your focus off yourself and onto the people you serve, you set yourself up for success. Move away from being a consumer to a producer. Do what you love, serve others what they love, get money in return. Most people believe that making money is just about receiving, receiving, receiving. But everything in life is about a fair exchange. Money is compensation for value given.

Always use your creativity to propose efficient solutions to problems and provide value to the situation. The challenge grows to constantly supplement each conversation, each setting, with value. It takes a lot of dedication and research to truly understand the desires and needs of your audience, consumer, or client. Be a diligent student of your industry. People will notice. It's funny because I often hear people say I want to be paid what I'm worth, but you can't put a dollar figure on your worth. The truth is you will never get paid what you're worth. Your worth more than $1 million or $5 million or $10 million or $100 million. I'm sure you wouldn't amputate your leg for a million dollars, right? So obviously you have innate worth. But the point is, the economy is predicated on a fair exchange of value and what value your bringing to the marketplace.

Recognize that your best ability is availability – showing up and letting people know they can depend on you. Give help or get help. In order to start shifting your mindset, think about the value you add and not in how often you agree, but how often you add unique value. The only thing more enticing than production is potential. Prove your impact by accomplishing something. Take the initiative, and you'll become indispensable. Come to the table knowing that you bring value to everything you touch. When it comes to creating value for others, you always have something to contribute. It's about adding value, always. You cannot plan the impact that you're going to have so ask yourself how you can add more value. Ask yourself how can you be a fountain and not a drain? Focus on impact because if all you're doing in a meeting or at work is agreeing, you're being redundant. If everyone is in lockstep, someone isn't adding value. Add value before you ask for value. Your job is to add something to the culture and contribute to society. Go somewhere where you are value added.

CHECK YOUR CHARACTER

Become attractive. In order to attain all that you want in your life, you must become attractive. I'm not talking about physical beauty, but rather the beauty you possess inside. For things to change in your life, you have to change. Success is something you attract by becoming an attractive person. It's not something you can pursue because what you pursue always eludes you like a butterfly. It's about character. Regard character over pedigree. Your life should be instructive. All you have in life is your reputation, and it's a very small world where everyone knows everyone. Deal with people fairly and well. Have a reputation for integrity. Integrity is about openness; being clear about what to say fearlessly and robustly. It's about authenticity and resilience. Let your values guide you through decisions. You have to make a short decision that reinforces a long-term belief. The way you treat yourself is the way people treat you. Keeping your commitments and maintaining your integrity and being honest are crucial to your moral intelligence. Your reputation must be protected. Guard your reputation with all that you have. Make a habit of being honest, reliable, and kind. Consider your choices. There are people by virtue and people by choice. Fame comes and goes, but quality stays around. So be quality. If quality slips, it doesn't really matter how good your ideas were. It's not what you do; it's how you do it that matters. Act with honesty and integrity. The message of *Enders Game* is that 'how' matters. Specifically, that how you win matters. It's not about wins and losses, or whether you're playing the worst team or the best team; it's about doing things the right way.

Stay humble and let your accomplishments speak for themselves. Being able to be proud of yourself at the end of the day, having family care for you and love you, that's success. Everything else is commentary. That's why it's so important you have integrity within you. This is the world we live in. Success will come and go, but integrity is forever. Success is not what you have; it's who you are that's the fortune of your worth. You want to be able to look yourself in the mirror every night and that demands strength of character. Something as small as opening a door for a lady reveals character and honor. Madame Necker said, "Fortune does not change men, but rather unmasks them." It just reveals what's really inside of you.

I once took some acting classes, and it was incredible for me because people think acting is like putting on a mask, but really it's taking a mask off. It's revealing something about you. So get to know yourself. Build a strong reputation. Always do the right thing and give a damn from now on. Do what is right and let the consequences follow. Achieve the outcomes that matter. Your most important values dictate culture. Be sincere and fair in everything you do. Freedom isn't just about doing what you like but doing what you ought to do or should do. Freedom is about choosing to do right. Just do right. Right may not be expedient; it may not be profitable, but it will let you sleep at night. Learn to align yourself with your values and beliefs, build courage, establish your identity, create boundaries, and find focus and direction.

We live in an instantaneous world of texting, twerking, and tweeting, where if something isn't trending, it's not happening, and it's easy to make a name for yourself. But to make that name mean something is the hard part. Now I don't care what others think of what I do, but I care very much about what I think I do, and that's character. Always keep yourself clean and bright. You are the window through which you see the world. Character is your impact on the world. Character and history do intersect. Your character will go down in history for better or for worse. So follow honor and live with integrity. Recognize that to whom much is given, much is required. One of the biggest misconceptions in this age is that it’s not wrong to do wrong. No. Do the right thing in everything you do. Integrity is the coin of the realm. No matter what happens, don't lose your integrity. You might cry, but hold onto it. You might go without, but hold onto it. You might suffer, but hold onto to it. You are who you are; don't lose yourself. In the *Count of Monte Cristo*, we see that Edmund Dantes was tip of the spear, the moral edifice, a paragon of virtue, and he was imprisoned for it. Naturally, he thought that when you do things right, people won't be sure you've done anything at all. But he learned to shine even when the spotlight was not on him. So the moral of the story is the whole world's watching you. Be careful what you say and be careful what you do. You never know when you will be called to testify. Sooner or later you will see there's a difference between knowing the path and walking the path.

Franklin Roosevelt said, "Man is at the bottom an animal, midway, a citizen, and at the top, divine. But the climate of this world is such that few ripen at the top." What he understood was that we live in an era of self-celebration and you almost have to have a degree of vanity to be successful. If we look at professional athletes or politicians, self-referential has become the norm. But here is the peril of hubris - Icarus flew too close to the sun. It was a failure to be more humble, to know what you don't know, and resist the mass of universal impulses. You may be brilliant, ambitious, and audacious, but there are other high IQ and creative professionals in this world too. Be kind and lose the hubris. The character of a person is how they treat someone who can do nothing for them. Treat people with respect, listen to them, care about them. Character is what you are as a person. Let your prayer and hope be for a clean heart.

DON'T JUXTAPOSE

We all want three things: **to be**, **to have**, or **to do**. We either want to be something, to have something, or to do something. So how do we go about getting it? *The Silence of the Lambs* says it best: We covet. And how do we begin to covet? Do we seek out things to covet? No. We covet what we see every day. We see someone else driving that sports car, and we want it. We see someone living in that big house, and we want it. We covet left, right, and center. Some people think success is all about money; it's not. It's about having the resources. Jim Carrey said, "I wish everyone could be rich and famous so they could realize it's not the answer." Success is about achieving what YOU want, as opposed to coveting what others have. Don't get in the habit of pursuing things you're not passionate about or as a means to validate your worth. Strive to be what you consider successful. The definition of success changes, so just follow your definition and never follow or envy someone else's path.

I remember reading an article awhile ago that said that women don't dress for men, but that women dress for other women (to compare). The article was very enlightening. It taught me just how important it is not to do things for comparison sake and to only go after what's yours in this world. Likewise, don't chase what's already chasing you. God has prepared blessings that have your name on them – not my name, but your name. They have already been set aside for you. One day you will come into what's already yours and what belongs to you. Think about Adam in the Garden of Eden. God made the garden beautiful with flowers and abundant fruit, and then placed Adam there. Adam didn't have to toil and work the garden; it was already prepared for him. Same as your life. There's provision already there. Everything you need for a victorious and abundant life is already here. You're going to come into your garden soon. You didn't earn it, you didn't deserve it; it's just the goodness of God bringing you into a prepared blessing. What God has in store for you is more than you could ask or think. You don't have to ask for the blessings; the blessings will come looking for you. Defeat, lack, and insecurity aren't looking for you; favor is looking for you. I believe there's so much in store for you – the people you're going to meet, the places you're going to go, the good breaks coming your way – you will be amazed.

We often get discouraged and say, "I don't have the training, talent or connections," "I come from the wrong family," or "It sounds good, but I don't believe it." However, God has the final say. The favor and blessings on your life are more significant than your circumstances. People may write you off, but that doesn't change what God has planned for you. The blessing God has for you will override any curse. I think about the oil that flowed for David in the Bible when he was anointed king; it did not flow to anyone else. You don't have to worry about someone else getting your blessing; the oil that's been prepared for you will not flow to anyone else. When it's time to be blessed, no one can take your blessing. God will open doors that no man can shut. People say, "Well Louis, my coworker got the promotion, and I worked harder." No, if the oil didn't flow, then it wasn't meant to be yours. That's their blessing. If you didn't get it, it wasn't supposed to be yours. Your oil will not flow for anyone else. The blessing that belongs to you will be your blessing; no one can take it. That house, that promotion, that husband, that wife – they have your name on them exclusively. That's why you don't have to worry. Nobody's going to get what belongs to you.

When you see someone being blessed, they move into a new house, they get a new contract, they get a new car, or they have a new baby, don't get jealous and say ‘I wish that had happened to me.' No, that doesn't have your name on it. If it was supposed to be yours, the oil would have flowed. You can be happy for them, knowing that what God has for you will be better because it's prepared specifically for you. If God were to give you what should not have been yours, it wouldn't be a blessing; it would be a burden. You're not anointed for it; it's not right for you. You may say ‘I wish I were married to him or her,’ but no. She's a blessing to him, but she would be a burden to you. She's not for you. God has your blessing specific for you – the right husband, the right job, the right connection, the right gifts, the right breaks. Nobody can take what's yours. Your oil is not going to flow to someone else.

Sometimes when we see God blessing someone else, we think they're taking up all of Gods favor, but no, he has an unlimited supply. If he did it for them, he can do it for you. Decide you're going to turn it around, not “God, why didn't you do it for me?” but rather, “God, I know you did it for them and I believe you can do it for me.” Even me. You don't have to covet what someone else has, their gifts or their promotions or anything they have because God has blessings prepared specifically for you. Lift your hands and say ‘God I pray for the blessings you have explicitly prepared for me.’ Your provision, favor, and abundance are already waiting for you, but like Elijah in 1 Kings 17:4, you have to go down to the brook, and the ravens will feed you there. There's a place specifically where you are commanded to be, and your blessings are waiting for you there. Get out of your comfort zone; leave your neck of the woods. Leave the worry, leave the doubt, leave the anger, leave the apoplexy, leave the resentment, leave anything abhorrent. There's more abundance waiting for you, but you have to leave your comfort zone. Stop being so afraid. Your place of blessing has changed and will change. Just know that if God is blessing your neighbor, it just means he's in your neighborhood.

When I was younger I used to be jealous until I realized that my problem was keeping score, and I would do a lot more winning if I didn't keep score. It's about getting ahead collectively, not individually. I am not envious of other people's successes anymore. I'm not envious anymore because what's mine is mine and what's for me is for me and what's for someone else is for someone else. Too many of us have an attitude of 'Schadenfreude' (pleasure derived from the misfortune of others). That's the wrong attitude. I was always taught to be happy and uplifting for people because when good happens to them, it means Good is afoot, and it can happen to me too. This is definitely a departure from what many may be used to. It takes so much energy to root against someone. Success is about all of us getting ahead. You'll get everything you want in life if you help other people get what they want. When the tide rises all ships rise with it. The keys to your future success lay in the past experiences of others; search for opportunities to expand both mental and spiritual horizons.

Joel Osteen says, "You don't have to be jealous or envious because what God has for you, nobody but you can glean it." If a door doesn't open, it's not your door. We keep trying to climb ladders that are not ours. We are guilty of trying to resurrect things God keeps trying to kill. Go after what's yours and what's for you. What's for you is for you, and what's for someone else is for them. You have to work too hard to get stuff that's not yours. If something's for you, even if someone else is holding it, they'll have to give it up. Focus on what's for you. A blessing for someone else could be a burden for someone else. What God has for you is for you and no one else can have that.

There's a story in the Bible of the Ark of the Covenant being stolen from Israelites by Philistines in 1 Samuel 4, but it brings nothing but plagues on the Philistines because it's not for them. Look at God taking the Israelites through the Red Sea, and Pharaoh and his army trying to catch them using Gods escape hatch for themselves in Exodus 14:28. Nope, what God has for you is for you. I want you to get in your mind what you want to leave behind – what anger, what ire, what hurt – and leave it there. You'll never experience life the way you're supposed to until you realize that you matter. You are powerful beyond measure. No one can do what you were born to do. We each have our own calling. All of us are born with a purpose. It's our job to manifest our greatness. It's not just possible for you to have your dream; it's necessary. Go for what's yours in the universe.

According to best-selling author Malcolm Gladwell, every startup founder wants to go toe to toe with the big dogs in his or her industry. But in the beginning, it's important not to compare yourself to your biggest competitors in your field. Rather, it's best to think of yourself as a large fish in a small pond.[26] Gladwell writes, "Our sense of our own self-worth and our own self-confidence is derived from judgments about our peer group." Gladwell discusses the currents that lead some underdogs to succeed and others not to succeed in his book, *David and Goliath*. Gladwell says, "if you put someone in a very highly competitive pond, they are going to reach very different conclusions about who they are and what they're capable of than if you put them in a less selective, smaller pond."[27] This big-fish-in-a-little-pond thought experiment Gladwell posits can help you build the self-confidence you need to persevere through all the challenges you face.

Naturally, humans want to compare themselves to their competitors, but it can be quite dangerous and damaging to be in a situation in which you are constantly paralleling yourself to only the best of the best. In that case, you can wrongly assume that you're dumb or behind. The key is to compare yourself to your goals, your dreams. In the end, we all face the same question: Did you run your race? Everyone is different. Everyone's goals and desires and life are different. Focus on you, your plan, and your desires. Compare your progress to your plan and nothing else. Ask how you are doing in relation to your goals, not to where someone else is. Focus on impressing only yourself. We would achieve more if we chased our dreams instead of our competition. It may seem that everyone else is in the catbird seat, but it may not be true. You're not really free until you realize you're not competing with anyone else. That's why in the end the race is eternally against yourself. Don't compare yourself with others, compare yourself to your goals. Stay running in your race and running in your lane. You can't outperform someone who's not even in your race. Stop competing and comparing and be fulfilled with what you have. You have what you need for your race, and I have what I need for my race. If you measure yourself against those around you, you will be drawn to dwell on your own flaws. This can be a damaging trait. The less you compare, the happier you will be.

In this social media age in which we always have a fear of missing out, but remember what Ralph Waldo Emerson said, "Life is a journey, not a destination." You don't get to the end of your life and say, 'Yay! I won my life!' Where you are is just a chapter of your life. Over time you realize it's less of a race and more of a journey. Life is something you experience, not complete. Life's just a series of milestones. Life is an odyssey. So forget about plotting out a well-planned life. Your life isn't a business plan. Life isn't a project to be completed or a canvas to be explored. Life is just a big story, a long story. Everything is just a step to the next thing. So don't think that just because you haven't done X by age Y, you're a failure. There's a great timeline that shows various people with things happening to them at various times in their life; one gets married at 22, another gets married at 45, one gets their first job at 16, the other gets it at 30. So no matter where you are, you're just on a different timeline.

In life, we spend a lot of time psyching ourselves out. We're our own worst critics. No matter how positive our intentions, or how driven, every day is not a good day, and when the bad days come they can be terrifying. Having ominous feelings is upsetting. But why is this clash happening? Humans have historically been terrible at understanding absolute values, and are better at understanding deceleration and acceleration, or *rate of change.* So in effect, your state of mind pegs itself by comparing if you are doing better or worse than yesterday, rather than overall. Losing perspective is easy, so try to be the best you can be rather than comparing yourself to others. Focus on only impressing yourself. Don't waste your time on jealousy. Sometimes your you're ahead, sometimes your you're behind. The race is long, and in the end, it's only with yourself.

Don't resent other people's success. Resentment is like anger that remains hidden and bottled up. Focusing on another person's success will not pave the way to your own success. Even if you become successful, you may never be content if you're always focusing on others. Comparing yourself to others only sets you up for disappointment and you will also lose when you do. Make a distinction between the inner scorecard and the external one. Judge yourself against your own standards, your potential. That's the only metric to measure yourself against.

Winning isn't enough. People can get lucky and win. People can be assholes and win. Anyone can win. But not everyone is the best version of themselves. Stop comparing yourself because we have very little (if any) of the information we would need to make a rational comparison. In most cases, we are evaluating our worst against other's best when we compare. If you tether your happiness to feeling superior to others, you will be frustrated a lot of the time.

Even if you believe you are doing better than your peers, sooner or later someone will overtake you. If not, age will catch up. It's understandable that comparison is tempting – we use it as a way to motivate ourselves – but you will soon find that the goalposts will constantly change on a wide timescale. More importantly, in the end, you can never win. Theodore Roosevelt said, "Comparison is the thief of joy." Don't waste your time comparing yourself to others. Instead, use people you admire as a source of inspiration. Comparison takes the fun out of life. This encourages us not to lose ourselves by comparing our lives to that of others. If you notice that you are chronically single and it appears that all of your friends are getting married, it might be difficult not to compare. But the real question is how is your relationship *with you* going? Just keep setting personal goals specific to yourself, and maintain eye contact with those goals.

So many people are competing with other people. They continuously check in with others and mimic and copy what's "working." Competing with others pulls you from your authentic zone. Someone else's success is not your failure. You are not doing poorly, because someone else is doing well. Success is personal, so you can't compare yourself to anyone because everyone is defining success differently. Your goals should be in proportion to where you are and where you want to go. Celebrate your success as it comes. Never be envious of someone else's accomplishments. Jealousy and envy are the egos which operate out of fear. Be happy for others because their success has nothing to do with you. People can say what they want, and they will. Don't let it distract you from being who you want to be. Even if others' approval of us is equally seismic, don't compare yourself; celebrate yourself.

The time is now to focus on being the best you can be and not living up or down to people's expectations of you. All you can do is be yourself. Recognize that everything is not for everyone, so it's asinine to try to make it. Focus on what you do best. Don't worry about what others are doing; you must embrace what is special about you. Don't abandon what's gotten you here. You can't control other people; you can only control yourself and your actions and responses. It's like running a race. Constantly looking back at other people and checking how far they are only takes energy away from you running your race. So don't worry about people. Stop worrying about the competition, trust yourself, and run your race. You need to run your race as hard as you can with everything you can for yourself. Stop worrying about the competition and who's out there and who's doing what. Run your race. You are responsible for the space you hold in this world. You need mental toughness and the ability to compartmentalize; you need to focus all of your energy on things you can control.

Look at the older brother of the prodigal son in Luke 15:11-32. When his younger brother returns, he gets jealous because his father never threw him a party, and the father says, "All that I have is thine." In other words, you can have a party too. You don't need to be jealous, it's here for you too. It's just like in Genesis 4:6, 7, when God asks Cain why his countenance has fallen. Cain is jealous of God's acceptance of his brother, Abel, and God says, "If you do well, will I not accept you?" I've learned from Romans 2:11 that

God is not a respecter of persons; he is a respecter of principles. If you see God blessing someone else, you can do what they do and get it too. What God was saying is if you do well, as Abel did, you can have what Abel has. There's no need to be jealous; if you do what's right, God will bless you. Cain did himself no favors, and it doesn't do you any good to compare yourself to others because you're missing out on your deliverance. Go after dreams, not people.

DEFINE SUCCESS

People ask me if I think I'm successful and I reply, "It depends on how you keep score." Know how the score is being kept in your life. How do you want to keep score? Is it by money? Prestige? Influence? It's incredibly important to define success for yourself. Only you and you alone know what will make you feel accomplished. So when you want to achieve a goal, whether it's running a marathon, or starting a new business, start with the end in mind. There is a difference between objective and subjective success – the difference between your quantifiable LinkedIn list of accomplishments and your day-to-day emotional, intellectual pursuits. Just like everyone else in the world, you only have 168 hours per week to allocate. So it's especially important strategically to spend your time on the objective goals that will bring you the most subjective satisfaction. However, the question is raised, what brings satisfaction? It's different for different people – even at the same workplace, even in the same role. Here's an insight that I've learned about success: You can't be successful at everything. It can't happen.

We hear a lot of talk about work-life balance. That's nonsense; you can't have it all. Any vision of success has to admit what it's losing out on. Any wise life will accept that there is going to be an element in which we are not succeeding. Many times our ideas of what it would mean to live successfully are not our own. So, I want to argue that we should not give up our ideas of success, but we should make sure they are our own. We are the authors of our ambitions. Probe away at your notions of success. Make sure that your view of success is your own.

When you think of success, how will you know if you're successful? Do you rely on objective metrics such as your job title, the size of your bank account, or the college you get into? Or do you focus much more on the subjective metrics, such as the satisfaction you receive from solving problems at work, how happy you are at home, or the love of your family? Make success possible for yourself. Whether you realize it or not, you're placing a huge emphasis on your definition of success:

- *Subjective success*: happy family, healthy marriage, well-adjusted children, fulfilling relationships, personal achievements (e.g., running a marathon), presence at children's' events
- *Objective success*: salary, job title, awards, accolades, et cetera

Subjective success is an individual's response to an objective situation. For example, a corporate attorney may work for a highly respected firm and receive a generous compensation package, but if his or her career falls short of becoming a Supreme Court justice or they lose the intellectual buzz from practicing law, they won't *feel* successful. Success doesn't always feel successful. When most people are asked how they define success, success factors like making a difference or working with a good team on mutual goals may come to mind. However, when it comes to personal success, rewarding relationships almost always tops the list.

Nonetheless, if you believe that having a high-powered career and a family too is "successful," it requires that you allocate your energy and time wisely, as opposed to grabbing every possible brass ring. In effect, if your definition of success is just a laundry list of extrinsic rewards, then it may not be at all realistic – or as satisfying as you would imagine. No one would spearhead a major business initiative without establishing clear metrics for success, based on a strong consensus and vision of what a "win" would look like. No army would go to war without knowing precisely what their objective is and what their definition of success would look like. This same principle should apply to managing your affairs in life and career. Life is too short to expend valuable energy chasing objective success metrics that don't affect your subjective bottom line. Just as you would on the job, make your professional and personal "wins" clear, meaningful, and achievable. That's how you ensure maximum return on your investment of effort.

I've learned that the concept of "having it all" isn't really achievable. Having it all is like speeding in a car. You can always go faster; a crash isn't guaranteed, but the situation is more fragile. An accident at 25mph is just that, an accident. An accident at 90mph is fatal. Since this concept of "having it all" is not achievable, it's better to pick the places in your life where you want to be great and then do that. You're not going to be great at everything, but direct your energy and efforts towards those things which you are. It's incredible how much insanity and stress we put on ourselves. We wake up in the morning with a deficit, saying I'm already behind so I have to work very hard just to catch up. We're insane about everything in our life. Insane about money, about balance, et cetera. But success is what you want it to be. Successful people know what they want to go after. They know what THEY want; not what OTHERS want for them. The reason you're not motivated is because you have the wrong motives. Ask yourself, what kind of success are you after?

Consider with me why do many people who are capable of success, fail to break through to the next level? The answer is success. Success can be a catalyst for failure. Successful people become distracted by trivial things. When it comes to organizing your life, there are two options: the disciplined pursuit of the essential or the undisciplined pursuit of the nonessential. This matters because if you don't prioritize your life, someone else will. My point is, figure out what is important to you and pursue that.

According to sociological theory, our reality is, for the most part, "socially constructed." We make things real via our interaction with them. Take for example money. We may believe that money is a real thing, but in reality, it is nothing more than just paper and metal. Inherently, paper and metal aren't 'money.' Money is a shared meaning or value we give the paper and metal. In a likewise fashion, your identity is socially constructed by your interactions with other people and the reactions you have to the expectations of society.

When you take these things too seriously – like your socioeconomic status or how physically attractive you are – you are living in *"The Matrix."*[28] All of these things are nothing more than social constructs – invisible walls – and when you see them for what they are, you can be free from them. That's why in the film *The Matrix*, Neo learns that there is 'no spoon.' Once you are liberated from that caged existence, you will enter a world of far greater possibilities.

The reason I believe I've been so successful in my life is not because of how smart I am. There have been people more intelligent than I, and had higher IQ's than I, but it's because of my EQ. My emotional intelligence. It's a lie we get told in school, that how well you do in school is how well you will do in life. It's how you manage yourself and how you handle relationships that predict true success. It's about having empathy for other people, realizing what other people are going through, and sensing what matters to them. That's success. Our success is not solely tied to our IQ, but empathy, compassion, and other emotional quotients. Daniel Goleman's book *Emotional Intelligence*, confirms this theory.[29] Your IQ is a threshold that gets you in the game. What you know can get your foot in the door, but then it's all about your EQ, how well you treat people, whether people like you, whether you fit well, how you manage relationships, et cetera. Your IQ can tell you what you can do, but not how to do it. EQ is more important than IQ. Be about making a change, not just counting it. Experience and emotions are your best investments. The orthodox measures of success – fancy cars and houses – are no longer relevant. Emotions, memories, experience, and knowledge are the things that matter. What you really want is money and meaning. It's ok to have things; you just can't let things have you.

In our society we have added years to life, but not life to years. For some, it's all about money all of the time. For others, it's all about others. We live in a society that has pegged specific emotional rewards to the acquisition of material goods. It's not the material goods we want; it's the rewards we want. It's not the sports car or fancy home we want, it's the prestige and acknowledgment that comes from it. I thought winning was the most important thing early in my career. Moreover, I was right because it identified me and was my identity. I thought if winning isn't so important, they shouldn't keep score. However, I have also found that there are some things worth 'losing' for, sacrificing for, namely my family and my relationships. Significance in life doesn't come from status, sex, or salary; it comes from giving our lives away so that we find meaning and we find significance. I'm not a nihilist who rejects all principles in the belief that life is meaningless. Our lives do matter. We can only achieve our dreams once we become confident enough to set our own definition of success and know that our path is different from others. You are living a different story in this world, so how can your success ideology be the same as others'? If you are confident enough to break the stereotypical definition of success constructed by society, you are one who will realize your dream.

Everyone's aim of success is different. My ceiling could be your floor, and your floor could my ceiling. What's important is that you're in control of your ceiling. Success is different for everyone, so define what success is for you. What's success to one person could be a failure for another. Success is different for everyone, and it's a constantly moving target. Just when you thought you made it, it changes. Anyone that thinks they've "made it" is kidding themselves. Your definition of success is going to change, a lot before it's all over. What's important to you or how you define success at 21 may not be what's important to you or how you define success at 45. So always ask yourself what does success look like for you. Be direct and uncompromising. No one can tell you what you want. You have to know what you want. It's not other's definitions of success you should be concerned with but your own. Make sure your definition of success work for you.

If you let success regularly be interpreted as reaching the next thing put in front of you, you will never get there because there will always be something next to achieve. So unless you consciously stop and ask yourself what you define as success, you may end up chasing it your entire life. Don't be like most people who are like a donkey chasing the proverbial carrot. You'll never reach it. You're going to find out very quickly that you've had everything you wanted all along. Don't live for power or prestige or accomplishments; those aren't always indicative of success. A life is distinct from and lasts longer than a career, and equal attention must be given to the foundation for a successful life. Your net worth is not your value; your self-worth is. You are not your valuables. Strive not to be a success, but to be of value.

Everyone seeks after success or happiness. Whether it's in the workplace, at home, as a mother, as a father, as a friend, we want to achieve it in all areas of our lives. People portray success because people want to be successful. In everything, people want to be successful. That's why people buy cars they can't afford, clothes, et cetera. But real success is subjective, not objective. Winston Churchill said “there are two kinds of success: initial and ultimate.” Ultimately, success is realizing worthy goals. Joshua 1:8 says that God wants you to have good success. So if there's something called ‘good success,’ there must be something known as ‘bad success.’ You can be successfully wrong. Good success is what we should be after. Get into Gods purpose for your life. Create brilliance. Like Goldilocks, there is a certain amount of success that is 'just right.' Understand that human beings are awful predictors of our own happiness. There is a wrong kind of success and a right kind of success. Go after the right brand of success. There is only one real success and that is to be able to spend your life your own way. Real success is living life on your own terms. In the beginning, it's all about necessity, but in the end, it's always about freedom to live your life on your terms. That’s the only success worthy of being minted.

5

HIGHER CALLING

"For I know the plans I have for you, declares the Lord. Plans to prosper you and not to harm you. To give you a future and a hope"
– Jeremiah 29:11

PURPOSE

There is a rising chorus throughout society that work must have meaning and for good reason. There are vast readings in literature that claim to create the conditions that can support meaningful work. This is an incredibly positive development because work is a huge part of our lives and meaning in life isn't just "nice-to-have." We need purpose and meaning in the same way we need oxygen. There are few things more life-enriching and life-prolonging than a human experience underscored with a sense of meaning. Meaning is what makes people thrive; it's important to performance and well-being.

Conversely, a lack of meaning can undermine people's ability to function on many levels ranging from mental and physical health to job performance. Studies have shown that people missing a sense of meaning in their lives have a higher chance of exhibiting chronic inflammatory stress responses associated with life-threatening diseases like heart disease and even certain cancers.[30] Questions about purpose come at certain points in our life. Sometimes it's a midlife crisis; maybe it's a job loss, a relationship ending, et cetera. However, across many occupations, the numbers of people failing to find meaning in what they do are skyrocketing. It's important to realize that meaning is something you create on your own. Even in jobs that may appear dismal from the outside, you learn to make your work more meaningful yourself. The trick is to link your personal values and motivations to the work you perform. People who find meaning in their work pay close attention to the elements of their work they find energizing and fulfilling, and systematically find ways to incorporate them into how they perform their work. Look to find opportunities to make an authentic connection with the people who benefit from your work. Since you have the ability to govern how you think about and can respond to the conditions you experience, you also have control over the meaning you derive from your work.

Purpose is a funny thing. At its root, purpose is nothing more than an intangible asset that everybody understands, and yet nobody can pinpoint. When we think about why an event happened the way it did, we conclude that "it was meant to happen." The truth is, it takes a certain level of passion, meaning, and fulfillment to lead with purpose. We are at our best when reaching for a higher purpose that ranges far beyond simplistic notions of making money or self-interest claims. Leading with purpose is at the heart of everything you should do because it is purpose that pulls you and passion that ignites you.

A Gallup 2013 State of the American Workplace study found that nearly 70% of working Americans were unfulfilled with their jobs, and 18% were unfulfilled to such an extent they were actively undermining their co-workers. This increase is a surge from the Conference Board that found 55% of Americans dissatisfied with their jobs in 2010. It is clearly evident that we live in a time of chronic dissatisfaction in the workplace. Now there are many explanations for this phenomenon, such as factors like sluggish economic recovery, frozen wages, or fewer opportunities for career advancement. However, I believe the real answer is that it's not necessarily clear how someone goes about designing a satisfying career in today's professional culture. This is especially true when lasting fulfillment is the goal. Many people accept that careers are no longer linear, and the archetypal career ladder is broken, but they still attempt to increase the "slope" of their career trajectory, patiently waiting until they are unhappy, keeping an eye out for other opportunities which may seem better than their current job, applying for a few, and taking the best options they can get. As a result, most people just end up with a career path entrenched in arbitrary events that end up as a circuitous path, and at worst, is nothing more than a series of unfulfilling jobs.

There is hope and a solution to this dismal cycle, though. Research from Cal Newport (*So Good They Can't Ignore You*), Daniel Pink (*Drive*), Tony Hsieh (*Delivering Happiness*), and Reid

Hoffman (*Startup of You*)[31] illustrate the three fundamental attributes of fulfilling work:

- Legacy – Reaching a higher mission, cause, and purpose. This underscores that in some way, the world will be better after you have completed your work.

- Mastery – The art of improving and getting better at the skills and talents you enjoy to the point that they are intertwined with your identity. Think of a Samurai or picture a Jedi; even a master blacksmith.

- Freedom – The ability to choose what projects you work on, whom you work with, and where and when you work each day, and being paid enough to support the lifestyle you want.

More importantly, the order of legacy, mastery, and freedom in that sequence is important. People are fulfilled more quickly once they first prioritize the impact they want to have (legacy), then from that knowledge understand the skills and talents they will need to have that impact (mastery), and ultimately, "exchange" those skills for more flexibility and higher pay (freedom). It's important to note that many people generally don't have only one purpose. The things and causes you're passionate about – women's health, childhood education, organic food, et cetera – will likely evolve over time. Once more, it's vitally important to develop a high degree of freedom, so you're able to chase down your purpose when it floats onto the next thing. This means being able to volunteer for a cause you care about on the side, go months without receiving a paycheck, or invest in nonconventional development opportunities.

WHAT IS PURPOSE?

Everyone is searching for meaning, purpose, significance, and value. I read a study that said the average person doesn't like 85% of their life. That's incredible to me. No wonder people ask themselves, "What if my life could be more?" Aren't you tired of the inertia in your life? The magnitude of your life cannot be the routine. I get up, I go to work, I come home, I sleep, and do it all over again. This is not as good as it gets; it can be better. Life can be more. Too many people feel alive but are not living. People say they are living, but in reality, they're just existing. Recognize that you're not an accident, and you matter. You matter to God, you matter to history, and you matter to me. There's a difference between the survival level of living, the success level of living, and the significant level of existing. You know which one you're at by figuring out what on earth you are here for. There are some smart people who can't figure out their own problems, and there are successful people who aren't fulfilled. It comes down to this issue of meaning, significance, and purpose: What am I here for? Where am I going? What am I best at? What am I passionate about? What is my plan for my life? Your purpose doesn't have to be something soft or overly lofty, just concrete enough to contain a plan and a vision.

We all have basic human needs, and chief among them is the art of fulfillment. Ask yourself, "What gives my life meaning?" "What gives each act of mine purpose?" "What's my purpose?" "What am I supposed to do?" Sometimes we find out; other times we stumble upon it. Sometimes we give up and say, "God, where you take me is where I'm supposed to be." In my own life, the more I thought about it, the more questions I had, like "Why do we exist?" "What is the aim of my life?" "What is my purpose?" "Is my passion my purpose?" "Where do I derive meaning?" The toughest question to ask is "Where do I belong?" That's because it's hard to know. Each person forges their own destiny and meaning, so before we dive into what purpose is, let's discuss what purpose is not.

Your purpose is not your values or mission. Now, I do advocate for people to have a personal mission statement because it will clarify goals and guide decision making. Many people have a **vision statement**, which may say what they want to be like in some years' time. This is an effort to move their thinking beyond day-to-day activity in a more concise, clear, and memorable way. As an example, the Swedish company Ericsson, defines its vision as being "the prime driver in an all-communicating world." There's also the **mission** that describes what business the organization is in (and what it isn't), both now and projecting into the future. For example, a consulting firm may define its own mission by the type of work it does, level of service it provides, or clients it caters to. Many people today try not to have work-life balance anymore, but rather, more life in their work; their "life's work." **Values** are related to the desired culture like Coca-Cola serving as a behavioral compass, having the courage to shape a better future and leveraging collective genius. Now, if values provide the compass, **principles** give the set of directions.

So how does purpose differ from vision, mission, values, or principles? Purpose says, "This is what I am doing for someone else." It is something that connects with the heart as well as the head. It's the philosophical heartbeat of our life. The truth is, why you lead your life determines how well you lead your life. People with internal, intrinsic motives often perform better than those with external, instrumental rationales for their actions. Living a life that is driven by purpose is a lot more meaningful and gratifying than meandering through life without direction. No matter what you want to be in society or business, first ask yourself, "Why do I want to be *fill in the blank*?" The answer will make a significant difference in how well you lead your life.

In American history, there was a prevailing doctrine called Manifest Destiny. It was the American belief during the 19th century that the United States was destined to stretch throughout the American continent. This belief carried America to be a global leader for the next century. This belief shepherded an era of immense progress in America. Likewise, you too have a destiny for your life. A destiny in which you don't want just a job; you want a calling. Since the dawn of time, humans have questioned their existence, and you are no different. We all have a desire for a meaningful life and a joyful life. We don't want apathy to rule our life or routine. The average life expectancy is now approaching 80, but how many of us live those years with purpose? How many of us live purposeless and depressed lives? Discovering your purpose – your driving force – is a scientifically proven way of escaping that emptiness. Research shows that people with a sense of purpose are indeed happier in their social, spiritual, and individual lives. Having a defined, actionable purpose can help improve cognitive function and increase overall wellbeing. People said Martin Luther King Jr. was ahead of his time, or Barack Obama was ahead of his time, but Benjamin Mays said at Martin Luther King Jr.'s funeral, "No man is ahead of his time. Every man is within his star, each in his time. Each man must respond to the call of God in his lifetime and not in somebody else's time." The Bible says in Esther 4:14 that this moment right here is the moment for which you were created. Not 15 years from now or 15 years ago, but right here, right now.

We all have a limited amount of time here to actualize ourselves. However, the question is who are you and what do you want to do with it? Align your personality with your purpose. Align your personality with your soul. Uncover what you are made for. Uncover just what you are here to do and what your race is to run. Your real job is to figure out why you're here and get on about the business of doing it.

WHY PURPOSE MATTERS

All of us are somewhere between our birth and our death. We're all moving towards our death, and so you want your life to mean something or at least have some purpose to your existence. All life is based on entropy, the principle that everything is on a march towards decay. I'll talk more about entropy a little later on. Actors always talk about "motivation." What is my character's motivation? Why do people do what they do? What's driving me? Too many people don't know why they do what they do; they don't know what their motivation is. Do you know why you do what you do? Patanjali lived around 100 B.C. in India. He put together the yoga sutras, the philosophy underlying the sun salutations that you may start the day with in your Yoga practice. Patanjali recognized the importance of having purpose, writing, “When some great purpose inspires you, some extraordinary project, all your thoughts break their bonds.”[32] He recognized that our minds transcend limitations, and our consciousness expands in every direction. Therefore, we find ourselves in a new, great, and wonderful world. When we live and act with purpose, dormant forces, faculties, and talents become alive, and we discover a self within us that is by far greater than we ever dreamed ourselves to be. Pretty epic, huh?

W. Clement Stone said, “Definiteness of purpose is the starting of all achievement.” The secret of success is consistency with purpose. Achievement is wonderful when you know why you're doing what you’re doing. Moreover, when you don't know, it can be a terrible trap. Purpose is the ‘why' side of life – why you do what you do, why you wake up early. A job is about a lot more than a paycheck. It's about dignity, identity. It's about being able to look your family in the eye and say things are going to be all right. Purpose makes you stop living to work, as is frequently done in our society, and start working to live. Recognize that if you live each day as though it were your last, one day it will be. So ask yourself if today were the last day of my life, would I want to do what I am going to do today? If the answer scares you, then it’s time for a change. I know you want to enjoy your day rather than just get through it. There's so much more to life than this life. The truth is if you don't have a cause, you can't have an effect. If you don't have a purpose or something to live for, you can't have an impact.

Too many of us have fuel but no fire. We have been well exposed to novelty, well educated, but there is no fire in the belly, with no isolated purpose to identify. No matter how hard you work, if you don't have purpose or spirit, you can see the air leave the balloon. God says in Zechariah 4:6, “It's not by might or by works, but by my spirit.” Your purpose is your spirit, and without it, you are like a balloon without air in it. You need more than shelter and food to survive; you need engagement, fellowship, meaning, purpose, love. You are not unlike any other living organism in nature; you need more than just water and sunshine to grow, you need harmony, balance, and purpose.

At our core, we crave meaning and belonging. We long for meaning, and we long to be where we are wanted. When people find purpose they find meaning, and when they find meaning they find significance. It's an existential threat to live without purpose. Everybody is dressed up and going nowhere in our world today. Everybody looks like something they are not. We focus on the external and not the internal. You can have more degrees than a thermometer, but if you don't have a purpose, you cannot do what you have been called to do. I can't promise you that life will be easy. I can't promise you that people won't hurt you or disappoint you. I can't promise you an unscathed life. I can't promise you a happily-ever-after life, but what I can promise you is it won't be a wasted one.

ME, MYSELF, AND WHY?

The only reason we are here is purpose; to figure out our why. We must have a goal, purpose, and theme to our lives. What am I meant for? What am I here for? Whom am I supposed to be? You are meant for your purpose, and you are to be the outcome of that pursuit. Find your 'why.' When it's 5 a.m. and you want to sleep in, remind yourself of why you're exercising, going to work, pursuing your career, et cetera. All of us are searching for something unforgettable and everlasting that's beyond us. Know your why.

When you know why you're doing something, you will get what you want a lot faster than if you don't know why. It's about your life's work, will, and purpose. Having a purpose is critical to being successful, whether in business or life. Work hard at something that matters to you; work hard to make a difference. Why do you want to be successful? Why do you want wealth? Are you good at your job, do you enjoy it, and do you find it meaningful? How will you serve the world? The effect you have on others is the most valuable currency there is. So ultimately, the two questions are: “Do you have a purpose?” and “Are you pursuing it?” If you answer yes to both questions, you are exactly whom you're supposed to be, and you are where you're supposed to be.

If you have the why, you'll always have a what and how. What's driving you? What's your gut telling you? What's your motivation? Find out now. Regain your motivation by understanding the big 'why' behind what you do. To be fully engaged with our lives we must have bigger and bolder goals. Why do you do what you do? Do you really know? The best way to discover purpose is to keep using two simple words "so that..." for example "I am a project manager so that I can help people achieve more so that their organization can attract more clients so that the difference they make is more impactful." This exercise will help you isolate your priorities and gain direction and enthusiasm to work on the things most important to you. Regain your motivation and purpose by saying, "I do what I do so that..."

Sigmund Freud said, “People need two things in life: love and meaningful work.” Early in my career I had the love. I just needed meaningful work. However, I realized pretty quickly, don't just do what you love. Love is a consequence of meaningful work instead of motivation for it. The problem with meanings is that they're Sisyphus-like: You're going up the hill looking for greater implications, and you never get there. Rather, if you pursue your purpose, your desires will follow. There are many people meandering around, without any idea about why they're doing what they're doing. To want to be ambitious, and to want to be successful are not enough; that's just desire. Alternatively, if you know what you want and understand why you're doing it, if you dedicate every breath in your body to it, if you believe your particular talent is worth developing and caring for, there's nothing you can't achieve. It's less about you and more about what's inside of you. Redefine what you want, then revisit and refocus on why you're here in the first place.

The purpose of your time here on earth is not primarily about acquiring possessions, attaining success, or experiencing happiness.

Those are secondary issues. Life is all about love – with God and with other people. Now, you may succeed in some areas, but if you fail to learn how to love God and love others, you have missed the reason God created you. We were created in love in order to love. So whether your life is long or short, it matters what it was lived for.

People ask me what their purpose is and what they are supposed to do. The only way to know what to do in life is to pay attention to the life you're living right now. You can't get it by listening to other people. You can't let the voices of the world drown out your own inner voice, that voice of consciousness. You have to decide for yourself that there's something more and listen to that calling and be guided by that. You deserve and are worthy of the best this world and creation has to offer. Look, it's bad enough to not get what you want, but it's worse not to know what you want and to find out after the journey that it wasn't what you wanted all along. Henry David Thoreau said, "Many men go fishing all of their life, not knowing that it is not fish they are after." It's imperative you know what you're after.

Most people do what they are taught and do what they see without ever knowing what it is they really want. Focus on your 'why.' Why are you here? Why are you doing what you're doing? While you're here on earth, figure out what your purpose is. You have to figure out and ask yourself first, "What is it that I want to do with my life?" Then ask why. "Why do I want _________ for my life, and what does it mean to me and for me?" Once you know that, everything else in life is there to help you reach that. Otherwise, if you don't know, you're going to end up being a tool helping someone else reach their goal. When you know why you're doing something, you will get what you're after a lot faster than if you don't. Having a purpose is essential for success in life. Don't think about what you want from life; think about what life wants from you.

Focus on the mission, not the position. God is not a booking agent, and he is not a talent agency. Position means nothing if you don't understand the mission. God will change your position to accomplish your mission. Don't get drunk off your position; pride comes before a fall. God has given you every dollar, every talent, every gift because he wants to trust you with the mission, not the position. I want to ask you if you see yourself on a mission? Most people pray for a position; they pray 'let me have power and favor.' However, God will not feed your insecurity. Until you understand the why of it, you won't get the what of it. More money for what, more people for what, more power for what. Most people are driven by ego. Until you are mission-driven, resources will be denied. Why do you want what you want? Is it more mission or more money, because if your money doesn't have a mission than it doesn't matter.

Go out there and find what you're looking for because only you know what you're looking for. I can't tell you what you want. You have to know, and only you know. The Japanese in Okinawa have a word for that, Ikigai, "the reason for which I wake in the morning." Without Ikigai, we cannot answer the questions: *Why do we exist? What is my purpose? Am I here by accident?* Uncover your deepest yearning and reason for living. There's always something within us that wants to be conscious of itself as us. There's something in us that wants to be expressed. It's easy to think about everything you're not. It's easy to say I've tried that before, and I failed. I'm not qualified enough. Quit focusing on what you're not and start focusing on what you can become. Efforts and courage are nothing without purpose and direction. Life is about following the path that was meant for you. Two moments matter most: the moment you were born, and the moment you realize why you were born. It's a great gift to be able to define what your purpose is. Don't force it, trust that it will come, leave room for inspiration, prepare yourself. We all have a destination, and it doesn't matter how you get there, what matters is that you go.

You Decide the Meaning

Every time I find the meaning of life, they change it. So you have to find your own meaning. The meaning of life is the meaning you decide to give it. The meaning of life comes from within. Nobody is going to tell you what life should mean to you; you have to decide that for yourself. **The question isn't what's the meaning of life, but rather what's the meaning of *my* life.** People should be less concerned with the meaning of life and more concerned with the meaning of their life. Love is just a word until someone comes by and gives it meaning. The same thing goes for life. Life is just a word until you give it meaning. The same thing goes for the word purpose. Each person determines the purpose and meaning of their life. You can't be the key to every door; so clarify your purpose. Know who you are and who you are not; know where you fit and where you don't. You can't be all things to all people. Each day is packed with questions of how to spend your time, money, emotions, and focus. You have to know everything that you want to do, and begin each day as if it were on purpose. We all face the eternal lament and want to know why things happen the way they do. However, think about what your motive is for action, not for yesterday, but today. The worst question you can ask yourself in your life is "How did I get here?" Have a direction for your life. Embrace who you were created to be. You were made to stand out. You were made to matter. Everybody's not supposed to be everything, so find your strike zone. Don't end up like *Macbeth* whereby "nothing became of his life like the leaving of it." Make your life memorable while you still have it.

Start With 'Why'

Start with 'why' to fulfill your destiny. When you start with 'why,' it gives your life new meaning. If you struggle knowing what you 'should' do, think about what you 'can' do and start there. We all have a yearning; what matters is that we listen to it. Some say the purpose of life is to find the purpose of life, and there's a lot of truth to it because to have a career with purpose you need insight, inspiration, and intention. In a world where it seems that people are needed but not necessary, we all want to live a full life and a better life, but how do we get there? How do we attain a properly balanced existence? The answer lies within, and we are here to unfold our souls.

Humans are wired for meaning and purpose, and your ability to push through tough situations is directly tied to that purpose. Any business, any flight plan always has a mission, and if you don't know your mission, you will lose direction quickly when things get hard. Let your 'why' drive you. If you have meaning in your life, you can survive anything. Moreover, without it, you'll never have the deep fulfillment we all hunger for. When the "WHY" is strong enough, you'll find the "HOW." Your "why" is your center of gravity. You need direction and a blueprint of where you're going. Energy follows motivation. It's not what you do; it's how you do it. It's not what you do; it's why you do it. Focus on your mission. Focus on your "why." What is the drive behind everything you do in life? You can take meaningful action once you're clear about where you're going. Stay fixed on your mission but flexible in how you get there. Don't be scared to change directions or explore new avenues quickly.

The very first command God gave Adam was to be fruitful. However, you cannot be fruitful if you haven't identified your seed. What's your seed, your gift? Your life's work should be a living organism and not all about the money. Your work should matter. Aristotle is one of the more famous ancient Greeks around 300 B.C. Aristotle was one of the first people who laid out ideas (which we now consider scientific) about the natural world, but he also gave an honest critique of living a capitalistic life 2,000 years before Karl Marx came on the stage. Aristotle is quoted as saying, "The life of money-making is one undertaken under compulsion, and wealth is evidently not the good we are seeking; for it is merely useful and for the sake of something else."[33]Aristotle recognized that living for money was not a smart call since money was only useful when leveraged as a tool to gain something else – such as security or status. Money will not make you happy. Money will help sustain you, reduce stress, and provide some amazing experiences in life, but your overall state of happiness needs to be anchored around a purpose. Money is a byproduct; it's not a purpose. Whether you're a company or just an individual, be purpose driven. You have to jettison the people and things out of your life that don't matter, and focus on what's meaningful for you. That's very liberating counsel because I don't think anybody can have it all, but you can have what you want if you focus on it and figure it out.

Know why you're doing what you're doing. Know what the vision for your life is. Successful people are successful because they do things which are important to them. You **win from within first**. The world's filled with people with passions and interests, but not much purpose. So many people want to be all-purpose and all-of-the-above. Make your work purpose driven and be internally motivated. You need to pull back a little at times and listen to your own drummer. Successful people do not love the world because they know the world will not love them back. They invest in people and invest in themselves; everything else is ancillary. Don't get caught up in the luxury of this world. Focus on what's lasting. I look at the Leprechaun from those Lucky Charms commercials. He does all that stuff – hopping around, being mischievous – and at the end of the day it's just sugary corn flakes; it's just cereal. Most success is just 'cereal.' Flaky and worthless. As stated before, there is a difference between success and significance. You get successful and very much so, and then at that point, there's no more margin for failure; only degrees of success. Live unattached and purpose grounded.

Hitch Your Wagon to a Star

I have found people have one pressing question regarding their purpose: "Does the work I do have any redeeming social value?" More specifically, "Does my work do any good in the world?" This is an age-old question that Karl Marx called the alienation of labor, in which the laborer does not see the fruits of their labor.[34] Furthermore, Greek mythology raises the example of Sisyphus, who was a former king punished by the gods and condemned to push an immense boulder up a hill and watch it roll down and do it forever.[35] The book of Ecclesiastes from the Bible states, "Yet when I surveyed all that my hands had done and that what I toiled to achieve, everything was meaningless, a chasing after the wind. – It did not profit me." This is why it's so important to have meaning. These Titans of the past illustrate to us that if you're not happy with what you're doing, every day will feel like punishment. You need reasons to keep going; you need purpose and meaning. Your 'why' is going to push you when you can't push yourself.

In Isaiah 6:1, God asks, "Whom shall I send?" and Isaiah says, "Here am I, use me, send me." God uses a lump of hot coal to purge his lips and cleanse him so he can be used. Volunteer your life to be of use. Live for the present; life is now. Be a part of something; don't live for yourself. My message to you is: it's not about you. Your 'why' can never be about you. It has to be about someone else, family, something bigger than just yourself. The purpose of our lives is to help others through it. Your job is to defend the truth, and it's to defend the facts. The sheer joy of doing what you believe is right is inexpressible. Attach yourself to a higher purpose. Get involved with something of worth. Pick something meaningful to accomplish and then attack it. Be focused and centered around how you want to change and impact the world, and use your platform to that end.

Use that platform; do not be used by it. Reach for the world that ought to be. We don’t have to live in an idealized world to reach for ideals that can make the world a better place. My prayer is always four words: **What's next; I'm available**. It's an acknowledgment that I don't belong to myself, and I'm here to serve. I am not my own; I belong to God. I am not somebody; I am somebody's. I'm not the choreographer of my life. There is something greater than myself that I am a part of, and it is also a part of me. I call that God. You are here for a reason, and you are co-creating that life with God.

The fact that you are here matters. All the events that had to come together just right, that one egg and that one sperm, of all the choices and opportunities, it chose you. All the circumstances that had to figure and reconfigure to get you to where you are today – wow! What a celebration. Look at our universe, where the earth is rotating, and it's also revolving around the sun, and the sun is in a more extensive system that is rotating; all of these rotations are symmetries. We're all a part of something larger than ourselves. Everything in the universe is a part of something larger than itself, even you. At the end of the day we are a bunch of little people in a big planet, in a vast galaxy, and before you know it we're going to be a bunch of dust. We are not that big a deal. The billionaires get buried next to the Uber drivers. Get over yourself. Every day, do your best to birth your gifts. We are so addicted to what the world thinks of us. Listen to your inner voice and be guided by that. We have an obligation to God and others. However, we also have a responsibility to ourselves. Your purpose is to make a difference with the time you have left. Don't just look for your blessing; hope to become a blessing for someone else. Change lives and save lives by sharing your life.

Recognize that you do revolve, just not around yourself. We're not the center of our universe we're apart of something much larger. Just like Copernicus, we are not the center of the universe. Giordano Bruno showed that the cosmos is infinite and we are part of that thread.[36] There is no up, no down, no left, no right, no center. Just an endless tapestry we happen to be a part of. You live in a world much bigger than yourself. You're not here by accident, you are called and led. So please trust me when I say this: The world has nothing to offer you. You don't need everything you want, and you shouldn't want everything you see. Reach for things higher, things not of this world. You belong to God and are blessed. In my own life I realized I was very blessed, but by the same measure I realized that to whom much is given, much is lost. I couldn't do everything that my friends were doing. I couldn't go everywhere, and I couldn't be just anything. I had a higher calling. You too have a higher purpose that transcends. Is there anything in your life that's bigger than you? That's bigger than the car you drive or the clothes you wear? Something bigger than what's sustaining you? Serve a higher purpose than yourself. If you wish to drown, don't torture yourself with shallow water. Die going after something more substantial than you. Reach for dreams bigger than you.

When you're at work, don't just give something for people to do, give them something to be. You need more than skill and talent; you need belief and buy-in. A belief that this is your purpose. When we are deeply involved in attempting to reach a goal or an activity that is difficult but well suited to our skills, we experience a joyful state called "flow." Get in your flow. Flow is the secret to joy. Flow is effortless and spontaneous; being still. Let it come to you. Everything goes right. Everything feels good, it's a rush. It's automatic without even thinking, like you're on automatic pilot; you don't have any thoughts. Ecstasy in Greek means to stand to the side of something, and it has become an analogy for a mental state. Essentially, it's stepping into an alternative reality.

Arthur Miller's famous play, *Death of a Salesman,* is one of my favorites. Miller's protagonist says at one point of frustration, "to suffer fifty weeks of the year for the sake of a two-week vacation, when all you really desire is to be outdoors, with your shirt off." So many people go through life on cruise control, never really doing what they want or becoming whom they want to be. However, I've found that if you're going to be happy, stop focusing on yourself. We are social beings. Think about it. People are happiest when they are in flow, absorbed with something, with other people, engaged in sports, focused on loved ones, discovering, learning.

Ultimately, love is the only way to self-actualization. Viktor E. Frankl said, "True meaning in life is to be discovered in the world rather than within man or his own psyche. I have termed this constitutive characteristic 'the self-transcendence of human existence.' The more one forgets himself—by giving himself to a cause to serve or another person to love—the more human he is, and the more he actualizes himself. What is called self-actualization is not an attainable aim at all, for the simple reason that the more one would strive for it, the more he would miss it. In other words, self-actualization is possible only as a side-effect of self-transcendence." Self-actualization means to fulfill your highest potential and to fully become what you can become. Self-actualization is about hitching your wagon to something bigger than yourself. Most people will never get beyond their own self-obsession. They get locked within the walls of their own suppressed emotions and socially composed reality. Your life doesn't have to be built around your own happiness; you can dedicate your life to something larger than yourself. In the process, you will find and become your actualized self.

What people want is to live and to be engaged with their own lives. To be a part of something more, something bigger than themselves. It's hard to be happy until you find something more important than yourself. So, hitch your wagon to something bigger than yourself. Attach yourself to a greater reality. Let your gift be guided by something more clear. I lived in Florence, Italy, for a summer and what these great giants of the past gave us was not just frescos, or sculptures, but experiences through a canvas of history. That's how you're remembered, by the experiences you offer people.

We want to be remembered and do things that are heightened in a certain way, yet grounded. We are not looking necessarily for fame and fortune, but just something that makes life meaningful and worth living. Let the focus of your life be beyond yourself. When you have a purpose, you have meaning. When you have meaning, you have significance. When you have significance, you have a reason. When you have a reason, you have success. People often debate: Should I live my life for now or should I live it for later (afterlife)? The answer is both. There's more to life than just being alive. If you think this life is it, that's all you live for. You smoke, you get wild, you don't realize that there's more to life than life. There's hope to live for, people to live for, dreams to live for, more to live for. Live a life larger than yourself. Our meaning of life is to attach and connect ourselves to some cause or purpose so that we feel that because we lived something was better; because we lived, that's meaning. You don't always have to wait on someone to call on you for you to engage. Join something, align yourself with some cause, and contribute your talents. Aligned is the new hustle. This is the new world order.

YOU'RE HERE FOR A REASON

At a certain point in our lives, we become what we do. We want our jobs and lives to fit us like tailored clothing, but it often seems that the secret to massive success and happiness is in finding purpose and working with meaning. Find a noble purpose. This is your call to action. It is the step which interweaves your core values into your day-to-day life. It provides you meaning and a reason to do your jobs. By doing so, you can formulate an "endgame" for yourself. You can examine just what you want your career to mean once it draws to a close. Many people spend their life on a career treadmill, not thinking about what their career will mean when they are done. Purpose is about bringing who you are to what you do. Find the intersection between your skills and your passions. My career now is no longer the reason for my being or my purpose, but now it's an expression of who I am. My job is to be fully me. You aren't what you do; you do what you are. Whomever you are do that. So if you believe you are having a rough day, place your hand over your heart. Do you feel that? You're alive for a purpose. Don't give up. What I am saying is if you are breathing and you're alive I want you to know you're not an accident. Your life isn't in vain. You have a purpose to fulfill.

We need to get in agreement with God. You can't come to God halfway. You have to give an entire dedication of yourself. You have to commit. Before I started my business, I asked God one question: "Is it mine?" Because I don't want to go after something that's not mine. Everyone has their own race, but you have to figure out what your 'own' is. Dig down deep; find what your lane is. To everyone whom God breathed life into he gave a purpose and a destiny. You have what you need for your race. Don't be jealous of what someone else has or is doing; you're not running their race, you're running your race. The Bible says in Acts 13:36, "David fulfilled the purpose for his generation." You are strong and well able; you can talk yourself into your dreams, or you can talk yourself out of your dreams. You are a hot commodity. So don't compare yourself to others; it's about doing your best with what you've been given. Work incredibly hard and just be the best you can be. Focus and be at peace with where you are. I'm not saying be content as in "I'm okay with what I have and I'll stop trying." However, just be at peace with where you are currently while still striving for more. Understand your divine purpose on this earth. Live now and get in alignment with whom you were created to be.

Human beings are determined creatures, and we have an internal calling to seek. Part of that seeking is understanding what we are created for. Every created thing is a solution. Everything solves a problem; your eyes solve a problem, my glass of water, my ears, my legs, et cetera. You’re put on this earth to solve problems. Stars were made to light up the night sky. What were you made to do? We have to ask what our purpose is, what our gifts are to share, then get on with it.

Everyone is looking for some purpose that will give meaning to their life. People need to be able to express, pursue, and exercise their purpose. People tell me, “I need to experience that my life matters, I just wish I knew what I was supposed to do.” I was there too. I was at a point in my life in which I needed some guidance and a sense of direction. Everyone has a need to answer basic questions like “Why am I alive and what does my life mean?” “What does my death mean?” “What's the purpose of my existence?” All of us have a specific purpose for our lives. However, the answer lies within you. Dig deep to find those answers. Human beings are the only beings who are conscious of their own death, and we are deeply afraid that our lives won’t matter. People don't believe because of needs, but we disbelieve because of needs. The opposite of depression isn't happiness, but vitality. The way your life has been going can be different. It doesn't have to be the way it's always been. It can be better. You can be more. Life can mean more. I cannot agree with the Zero Theorem that says "All is for nothing: everything adds up to zero. Life has no purpose." It does.

God says in John 15:16, "You did not choose Me, but I chose you and appointed you that you should go and bear fruit and that your fruit should remain, that whatever you ask the Father in My Name He may give you." You're not just another link in the chain; you have a purpose. Our lives are not meant to be as a leaf blown by the wind or a twig on the tide. We are not on this earth to just be on this earth. There is a purpose and direction to our lives. You were put on Earth to fulfill a specific purpose; you only need to name it to achieve it. As you embark on your life, I challenge you to do the work that matters. The goal is living a life well. To fulfill a divine purpose, you have to answer when you're called. I am imploring you to answer the call on your life. You have visions that can change the world. You are well positioned, so don't be afraid to dream out loud. Believe that there is a reason you are here, and your job is to still the mind and feel that.

Live With Intention

If there is a law, canon, code, treatise, or mantra I live by, it's the Sir Isaac Newton's third law of motion in physics: For every action, there is an equal and opposite reaction. Before you do anything, say anything, hear anything, make sure you have thought out your intentions. I do not do anything unless I am entirely clear as to why I am doing it, because what I'm sending out comes right back to me. What propels the action is the intention. It's the intention and purpose that drive the results and outcomes. Stay centered, connect, and always act with purpose. Don't say just anything, be purposeful. Be intentional with your actions and with your life. Live intentionally, every day and each moment with purpose.

The conventional thinking is that you have to live fast and die young. However, that's not the case. You can live with purpose and direction and that starts by living with intention. Stop asking what you should be doing and start understanding whom you want to be. Look, sometimes the truth is just staring at you in the face. When things get tough, identify your purpose. Purpose provides focus; it offers direction and guides decision making. Your purpose is the underlying belief for being and the why for why you're doing whatever you're doing. We're not on earth by accident. I exist to figure out why I exist. I didn't look far enough, and I didn't look deep enough. You can have gifts and talents, but your character is what matters. You're asking for more, but can God trust you with more? What have you done with what you've already been given? This is your wakeup call, and I'm sounding the alarm. What's your target? What are you after? You don't form it; you uncover it. I want you to have a sense of direction in your life. When you live with purpose, you're no longer the artist; you're the art.

Daniel Pink writes in his book, *Drive,* that purpose is self-direction, learning, and creating.[37] However, can you see the purpose of your work? There are three main ways to view the world regarding meaning, purpose, or significance in work. If you can triangulate across them, you will be well served. First is the view that no work has any purpose, second is the view that some work has purpose, and finally, all work has purpose. The first view is one that many people hold onto and they believe work has no significance and eventually bliss will come when their done working. The second view is also popular with people who are more mission-oriented and future-looking. But as for me, I believe that all work has a tremendous purpose, meaning, and significance, but only if you live intentionally. Everything you do should be an outgrowth of your purpose. All roads need to lead to Rome; all paths and activities you undertake should lead to the center of things. As a point of history, this was actually true during the Roman Empire when the empire's roads radiated out from the capital city, Rome. Everything you do should emanate from your purpose.

If you don't know what you are willing to fight for and why, the chances are that you will quit fighting when it gets tough. This is why I referenced the 1999 movie, *The Matrix*, earlier. It's all about consciousness and the idea of "waking up." Who am I? Why am I here? This is as the Buddhists call the birth of consciousness. What do people gain when they are around you? What do people lose when you're not around? It's about living on purpose intentionally. It's so important to pay attention; to know what you're doing and why you're doing it. Many people don't understand their purpose; if you don't know your purpose, your immediate goal is to figure it out. Otherwise, you're just wandering around. Develop what God has put into you. Don't just be the trend of the week; have a lasting purpose.

We need total alignment with our purpose here on Earth. You had a purpose before anyone had an opinion. Ignite your purpose and set your life on fire. Be the most compelling person; compel people with the 'why.' The 'why' you're doing 'what' you’re doing. Have a clear purpose and map your meaning. Your life may have become robotic, and perhaps you just become numb, and you just get through the day, and you don't live with purpose, but we're called to live with purpose and intention. You may be tired of working on things that don't mean anything to you, and not pursuing things that you're passionate about. I know you want to go higher and higher. Move forward and go upwards. If you're not making someone else's life better, you're wasting your time, and time is the most precious gift. Let your purpose guide your work.

I believe that forty days is the amount of time required for transformation. Noah had 40 days with the flood, Moses had 40 years in the wilderness, Jesus had 40 days on the mount of temptation. For some of us, this is our 40th moment. It's our day of realizing we haven't been living the life we were called for. Let today be the day you live with intention and purpose. Be deliberate in your actions and pace your growth with purpose. You can't question it; you can only go towards it. Your goal can't be to work a job but rather to pursue a calling. Your calling and what you choose to do are two different things, and when you don't know what you're doing, it's fatal. So understand what you're doing or aiming towards. A definite purpose needs a definite plan that needs to be followed up by definite action every day.

Fear of Being Forgotten

If you miraculously disappeared, how long would it take before people knew you were gone? How long before you were missed? Personally, that triggered the question in me: "Do I even matter?" In the lives of many people, they're not asking what the meaning of life is; they're asking if their lives matter, if they have a contribution to make. So many people are aimless. They don't know what they're doing, and they do what's necessary to get by. Mortality scares us; the mere thought that we will die has a chilling effect for us because there is nothing to prove that we ever existed. That's why we say, "publish or perish." People want to be remembered. Think about it. People put their names on schools, buildings, or other places because they don't want to be forgotten, and there is nothing to prove we ever existed. If you're going to be remembered, put your name in literature, write literature, put your name on education buildings. Publishing is a way to live your life beyond yourself. Life is finite but if you want immortality, do something meaningful with your life that's lasting. Our own realization of mortality is a life shifting experience. Mortality is most alarming to us because we're only here for a brief moment and there is nothing to show we lived or existed. People want to be remembered. Ask yourself how you want to be remembered.

We are digitally curating ourselves. We have to record, post, and tweet every waking moment of what we do because we want to be remembered, relevant, and revered, and we fear becoming obsolete. Our deepest fear is being forgotten. Our fear is not being a failure, but being forgotten. I'm reminded of the 2007 New England Patriots who went undefeated in their season but lost in the Super Bowl. The season wasn't a failure, but their seasonal success was forgotten and all that is remembered was the Super Bowl loss. If you're walking on the beach and you don't leave any footprints, no one will ever know you were there. I believe that oblivion scares us. People want to be memorable and not forgettable. All arguments and global conflicts are the same: did you hear me, did you see me, and did what I said mean anything to you?

YOUR TIME IS LIMITED

There is a concept that is crucial to chemistry and physics. It helps explain why chemical processes go in one way and not the other. It explains why ice melts, why cream metastasizes in coffee, and why air leaks from a punctuated tire. It's called **entrop**y. All life is based on this principle. The entire world operates on this universal law of entropy. Entropy means that everything in the world is in a state of decline and decay. There's only one exception, the human spirit, which can evolve and ascend the upward staircase. I think it's why we love athletes, champions, or Olympians; it reminds us of what we're capable of. It's why we worship ourselves, and why all of our heroes are human heroes. However, we hardly know who we are. Even time is just an illusion; it's a social construct. Time isn't limited, going from January to December or noon to midnight. Time goes forward and backward. Time is elastic; it moves slowly when you're doing something you don't like, and moves faster when you're enjoying what you're doing. So it begs the question, how do we behave inside this body inside of time? How do we navigate that fate of mortality? How do we use this time we've been afforded? How do we live it successfully? I think of aging as an arch rather than a staircase. You're born, you peak, then you die into decrepitude. I see age not as pathology but as potential. This is not for the lucky few, but for all of us. It's what David Brooks calls the odyssey years.[38] We are continually searching and soul searching. We want our voices to be heard, and we want our words to be celebrated. We want to see if our voice is wanted and needed out there.

Here in America, we're just living our lives, and there are other people around the world fighting for theirs. So don't take your existence for granted. Your time is limited; use your time to pursue noble, necessary, and worthwhile goals. All you have to do is decide what to do with the time that is given to you. That's the only control there is. Decide now to choose the hard path that leads to the life you want. If you can't find something to live for, then you'd better find something to die for. A better life, true living, takes place at a different altitude.

In Luke 12:13-21, Jesus tells a rich man, "You fool, this night your life will be required of you." Jesus is saying that a man's life is more than all he can accumulate for himself. Jesus is telling this man he is a fool for putting his hope in things he could never enjoy or could save him. The rich man needed to know what Matthew 6 instructs, "Lay not up for yourself treasures on earth where moth and dust collect and thieves steal, but lay up your treasures in heaven." Paul writes in Colossians 3:2, "Set your thoughts on things above, not on earth." The Bible warns us in Job 14 that "The years of our lives are cut down like a flower." James 4:14 goes further adding, "Your life is a vapor that appears for a little and then vanishes." Our time is short on this earth; we are to maximize it.

SAY 'YES' – TO GOD's WILL

I have always been impressed with the biblical account of Moses in Exodus, because Moses is us. He's an ordinary man on an ordinary day, and has an extraordinary experience. There's a bush on fire, but not being consumed. Moses is a reluctant protagonist whose energies and efforts made a difference. There is a similar journey that each of us must take. Joseph Campbell would call this the hero's journey.[39] That brings us from our local temporal ego point of view – our self – to an understanding that of a person's wholeness. Moses didn't think he was worthy, but that unwillingness left a space for God to work. Moses is both you and me; it's a meta-story. He shudders and says, "Who am I to do this? I can't lead," and God finally says he will get Moses' brother to help him. That's like all of us. We may have a dream or vision for our lives, and we say, 'Who am I to do this? I'm not up to it.' There's a destiny within all of us. Something is calling all of us, and we are not presently the person who can fulfill it; we grow into it and say yes to it. God does not call the qualified; he qualifies the called. So that when you are called, God will qualify you when you say yes. All you have to do is say, 'yes.' Yes to your will God, yes to what you have for me. I didn't have the money or the resources, but when I said 'yes' money showed up, answers showed up, people showed up. Moreover, then I changed and I grew. Those people who say 'yes' today to the vision laid before them aren't the same people as they were before.

We're continually growing, evolving, and unfolding based on our ability, willingness, and capacity to say 'yes.' Say 'yes' to your own purpose, yes to your own destiny, yes to your own discovery. Moses had a speech impediment, so why would God call him? We all have impediments, but God will use us and it to deliver his will. Moses learned, and so will you, that you don't decide your assignment; you discover it. The apple seed doesn't ask the grape seed what it should be. That's why you crave what you're created for.

Let your personal mantra be "I am the temple; I am the vessel." Dip into your soul to be your true self and all that there is. The difficulty is this: We're a constellation of different identities that have emerged for various reasons. We're fathers, we're mothers, we're brothers, we're employers we're employees, and all of these identities are pulling upon our energy for their survival. However, there is a central identity, which is the I Am presence. Also, this identity invites us to be more of ourselves. Remember, it's the still small voice; we have to get quiet enough to hear it and distinguish the noise from the signal. At your fingertips is a whole world of creation. Within us is the ego, the pharaoh who advocates for the circumstances we know, and our intelligent brain. But also within us is the prophetic side that does have a destiny, that does have a call to make a difference with good. Align the pharaoh part with the heart. That's how you align God's will with our own.

I'm not a statistic. Statistics say I'm supposed to be dead or in jail, but God had other plans for me. I'm happy where I am. It wasn't easy, but it was worth it. My prayer to God is: "tie me to the altar and do what you want to do in my life. Bless me, Lord; send your fire. Whatever you have for me, Lord, I want. Do your will in my life. Whatever you do for me, I'll thank you, and I'll praise you; I'll lift your name." When God has called you into a place, you don't have to kiss up, you don't have to suck up, and you don't have to play up. When you wait on the Lord, he'll bring you to where you need to be. You don't have to know the right people; it's about God's purpose for you. God's purpose for you doesn't change.

I have a GPS in my car, and sometimes it will reroute you, but the destination remains the same. You may be redirected or rerouted, but your purpose is still the same. God may change methods or directions, but the destination for your life remains the same. I have something more important to live for than the moment. Your life is not meant to be as the lives of other people. You have been set aside for God's use and God's protection and direction. The Bible in 2 Timothy 2:20 talks about vessels of wood, silver, and gold being set aside for particular purposes. The script for your life has already been written. All you have to do is play your role. Who knows what God's use is for anyone in this world. It's up to us to encourage and help one another. Who knows; others may be sent here to help you or answer your prayers.

I spent my life looking for answers, but in the face of God, there are no questions. Many times life speaks to us in signs. There's a heart calling on your life, but that's only for you and your purpose.

Be aware that you have a purpose that you may not have discovered. Watching your dream unfold in your life may be something you can't imagine. Believe in yourself anyway. Don't sell your own self short. Don't give up on your beliefs. When you get to the point where you say, "What do I do? the bigger question is "God, what would you have me do?" Then surrender to his will and let him flow and move you where you need to be. It will come, but you must surrender. Giacomo Casanova said, "I don't conquer; I submit." It's time to submit to what's for us.

I was watching a lady on *American Idol* who had been on for the 7th time, and still had not made it past the auditioning round. The conventional thinking says, maybe this isn't for you. Maybe there's something else for her. We are so busy wanting the talents of others. Not everyone is meant to be a singer, and not everyone is meant to be a pro-athlete. You can't be successful at everything. Any wise, successful vision has to know what it's losing out on. You may want to be the guru of this and the ninja of that, or want to be a Swiss Army knife. But it's better to ask what's for me. Where am I supposed to be planted? You belong somewhere, not everywhere. You can't be everything to everybody; otherwise, you end up being nothing to nobody. Become whom you were destined to be.

I like watching ESPN. They always say 'He's a great athlete,' or 'She's a great athlete,' but being a great athlete is sport specific. Someone may be a great athlete for track and field, or a great athlete for swimming. They can run very fast in a straight line, but they may not be elusive as is needed in football or some other sport. Maybe in another sport, that skill or talent wouldn't be as advantageous. The point is don't keep up; set the pace in your lane.

Where you are matters as much as what you are. You don't belong everywhere; you belong somewhere. There are some places you don't belong. Look at the fish. It looks stupid, can't walk, can't talk, can't fly, but when it's in the water, in its environment, it thrives and has no rivals. You are no different, and there's a place for you. I take trains a lot when I'm in New York. There are various destinations and different platforms for each train; the key is to know that the train goes where the tracks go. Make sure you're on the right train. Trust the tracks, but you get off when its right for you. The elevator is there, but you decide when and where to get off. Everyone isn't supposed to go to every stop. What's your stop? Where are you headed?

In my own life, I don't want to emulate anyone else. There are definitely people I look up to, but I believe there is a path for me and me alone, which is alongside others. You can't be everyone else; you have to do what you were called to do, and be whom you were called to be. Follow your path. Whatever your path, be open to the journey. This will not be a process that concludes in a week, but the more open you are to the journey, the more opportunity you will see around you. Everything is not linear. Finding purpose and meaning is an intensely complex process that is full of many detours and many great success stories. Being open to the journey itself as opposed to a fixated destination is wise. Think more expansively about possibilities by looking up, sideways, and diagonally. So when you ask yourself, “What will I be?” Declare, ‘I will be still, I will be patient, I will be hopeful, I will be committed, I will be open.’

Remember that when it is none of you, it is all of God. When it is all of you, it is none of God. So stop trying to do it all on your own; let God in. Look at Moses, who stuttered and said I can’t do it because I can’t speak. That's when God steps in and blesses. It can't be your intellect, and it can't be because you look good; it has to be God's fire. It can't be your own fire. Leviticus 10 shows us what happens when we try to do things on our own, and we don't follow God's instructions. We get burned up! It has to be what God wants for you. That's why whatever you’re doing isn't working; because if you started it, you’ve got to finish it. However, if God started it, he has to finish it. Give it to God. That's what Paul means when he writes in Philippians 1:6, “He who has begun a good work in you will see it to completion.” If you let God light the fire in your life, there's no devil in hell that can stop you. You may have run, but it was God who gave you legs and the idea to run. You didn't do this; it was God. It was God who unhooked you from things, it was God who brought you through, and it was God who set you free. There is nothing you did that made God choose you. It's not because of your strength, your righteousness, your weakness, or anything. God chose you for such a time as this before you were even born.

I want to tell you how to beat the odds. I don't advocate gambling. Since all things belong to God and all things that have been given have been given to us by God, it is poor stewardship to gamble what has been given to us. In places like Las Vegas and Macau, with the billion-dollar casinos and hotels, it is hard to see the odds ever being in your favor; it is in favor of them. Whether the lottery, dice, or roulette, you can gamble on pretty much anything. Professional receivers of bets, called bookmakers, place the likelihood of winning and losing depending on the event. Each participant has odds placed on them. But let me ask you some serious questions. Will you win the contest of life? What are the odds? If a bookmaker were to take the odds of your life as a whole or part, what are the odds he would set? Will it be a happy life? What are the odds? Will your marriage be happy? What are the odds? Will you overcome bad habits? What are the odds? Will your life make a difference; will the world be better because you lived? What are the odds? As you near the end of your life, will you be a success or will you be a failure? What are the odds? What are the odds that your life matters? That your life makes a difference? Some people say, 'I've got it made; I got my education, I got a new car, I'm sophisticated in my trade,' but many people who think they've got their act together and believe that the odds are on their side soon find out the odds are against them. Many people who decide to live outside of God's will and whose objectives are contrary to God's soon find out the odds are overwhelmingly against them. The odds are against us because we live in a physical world; the odds are against us because life is unpredictable and so many things can go wrong, The odds are against us because we are error-prone and inclined to make mistakes. We need to find a way to beat the odds, so our lives are not entrenched in sorrow. It's hard to place the odds on your life because life is unpredictable. The only certainty to beating the odds is staying in God's will.

YOUR MISSION, SHOULD YOU CHOOSE TO ACCEPT IT...

People ask me all the time what my purpose is and how they can find their purpose. No one can tell you what your purpose is or what it is going to be. You have to know for yourself. You have to ask the questions of yourself. Ask what's trying to unfold in you, what's trying to emerge. Then move in that direction; that's how you find your purpose. The meaning of your life is yours to decide. Think about the meaning of an ant's life after you have stepped on it. Stop worrying about finding a purpose and way of life, and just do. Our purpose is continuously unfolding in the moment. Think not so much of your life's purpose, but your purpose for this moment. Resolve to find your purpose deep within you. Ultimately you will find that the world is not enough; there's always more to want. Keep on keeping on, dig in until you gut it out. You have it, and you keep going until you realize your purpose. Our purpose need not be an existential crisis. Our purpose is to learn from the past and shape the future. Mahatma Gandhi said, "Whatever you do in life will be insignificant, but it's important that you do it." We want to be alive and full of life, but when all we do is live for ourselves, it doesn't net those results. We call it the search for meaning, but we should call it forging meaning.

I think about Nietzsche who said, "truth is dead; knowledge is power" or Atlas, who carried the world, creating his own meaning, and subsequently carried his own meaning.

Don't be scared if you don't know who you are or what you want. Instead, find out. Start by asking the right questions and then experiment with opportunities that align with your interests. There is a huge experimental cycle when it comes to finding your purpose. You don't just wake up and say ok my destiny is X. You need bounded rationality, so instead of saying “I can be every possible thing in the world,” say I'm more of a math guy; my destiny is within that, or I'm more of a people person; my destiny is within that. Find your destiny there. Experimenting with what you’re good at goes hand in glove because the kind of person you are points to the things you're good at.

Keep experimenting with new things, and don't try to think about it in advance because you don't know what you don't know. You have to try different things out and see which flavors you prefer. Thomas Edison taught us that whoever experiments most wins. Look at every role and every job like a treasure map. Every detail matters and points you in the right direction and tells you where you need to go. You start with a few choices (i.e., I need to learn the piano; I need to learn Mandarin, et cetera), but it's like painting. You start painting but after a while the painting starts telling you what to do, and it starts to create itself in a way. Similarly, each situation is different, but every situation will tell you what you need to do. Even when you pray to God, eventually the answer you may get is “Stop asking me what to do. Stop waiting to be told what to do. Look around and see where you can be value added. That's what I want you to do.” See problems and implement solutions. We are called to implement a remedy for challenges. However, stop looking to others for meaning because your meaning can be whatever you want it to be. It's like my former boss said, “No one is going to tell you what to do; look around you and see what needs to be done and where you can be value added, then do that.” It's like a company that hires you. They are paying you money for a return on their investment. God has blessed you and wants a return on the investment. You're going to get out of this life what you put into it. Life is what you make it. The question is what are you going to do with the rest of your life, so you don't end up with regrets at the end?

6

CIRCLE OF INFLUENCE

"Show me who your friends are, and I will tell you what you are."
– Vladimir Lenin

BUILD A TEAM AROUND YOU

The United States Military has a 'Force Structure,' which is the combat-capable division that organizes for operations and is basically the brain headquarters where they allocate resources accordingly. In this headquarters, we see a team dedicated to achieving the best outcome. This force structure only works when the best and brightest are providing the best counsel. This force structure reminds us to *always have the smartest minds and people around you and never be the smartest in the room.* You don't have to have all the answers; you just need to surround yourself with the people who do. Surround yourself with people who have domain expertise. I didn't go to an Ivy League school, but some of my associates did. I make sure to surround myself with objective people so that their loyalty isn't being divided. That's what happens when you hire only friends or only work with family; there's too much history there and not enough objective counsel. Make sure you get people with different viewpoints, who serve as counterweights to balance the discussion.

Surround yourself with people better than you in areas in which you aren't proficient. Add stellar people to your roster, and encamp yourself with top talent. You can never have enough spark plugs around you. Unfortunately, that's not always the prevailing wisdom in this age. It seems that there's too much nepotism in this world and people getting ahead only because of their connections rather than their expertise. To maximize your potential, stop running your life off the buddy system. Start calling people because they're effective and because they can get the job done. Find people who have character, find people you can trust, find people who are committed, find people who are disciplined. This is important because someone can only lift you only as high as they are. You can only know what someone else knows, so be around people who know more, if not the most. The people around you have a considerable influence on the decisions you make because they can get in your ear. If they're right, it's a blessing, but if they're wrong, it's a curse. Hearing is important, and what goes into your ear matters; so much so the Bible says in Romans 10:17, that "faith comes by hearing and hearing by the word of God." In other words, we have to be careful about what we listen to. People are influenced by word of mouth. A friend may tell you I liked that restaurant, or you should try this, that, or the other. So be careful who has your ear.

Hang out with friends, but work with talented people. I work with many talented people, and they make me twice as good as I think I am. Create the most empowering environment around yourself. If you are around chickens, you end up being a chicken. If you are with eagles, you end up an eagle sooner or later. A person is known by the company they keep. You are your environment, and that is the most critical and significant influence. The truth is, you are the average of the three people you spend the most time with. Stick close to those who inspire you. We look to the attributes in others we most admire, so admire high caliber characteristics. Optimize for working with great people, people with integrity, people with values. It's important to listen to people, but they need to be the right people. The point is to stay out of your own way. Nobody knows everything, so be open to overtures to receiving help from those who are better than you in certain areas in which you are weak. There is no shame in getting help, so get the help that's needed.

TEAMWORK

Physiology tells us that our senses, by design, absorb massive amounts of information in relation to where we are, how we feel, and what we're doing. These stimuli follow a different neural pathway in each of us. We all make sense of them differently. As a result, we go through life understanding the world and influencing our behavior as though we're at the center of reality and everything around us derives its importance according to how it fits into our own narrative. This view warps our perception of our surroundings and how they unfold. For example, in cosmology, the Copernican Model states that Earth has no privileged position in the universe. Despite Earth's importance to us, on a grander scale, it's very unimportant. The same reasoning applies to people. In spite of the intensity with which we feel and sense, much of what happens in the broader world isn't just about us. There's a much larger picture and much more taking place. Success is about all of us getting ahead. Too many people have a Genghis Khan viewpoint who once said, "It's not sufficient that I succeed; everyone else must fail." That's the wrong outlook. Real success is about all of us getting ahead together. If you want to win in the 21st century, empower others. Make sure others are better than you. Lift each other up. Be a force multiplier.

I played a ton of basketball in high school. The biggest lesson I learned is that on the basketball court five become one and you need to play as a unit. It doesn't matter how good you are, and I don't care if your Michael Jordan; you still have to pass the ball. You need to get help. "Do-it-yourself-ing" is a trap to think you can go it alone without a support system and without supporting others. Think about the story in Mark 5:1 in which a man had a legion of demons in him, and Jesus cast them out to a group of pigs, and the pigs ended up drowning. No wonder why the man wasn't victorious, no wonder why he couldn't get loose, no wonder why he couldn't be free; he was carrying too much on his own. We need to share the burden. Teamwork is everything. Teamwork makes the dream work. No one can achieve success alone. You may be able to dream alone, build alone, and strive alone, but success requires the help and support of others.

I used to think I made my success happen, but I did not alone make my success happen. I had help from others. You always need others; you might get it started by yourself, but you need others to finish it. Building a team is essential. Any kind of vision needs people. Galvanize a cadre of people around your idea or goal. Having an ecosystem of supporters is critically vital for success. Nothing in life is achieved alone. Success isn't a solo act. Teamwork divides the risk and multiplies the reward. It takes a coordinated effort. A smart person only can provide solutions. You can call it bench strength, call it intellectual infrastructure around you, call it whatever you want, but surround yourself with trusted advisors. As Henry Ford says, "Coming together is the beginning. Keeping together is progress. Working together is the success." You're not a one-ring circus; don't try to do everything yourself. We come into this world needing others, and then we are told its braver to go it alone. However, the truth is the only path to fulfillment is through others. You always need other people. You may have the vision, but your provision comes from other people. The Bible says in Luke 6:38 "Pressed down, shaken together shall men give unto thy bosom." Your blessings always come from other people.

Early in my career, I was determined to be independent and create my own success, and I thought this meant learning everything on my own. However, the reality is, you can't be an expert at everything, so you have to surround yourself with brilliant, diverse people and not be afraid to ask questions. Everyone says they want to 'win,' but most say 'I want to win my way. I only want to win if I get the credit, if I'm the star player, and if I get to score the baskets.' However, sometimes winning means not winning your way. Sometimes winning is about sacrificing your paradigms for better ones, and that requires humbling yourself to get help. Help is often hard to ask for but easy to give. It's incredibly difficult asking for help (especially for men). It's hard admitting weakness and failure, but I want to encourage you to cultivate your personal advisory board who can adequately guide your career goals. Be open to contrary opinions, and recognize that their advice and connections are invaluable.

Be like an infant. Nobody is needier and has less to give than an infant. The difference between infants and adults is that infants communicate helplessness without choosing to. You must be like an infant. You are helpless, so admit it. Learn to receive what you cannot provide for yourself. Think about the poem titled *Footprints in the Sand*, in which the author says when he saw one set of footprints, he was carried. No one gets through this life alone. We need each other. Seek help and advice. If you come with an idea or vision, people will help you. Abandon the blame and the shame. Stop blaming other people, blaming circumstances; stop being prideful and ask for help. Don’t go solo all the way. Doing it alone limits your growth potential.

Do you know why we work together? Because one hand clapping doesn't make any noise. You need two because one cannot multiply. God created us so that we couldn't survive without each other. You encourage me, and I will encourage you. Iron sharpens iron, diamond cuts diamond, one hand washes the other. 1 Thessalonians 5:11 says, "Encourage one another and build each other up." It's ok for us to challenge one another as long as it's not threatening. Growing alone is hard. People grow best in a community. We’ve got to do it together. Individually, threads are weak, but together they're strong rope. None of us is going to make it on our own. We need each other. None of us is smarter or greater than all of us.

The acronym 'OPM' shouldn't just be other people's money; it should be other people's mindset; learning from other people's mistakes, and other people's manpower. You cannot achieve your vision alone or in a vacuum. Understand the power of leverage. Do what you do best and get others to do the rest. You need to know what you're good at and what you need help with to properly meet your goals. It takes some advocates on your behalf to reach your success. At one point or another, you're going to need advocates to go to bat for you. I love watching football and I can tell you it's easier to score a touchdown if you have blockers and tackles in front of you. So who's blocking for you? Who's making your success possible? Our culture likes to acknowledge people who go it alone, but that's not how life works. Anything worth doing in life takes a village. It's about relationships, and you do that by investing time and energy into them.

NETWORK

All things are drawn to what is like them, and we tend to hang around people who like what we like and are interested in the same hobbies as we are. However, it's essential to extend your sphere of influence and network. We are all 6 degrees of separation from each other in this world and the more extensive our network, the greater our influence. People and relationships are extremely important. Invest in the right relationships and give them time and attention. What I've learned is that we have to help each other in life. Understand that friends come and go, but a precious few you should hold onto.

Shift your circle of influence. There comes a moment in everyone's life when you realize who matters, who never did, and who always will. So hang out with people who inspire you. Whether it's friends, family, or colleagues who think you are crazy and offer no support, you can always find support from your networking groups, support groups, and other community resources. Go where you are celebrated and not tolerated. Take the time to build relationships so that when you have ideas, you can bring them to your relationships and get more done. You'll have more influence. Leverage your networks and add value to everyone in your network. Relationships are the key to success. Real success takes real relationships in the real world in real time − not behind a computer. Build relationships. Having that social connection is essential.

Your most important asset is your network. Identify your circle of influence. Who are they today? Are they guiding you rightly? Don't just use all of your brain, but use all that you can borrow. Tap the brain trusts of other people; extend your sphere of influence and access. Access is power. It's all about who you know and who knows you. It's not what you know; it's who you know. In our society, we derive status from proximity to power. Someone says they went to school with Bill Gates, or their cousin is married to a Royal, or they played in a band with Paul McCartney, et cetera.

Nevertheless, the truth is you're not going to be successful just because of other people's success; you're going to be successful because of your own success. You may be around successful people and they may hold your hand, but you still have to take the steps yourself. You still have to actuate your success even though you need other people. But your network makes it a lot easier.

FIND A MENTOR

People often say to be around like-minded people, but sometimes when you are around like-minded people, you don't always receive unbiased information and sometimes you receive false encouragement. However, the problem with false encouragement is advice is a form of nostalgia, and you have to be careful from whom you derive input, and especially never take advice from someone who has to live with the consequences. The art of taking advice isn't what you ask; it's whom you ask. Get some real unbiased advice from people who've done it. By ‘it' I mean whatever it is you want to accomplish. To know the road ahead; ask those coming back. Surround yourself with the people who have been where you're trying to go because forewarned is forearmed. When you see someone who has what you want, you should ask him or her how they got it.

Everyone needs a sensei. Find a mentor, coach, confidant, or advisor with whom you can be an understudy. There are incredibly smart people who will help you if you ask. There are always people who will help you and are willing to help you. You don't have to know it all or have all the answers; you just have to find the people who do. You need honest friends and true people around you. I always ask my mentors to tell me how to overcome what I'm confronted by so I can deal with it. However, I tell them I need you to be honest and be open with me. You have to know what you're good at and what you're not good at and ask for support for those areas in which you're not good. We need thinking partners who aren't echo chambers. We need people around us who challenge us.

Find someone who complements you. If you're creative, find someone logical, and vice versa. Olivia Goldsmith said, "People seldom improve when they have no other model but themselves to copy." Be highly open to suggestion. Say ‘no' to "Yes men." Get an honest dialogue around your ideas. Don't keep your dreams and ideas in your head; put them out there. Have a dialogue surrounding them, let people offer insight and suggestions. You need access to a wider network and constant feedback. It’s time for a painful and honest reckoning, a true hard reset. Get honest feedback and true insight about who you are especially from those around you. Each of us seems to think we are an expert by merely being conscious, but someone who is his own lawyer has a fool for a client. You need objective counsel…always.

I am extremely grateful for one of my mentors. He is such a rainmaker, and he has forgotten more than I'll ever know. However, a recent experience together was a fascinating experience for me, to learn from him, especially at a time when I was in need of a kind sage. It was like lifting the hood on a car and seeing how the engine works, or discovering the Dead Sea scrolls. He told me you have to plan for the success you want to have. He continued, saying, "you look, but don't see. You have to learn to see the invisible. To see what others don't. See every crack, every detail. Learn to see and not just look at myself or other people. See every detail of you." I mentioned earlier that I am in New York often, and the most significant thing New York teaches me is that if you don't care, no one else will. Everyone has their own dreams, details, and distractions to contend with. If you want them to care about your story, you have to make them care. More importantly, learn something from everyone you meet.

Every person you will ever meet knows something you don't. This is a hard concept for many of us know-it-alls. In today's world, auto mechanics write code and debug software. Bricklayers have an intimate knowledge of the strength of materials. Cooks understand the use of copper to control egg proteins. Respect their knowledge and learn from them. Learn from other people; learn who to trust, and learn who not to trust. Observation is a big part of observation because everyone's a teacher. Ultimately, everyone can teach you one of two things: what to do or what not to do. So my message to you is learn from not just what you do but whom you do it with. The real value of surrounding yourself with a great peer group is vital for the short and long haul.

Finally, people don't need just mentorship; they need sponsorship. They need someone to say, "I want you to work alongside me," or “I see potential in you, and I will pay for your classes to get you where you want to go.” People need someone to bankroll their advancement if need be, and physically drag them up the corporate ladder. So find sponsors, not just mentors. Learn from mistakes, but you don't have to only learn from yours. Think about the mentors and people in your life. No wonder why we feel lost so often; we have to think about who's guiding our way. Find people who have done it before, who can shorten the path for you, and who can keep you from falling.

Meet influencers, powerful people, and dynamic investors – network! You have to reverse engineer their success. Look at what they do to become A-list celebrities, or billionaires, or millionaires. Modeling success leads to success. That's why you need mentors. It takes one to know one. Adopt mentors and leverage them. It's just like in sports; it doesn't matter how talented you are. If you don't have a coach, it won't matter. Good players can't overcome bad coaching. Surround yourself with people who remind you of the future, not the past. If you surround yourself with people who remind you of your past, you'll have a hard time progressing. It takes an armada of advisors to make it; just make sure it's the right advisors.

ELIMINATE TOXIC PEOPLE

I no longer have the patience for certain things, not because I'm arrogant but because I've reached a point in my life where I don't want to waste more time on what displeases me or hurts me. This is my time now. I have no patience for cynicism, excessive criticism and demands of any nature. I lost the will to please those who do not like me, to love those who do not love me and smile at those who do not want to smile at me. I no longer spend a single minute on those who lie or want to manipulate. I decided not to exist anymore with pretense, hypocrisy, dishonesty and cheap praise. I don't tolerate selective erudition or academic arrogance. I hate conflict and comparisons. I believe in a world of opposites, and that's why I avoid a world of opposites, and that's why invalid people with rigid and inflexible personalities. In friendship, I dislike the lack of loyalty and betrayal. I do not get along with those who do not know how to give a compliment or a word of encouragement. Exaggerations bore me, and I have difficulty accepting those who do not like animals. And on top of everything I do not have the patience for anyone who does not deserve my patience.

- Meryl Streep

I love this quote from Meryl Streep because her message is so sublime: Limit what you tolerate. Don't tolerate incompetent or unhelpful people. Don't tolerate an absence of results. Sir Isaac Newton's first law of thermodynamics said: "Energy is neither lost nor destroyed; it is merely transferred from one party to the next." Make sure you're getting positive energy from those around you. Otherwise, you're losing energy. I learned very quickly there are two types of things in this world impacting me: things that nourish me and things that drain me. The world is full of so much clutter and noise, and frankly, it's draining. Surround yourself with people and things that nourish you. Don't be around people who cheat the process and cheat themselves out of the best. It's kind of like *The Milgrim Experiment* in which someone applies shocks to an unidentified individual. It's all about the rationalization that you're not doing anything wrong. When the moral axis keeps moving every time you do something more maniacal, it becomes a matter of degrees. Don't surround yourself with people like that. Surround yourself with positive like-minded people. Ditch people weighing you down and not in your corner because they're making this journey more difficult than it should be.

Don't tolerate bozos around you. Weed them out from around you. You'll never be perfect at it but don't let bozos or anyone else steal energy from you. Stamp them out immediately. I have a friend who is a pilot. He says there are four forces of flight: lift, weight, thrust, and drag. In life, people fall in these four categories too. People who lift you, people who weigh you down, people who thrust you forward, and people who drag you back. Eliminate those who are weights and drags.

Consider with me the power of influence. Notice if you're walking with someone, how you adjust to their pace, or how they adjust to yours. Alternatively, how in school, your GPA was the average of your three closest friends. The power of influence is so great that your income will be the average of your three closest friends. If your three friends are broke, you'll be the fourth. I tell people who want to become successful, show me your cellphone. Because if I see your cellphone, I know who you talk to. You are whom you hang around. You are whom you associate with. If you hang around losers, you'll be a loser. If you hang around winners, you'll be a winner.

Success begins with finding the right people. Choose your friends carefully. Relationships and loyalty are the bedrock of success. When the character of a person is not clear to you, look at their friends. People are only as successful as the people with whom they choose to associate. Successful people arm themselves with mentors, and they locate people who can serve as resources. Don't hang around negative people. Go where the joy is. Go where there's oxygen. Hang around people smarter than you, better than you. Think about this: Wherever you work you will be entering a culture. Ask yourself if that is a culture you want to be a part of, because there are some work cultures you don't want any part of.

I was fortunate to live in Shanghai, China for a little less than two years, study the culture, and travel throughout Asia. I must say I loved it and I love every time I go back to Asia. I felt baptized in that culture. I loved China because it's such an optimistic culture. Everything is about good luck, good fortune, health, peace, destiny, balance, Zen, prosperity, tranquility, wisdom, love, beauty. I love being around optimistic people because I start thinking about what's possible for me. Also, isn't that what we all want? Positive relationships bring out the best in us and challenge us to imagine our lives a little bigger and better. In many western cultures, it's hard to find that level of optimism, and we learn to function in our dysfunction. It never ceases to amaze me. We all love ourselves more than other people but care about their opinion more than our own. We get used to the negative words people say about us, and we believe it. However, you can't let people determine your mental state because most people are half crazy anyway. Sometimes it feels like we're living in a mental hospital in this world. Don't associate with people who are going to drag you down emotionally. Stop caring what others think of you. In John 15, Jesus said, "They hated me without a cause." People don't need a reason to hate you, so stop trying to make sense of it. Demonic things don't make sense. Just continue doing right and keep having peace in your heart.

Focus on simulating higher levels of enjoyment and activity. This isn't just a function of our physical health but of our mental state as well. There is one thing I have realized from being around sincerely positive people: They don't hang around negative people. Complainers are radioactive because they wallow in their problems and don't want to focus on solutions. They want others to join their pity party so they can feel better about themselves. Most people feel pressure to listen to complainers because they don't want to be seen as callous or rude, but there's a thin line between lending a supportive ear and being drawn into their negative emotional spiral. The best way you can avoid getting drawn in is by setting boundaries and distancing yourself when necessary. It's no different then if you were not a smoker and a person were smoking. Would you sit there all morning, inhaling the second-hand smoke? Of course not. You would distance yourself, and you should do likewise with complainers. If you want people to get out of your head, shut the door.

I've come to realize that success doesn't change you, it changes the people around you. It’s critical to know who you are inside and out, and to know the people around you. True friends who genuinely care about you aren't interested in your accomplishments and possessions; they're interested in you. False friends say they will be there through thick and thin, but when things get thick, they get thin. Believe what you see; trust what you see. When people show you who they are, believe them because the people around you matter. In any job, ask yourself if this is a great ensemble to be a part of. If not, move on. Banish toxicity everywhere in your life. When I stopped spending so much time with toxic people, I found my life improved beyond measure. Toxic people do nothing more than bring you down, and you can't flourish with them in your life. List these people and stop associating with them, or at a minimum limit the time you spend with them. I worked in management, and I can tell you it's better to get rid of people too soon than to get rid of them too late. There are some people you don't need to have in your life, even as friends or employees. A sad truth in life for athletes is you either leave the game (i.e., retire or move on), or the game leaves you. It's the same truth for us.

So be very cautious from whom you take advice. It's impossible to learn about real estate investing from someone who has never done it. Be confident in what you're doing, and learn to ignore critics. All of us need trusted advisors who can help us go farther and become better, but remember that everyone with an opinion doesn't deserve to occupy that trusted role (nor does everyone with a social media account). I've always been amazed when someone with 25 followers on Twitter slams someone doing good in the world. Strategically ignore these people and move on. I have come to find there are two types of people who will tell you that you cannot make it to becoming the success you want to be: those who are afraid to try for themselves, and those who are afraid you will succeed. Don't have time for either types of people. Don't have time to be around people who are broke, wishing they had something to eat. If I can walk and I hang around a bunch of people who are crippled, and I start acting crippled, then crippled looks normal. Don't fall for that old okey-doke.

Surround yourself with people who can do what you can't do. Surround yourself with those who are not limited in the same areas you are limited. Surround yourself with people who want you to succeed. Find collaborators. Enlist likeminded friends, colleagues, and family members who will hold you accountable, share their insights, and celebrate your achievements. Psychology tells us that much of our influence comes from outside our conscious awareness. Most of the time it doesn't matter where inspiration comes from, but it matters you know what or who is influencing you. We become like the people we associate with frequently, that's why winners like to be with other winners. Don't hang around bottom feeders. Never plan a future with people who don't have future plans.

For some of you, your circle of friends has become a noose and is constricting your blood flow. Listen, people come into your life for four reasons: to add, subtract, multiply, or divide. Now is the time to set your life on fire. Find people who fan your flames. Keep distance from those who inject negativity in your life and surround yourself with people who give you hope for life and can bring peace in your life. You're only as good as those you associate with. You should always strive to surround yourself with people who inspire you, people who make you want to be better. The chances are that you already do. But what about the people who drag you down? Are you allowing them to be a part of your life? Any person who makes you feel worthless, anxious, or uninspired is wasting your time and possibly making you more like them. Cut these people loose; life is too short to associate with people like that. Divorce yourself from toxic situations like that, and from people who traffic in hatred; otherwise, you end up like Julius Caesar surrounded by enemies.

Regrettably, people are jealous, and if you're not careful, it may be a fact learned too late. People want what's best for you, just as long as it's not better than what's for them. Surround yourself with people who want you at your best. I am of the mindset that if you can't handle me at 100-proof, pass the cup! In this age we know that technology comes from innovation, and innovation is not achieved by imitating the success of others. If people are trying to beat you down and treat you less than you are, you've got to elevate yourself and remind yourself of who you are. Social media is a distortion of reality because we post only our best photos of ourselves, our favorite activities only when we're happy, et cetera. So if you go on social media too much, it can be depressing. Leave that behind.

Eliminate negative people from your network. Some relationships are just combustible. It's not so much cause and effect as it is an association. Simply because you trust someone doesn't mean you can depend on them as well. Delivery and trust are separate — you're always only one person away from a breakthrough. Negative people have a problem for every solution. Successful people leave their loser friends behind. Don't waste your time sitting down listening to people who have no idea about anything. Avoid losers and treat them like the plague. Don't let negative people tell you how the world is supposed to be. Find out for yourself. Get rid of negative do-nothing people from your life because it's necessary we achieve our full potential. The Bible says in 1 Corinthians 15:33, "Bad company corrupts good character." Don't worry about having good seed, worry about finding good ground. It's your environment that matters. You can have good seed, but if the soil is rotten, it doesn't matter. Thermodynamics says that if you place a hot pie on a window outside in the winter, the temperature of the pie will cool to the same temperature as outside. You become like your surroundings. You are a product of your environment – choose yours carefully. Surround yourself with doers, believers, and dreamers.

George Washington is one of the best-known men in all of American history, who knew the importance of choosing your company wisely. Washington led a courageous life of risk, sacrifice, and service to his ideals, underscored by the belief that it was better to forge a path alone than to wait on the sidelines with the wrong company. Successful people don't spend time with naysayers or critics, but instead, forge their own path and live their own vision, especially in periods of doubt or isolation. There are so many people in this world peddling fear, trying to make you afraid of everything that goes bump in the night and every boogie man hiding in closets. Don't listen to people who are peddling fear; listen to your better angels. Know that "the wealth of the wicked is stored up for the righteous" (Proverbs 13:22). Trust and expect betrayal. That’s the lesson of the Trojan War: Beware of Greeks bearing gifts. It's like in Jiu-Jitsu – it’s not the one you see coming that hurts you; it's the one you don't see – the person you least expect. Be skeptical because everyone's nice until you get to know them (be careful whom you trust).

You need to be too busy for games. I was once dating a girl, whom I told she better be sure about us, because I have a plan for my life. You need to assess, evaluate, and examine those relationships. Then purge the bad ones. Not everyone likes me, but not everyone matters. Some people will always try to undermine you. I could walk on water, and some people would say it's because I can't swim. Go figure. Be around people who will uplift you and encourage you. The last thing we need is other people's judgment; we need encouragement. Surround yourself with people who challenge you and hold you accountable. I wrote another book with a theme of how to be successful, and the publisher wanted me to change it to *How to Get Successful.* The problem with that is anybody can **get** rich/successful, but it takes much more to **be** rich/successful and deal with all of the vultures, parasites, people asking you for money, and all it entails. It takes a different skillset to be successful than it does to get successful. You have to eliminate the toxicity in your environment. You can do it because you have more control over your situation than you like to think.

IGNORE THE NAYSAYERS

- "Everything that can be invented has been invented." Charles H. Duell, Commissioner, U.S. Office of Patents, 1899.
- "Who wants to hear actors talk?" H. M. Warner, Warner Brothers, 1927.

- "A cookie store is a bad idea. Besides, the market research reports say America likes crispy cookies, not soft and chewy cookies like you make." *Response to Debbi Fields' idea of starting Mrs. Fields' Cookies.*
- "I think there is a world market for maybe five computers." *Thomas Watson, chairman of IBM, 1943.*
- "We don't like their sound, and guitar music is on the way out." *Decca Recording Co., rejecting the Beatles, 1962.*

If there is one thing I know for sure, it's don't listen to people or naysayers. People will take what you love and try to crush your spirits with it. Don't give them that power. People can't keep you from your destiny. Don't let people get you down; they don't have a heaven or hell to put you in. You don't have to respond to the naysayers or haters; just continue to wake up each morning and be your best self. If somebody says 'no,' you're talking to the wrong person. Someone telling you that you can't do it is the best insurance policy for success. Frank Sinatra said, "Success is the best revenge." I would go further and say living well is the best revenge. Don't shoot down. Don't go to their level. Boxers know that you don't punch down. You don't go low. Fight your own equal.

In fact, having haters is a good thing because you're nobody until someone hates you. If you don't have enemies, you're doing something wrong. People don't talk about, hate on, or get jealous of mediocre people. Haters are a gift because they are your biggest testimony. Think about it; nobody robs a house with nothing in it. If people are coming after you, it means you've got something. Ali G.

said, “Video games have taught me that if you encounter enemies, you’re going the right way.” Keep your enemies ahead of you and not behind you because it's better to get ahead than to get even. Keep your enemies close to you. It's better to have them inside your tent pissing out, than outside pissing in.

It's one thing for people to say things about you which aren't true, it's another thing for people to hold your past against you. You are not your past. Move on from those types of people. Some people will want to go back in time and unearth all kind of dirty stuff about you. It's not what people call you; it's what you respond to. People will either attack you or alienate you. Regardless, you can’t let hatred and bigotry stop you from doing what you need to do. Someone’s opinion of you doesn’t have to be your reality. More importantly, someone’s opinion of you is none of your business. People will hurt you, and people will let you down. If you're on the West Coast people will stab you in the back, and if you're on the East Coast people will stab you in the chest. It doesn't matter; you keep putting out good. Keep doing right. Keep your head held high, and believe in what you're doing. Aim high and tune out the naysayers. Average people concern themselves with the opinions of others because they're afraid of looking stupid and fearful of disapproval. From now on, be successful, and frame the naysayers as nothing but noise. As the saying goes, “The dogs bark but the caravan moves on.”

We have a tendency to hold onto things, specifically emotionally, and it creates density in our bodies. Things western medicine calls cancer, disease, stress, depression, etc. When we go on the plane we have a physical response to something happening emotionally. We have sweaty palms, etc. emotional blockages lead to physical blockages. We have to let those emotional blockages go, especially the blockages in our subconscious, things which we have buried away. We have to let those things go. When others hurt us or begin to doubt us, the best revenge is to move on, get over it, and continue to succeed. You can still write your own destiny. You can overcome; you can triumph. The trick is not minding that it hurts, not letting it affect you. You have to be delivered from people before you can go to people. Don't care what other people think of you; overcome anyway. Do your job and don't let anyone stop you by what they think of you or anything else. You don't need to dignify what they say with a response. Hold fast and withstand the attacks of your enemies, knowing that in the end truth will out. You don't have to trust or like anybody; you just need to deal with people and move on.

UTILIZE YOUR SUPPORT SYSTEM

I asked my parents once what the most important thing is when it comes to raising kids and they said, “The important thing is never criticize; always encourage.” There are going to be peaks and valleys in your life, and you have to have people around you to encourage you, to help you, to lift you. Most people know what they're doing wrong, and they don't need other people pushing them lower. They need to be lifted up. I think people in all walks of life think they have to do it all on their own, but it always helps to talk about the problems and challenges in your life with others. Have a support system around you and stay on the same wavelength as them.

I spent some time working politics in the United States Congress and United Kingdom Parliament, and politics is all about coalition building. Build strong coalitions in your life. Focus on the people in your life and the ones who say 'yes' to you. Your life isn't made up of the people who aren't in it. Don't waste time on people who make no difference in your life. Dig your well before you need it; have your support system in place before you need them. Get your support group now, because when crisis hits, it will be too late. If you have to ask for help, it's already too late. Know that you are not alone. There are people out there who love and care about your wellbeing; and I am one of them. Get in touch with those people. Nurture empowered relationships. You will fail at many things, and you have to learn when things go wrong, you'll have people saying you can't do it. But you have to push through those barriers and ask for help and drum up support if needed. Always go to something bigger than yourself. You may have been so committed to you that you have never immersed yourself beyond yourself. People can't tell you anything because you are your own physician. Immerse yourself beyond yourself, and you will redefine yourself. Attach yourself to a higher purpose with people who can get you there.

There's a difference between people with you and people for you. Surround yourself with both kinds of people. When it comes to being productive, you have to recognize your weaknesses and ask for help when you need it. When a situation becomes overwhelming, this means tapping into your support system. Whether inside or outside of work, your support system is on your team, rooting for you, and ready to help you get the best from a challenging situation. Identify those people in your life and seek the insight and assistance you need. Building a strong support system is the key to making incremental change.

Keep people who ground you around you. Stay away from the snakes in the grass, and stay close to your secure enclave because the people around you matter. No man is an island. Everyone needs somebody they can trust and who they can call on when they're feeling under pressure. Find someone whose judgment you trust who can listen and provide you sound counsel. Don't diagnose yourself; enlist support. Merely venting your frustrations aloud can sometimes help you regroup, and at other times give you a new perspective. Even something as little as talking about your concerns and worries can provide an outlet for your stress and anxiety to escape while reframing your view on the situation. Most of the time, someone who isn't emotionally invested in the situation will be able to see the dilemma from an alternate perspective, and can help you find a potential solution. By reaching out to people you trust and respect, you'll feel more connected and grounded and in control of your stress and anxiety.

7

LEVEL UP

"Life is a traveling to the edge of knowledge, then a leap taken."
– D. H. Lawrence

PERSONAL DEVELOPMENT

One of my favorite movies is *An Officer and a Gentleman*. It stars Richard Gere as a guy named Zack Mayo, trying to become a pilot. Mayo is the best in his class, flies jets, runs the fastest, is the strongest, but if that were the only thing important the movie would've been called just *An Officer*. However, it's called *An Officer and a Gentleman* because Zack still has some things to learn; namely how to be a gentleman. Like Zack Mayo, we all have more things we can learn and things we can improve upon. No matter how smart you are, the more you know, the less you will understand. So no matter how smart you are, you always have a lot to learn, and I'm not talking about learning that a thesaurus is not a dinosaur, but truly getting to the core of self-improvement.

Part of the magic of God's grace is recognizing that he's given us the chance where we've been lost to find our best selves.

This grace wasn’t earned, but we got it all the same. From an early age, personal development is at the core of our lives. Consider a child. You don't really instill anything in a child; you just encourage his or her development. Personal development is the central mission of our lives, constantly seeking to expand our human capital. All of us are in need of development.

In order to grow as an individual, you need to understand where you came from, who you are, where you're going, and why all things happen. Every generation needs to build and go further than the previous one. Successful people are always looking for ways to improve themselves, whether it’s reading daily, limiting the time they spend watching television, or upgrading their skills. They don't spend their time on activities that won't bring them closer to their goals. Time is too valuable a commodity to waste on activities that will not move the needle on their goals. Committing to self-improvement means you engage in activities every day that stretch you. It's not always easy, but we grow from things that pose a challenge. Successful people know that the world is a tough place and if you're not careful it can chew you up and spit you out. However, if you work hard and commit to excellence, you can hit it big. Greatness is within all of our grasps.

Trappist monks are the most successful businessmen because for over 1000 years they have dedicated their entire lives to personal development. For example, being on time for work isn't just a part of the job description; it's a way to build self-discipline. In other words, being on time is not a result of a monk’s personal development, it is a form of personal development. Even their personal and business lives are all subsets of their overarching mission: *becoming the best human being they can be*. These monks show us we should be self-disciplined. We should be avid readers to increase verbal skills, articulate thoughts, enhance problem-solving skills, increase concentration, improve writing skills, and improve memory. More importantly, we should think about thinking (metacognition – the self-awareness of one's knowledge). Metacognition encourages critical thinking and helps maximize cognitive skills.

To improve yourself, you have to understand that first and foremost, you have to get better for yourself. Your first responsibility has to always be to yourself. Some people feel thwarted and unsuccessful because they put off investing in themselves and neglect their own needs. Everyone has a limited amount of time, money, and resources that they can actualize themselves. That's why you should focus your energies on opportunities that will set you apart from others. In other words, innovate where you differentiate. Innovate and continuously move the ball forward in your life.

In 1 Corinthians 13:11, Paul says, "When I was a child, I spoke as a child, understood as a child, and thought as a child." Personal development always comes down to how we **speak, understand,** and **think**. You know you're maturing by how you speak, how you understand, and how you think. However, Paul says, "When I became a man, I put aside childish things." What we're dealing with is an immature inner life. There's a child inside. You might be an adult, but inside you're still a child. You're speaking as a child, thinking as a child, understanding as a child. Too many people have not outgrown this dysfunctional system. People can be developed outwardly but not inwardly. The author is telling us if you don't put it away, it will put you away (and by "it" I mean the systems of being a child: speaking as a child, understanding as a child, and thinking as a child). You can't put something away if you're holding onto it. So, if you don't put it away, it will put away promotions, it will put away love, and it will put away blessings.

Eli Cohen said, "Without continuous personal development, you are now all that you will ever become, and hell starts when the person you are meets the person you could have been." Give yourself the space you need to develop into the best person you can be. You're not born one. Nobody is born a success; you are born a person. So you have to learn and grow into that success you envision. You have to tend to and work on it every day to develop that championship pedigree. There's more to learn and there are more dimensions for you to develop.

Life is a journey; the beginning is just the beginning. No matter how we start in life, it's a long path to actualization. The truth is you can never be the best, the only thing you can be the best at is developing yourself. Moreover, we do that by learning, unlearning, and relearning. You're always learning. Leo da Vinci on his deathbed said, "Art is never finished, only abandoned." Nothing is ever complete. You're always getting better, and you can always be better. There is no real ending; it's just the place where you stop the story. There is no winning or losing; just growing and more journey. Douglas Pagels said, "Sometimes it's important to work for that pot of gold. But other times it's essential to take time off and to make sure that your most important decision in the day simply consists of choosing which color to slide down on the rainbow."

With all of that being said, I'm here to help you get the most out of yourself. So if your idea of 'more' is a day off from work, this chapter isn't for you. If your idea of 'more' is having dessert with dinner, this chapter isn't for you. However, if you want to go to France for a year to study wines, or study Asian culture, own your own business, or write your own checks, this is for you. This is about a higher level of achievement with no ceiling and no floor.

Successful people are committed to personal development, and they dread obsolescence. They know everything can be improved, even themselves. They know, as Jim Rohn said, "Your income rarely exceeds your personal development." Lots of research shows that if we don't have a clear important objective for growth, we're less likely to invest the time it takes to learn and grow; purposeful growth is critical. Sometimes even therapy helps. Obtaining therapy is a way to focus on you and you only, without feeling guilty or selfish. You don't need to ask your therapist how you're doing; you get to focus on yourself, and it's so life-changing. Therapy teaches you that you have to realize that you do this for yourself; you don't do this for anybody else. Therapy allows you to work <u>on</u> your life versus <u>in</u> your life. When you commit to self-observation, learning, and growth, it can feed a greater sense of control in your life. Some of the best employees I've had worked <u>on</u> the systems they labored <u>in</u>. We can work <u>on</u> our best lives by self-questioning and improving in increments.

The body responds to progression. You can't just pound it and expect results; you have to implement change and resistance gradually. Now, while these rules aren't necessarily hard and fast, they are guiding principles. Success is not always about talent; it's about dependability, consistency, and a willingness to improve. We are all under construction. However, the thing about construction zones is that you don't know if something is being torn down or built up. Just make sure you're being built up. Always think about how you could be doing things better, and always question yourself. It's not just about how good you are now; it's how good you're going to be that matters. I live in Los Angeles and everyday it teaches me that it's not enough to be technical (skill-function); knowing how to perform matters. Whatever you do should be a performance, and you have to be your best at all times. I love attending the Los Angeles Lakers or Los Angeles Dodgers games, I see that one is always performing; the theatre of it all matters. So here's a quick rundown to get started on personal development:

Build a Good Environment

Any success is created by making consistently great choices and building a disciplined environment. Design your environment to set you up for success. Create a winning environment through ongoing learning, growth, and discipline. Prime your environment. We humans are weak, so environment design is our best lever to change habits.

Trust the Process

Create disciplined morning and evening routines and stay faithful in the routine. Sometimes it feels like our lives are going in circles and we're just going round and round, not making any progress; but remain faithful. When David was anointed king, he was just a shepherd boy. He didn't immediately go to the palace; he had to go back to the field for 13 more years before he was actually made king. Like David, you also may have a king's anointing on you, but stay faithful in the shepherd fields. If God can trust you in the shepherd fields, he can trust you in the palace. The Bible says God is the potter and we are the clay. Like a potter's wheel, God places us on the wheel and spins us around. It feels like we're not making any progress, but what the clay doesn't realize is that it's going up higher. Our character is being built, and resilience is being constructed. So when things feel like they're spinning out of control, remember, things are spinning in control.

In Joshua 6:2 When Joshua led the Israelites up to the walls of Jericho, God told them to walk around seven times and not say anything. I believe God told them not to speak because if they did, they would've talked themselves out of their miracle. I'm sure they would've said, "Why are we walking around this wall? Nothing's happening." Even in your routine, zip it; trust the process. When they got done, they shouted with trumpets, and the walls came down. Even when Moses was a baby, he had to be hidden for three months because Pharaoh decreed all male babies to be killed. The Bible says in Exodus 2:3 when Moses could be hidden no more he was sent in a basket down the Nile, all the way to Pharaoh's home, and adopted there. So you may be hidden now and overlooked, and God has placed something in you, but stay faithful in the routine, and know that you are being built up. God is preparing you to be king. The routine is just a test. Even when it looks like nothing is happening, like a seed planted and consistently watered, growth is taking place.

Track Your Progress

When you have your process, implement a morning and evening routine. Having a morning and evening ritual is essential. There has been plenty of research that illustrates that having rituals can really improve your life. The Stoics encouraged this. One ritual gets you ready for the day, whereas the other ritual allows you to reflect on how things went, and figure out what to improve. The Stoics did not believe in the ethereal or perfection; they believed we are all a work-in-progress. You can always get better. So long as you live, keep learning how to live. The Stoics lesson is simple: Plan for the day, then reflect on the day. You need to track your progress, measure your improvement, and have specific goals. If you study your choices and consistently make efforts to improve, success becomes inevitable. So review and revise regularly. What's important is to look forward with enthusiasm and build upon your gains.

GROWTH MINDSET

Many studies have proven that there is a true power that comes from believing you can improve. People with a growth mindset (as opposed to fixed mindset) know that their abilities, skills, and talents are not predetermined. They recognize that they can grow, learn, and reach new heights in their potential. Those who possess a growth mindset approach their work with more positivity, motivation, and ability to succeed. Psychologist Carol Dweck of Stanford University has studied and proven that your attitude is a better predictor of your success than your IQ. Dweck found that people fall into one of two categories: ***a fixed mindset*** or a ***growth mindset***. With a fixed mindset, you believe you are who you are and cannot change. Now, this creates problems when that person is challenged because anything that appears to be more than they can handle will leave them feeling overwhelmed and hopeless.

Conversely, people with a growth mindset believe they can improve with effort. It is the belief that abilities can be developed through learning and practice. Even when a growth mindset individual has a lower IQ, they outperform those with a fixed mindset because they are willing to embrace challenges, seeing them as opportunities to learn something new.[40]

Many people think of IQ like a genetic trait, similar to eye color – something you're born with and stuck with forever. However, studies (notably, Sue Shellenbarger's on *Lunch Break*) have shown mounting evidence that IQ can change over a lifetime.[41] Our IQ can rise and even fall over the years. There are multiple myths about IQ, like the notion that IQ is a fixed number or some crystal ball indicating future performance. But that's incorrect. Your talent and intelligence are NOT fixed traits. They can be developed at any age and in any direction. Your genetics are not your fate.

Conventional wisdom would presume that having an ability such as being smart inspires confidence. But this is true only when the going is easy. The deciding factor in life is how you handle challenges and setbacks. Those with a growth mindset welcome setbacks with open arms. According to Dweck, success in life is all about how you deal with failure. She describes the approach people with a growth mindset have: Failure is information – we label it a failure, but it's more like, "This didn't work, and I'm a problem solver, so I'll try something else." Irrespective of which side of the aisle you fall on, there are changes you can make to develop a growth mindset: You can change your attitude. Attitude is more important than intelligence. To get better at anything, you must first believe that you can get better. People with a fixed mindset see their abilities as a fixed trait while people with a growth mindset see them as malleable. Fixed mindsets attribute failure to a lack of innate ability, get beaten down by it, and become more risk-averse and self-conscious.

On the other hand, people with growth mindsets learn from their experiences and don't attribute failure to a fixed trait. This allows them to be able to analyze problems more profoundly and bounce back more effectively. Therefore, there's truth in what doesn't kill you only making you stronger. Seneca expounds writing, "A good man dyes events with his own color and turns whatever happens to him to his own benefit." Don't complain when things don't go your way. Complaining is a visible sign of a fixed mindset. Whereas a growth mindset looks for opportunity in everything, so there's no time for complaints. Everyone faces unanticipated adversity. However, people with a growth-oriented mindset embrace adversity as a means for improvement, instead of something that holds them back. We live in a society that measures the wrong metrics. Have a growth mindset, believe that the ability to learn can be achieved with effort at any stage, and remember that becoming is better than being.

There are many studies that have proven that there is a true power that comes from believing that you can improve. People with a growth mindset, as opposed to fixed mindset, know that their abilities, skills, and talents are not predetermined. They recognize that they are able to grow, learn, and reach new heights in their potential. Those who possess a growth mindset approach their work with more positivity, motivation, and ability to succeed. The journalist Annie Murphy Paul says intelligence is affected by the context in which we put it to use. She says situations can make us smarter (situational intelligence is the only kind of intelligence there is), and beliefs can make us smarter (e.g., fixed and growth mindsets).

Beliefs matter because they influence how we think about our own abilities, how we perceive the world around us, and how we act when faced with a challenge. Expertise can make us smarter. Experts don't just know more, they know differently in ways that allow them to think and act intelligently within their domain of expertise. Also, attention can make us smarter. Focused attention is critical. In addition, emotions can make us smarter. When in a positive mood, we tend to think more expansively and creatively. When we feel anxious, it makes us less intelligent. Additionally, technology can make us smarter, and our bodies can make us smarter. Proper nutrition, adequate sleep, regular exercise, moderate stress all make the brain work better. Finally, relationships can make us smarter.

There used to be a belief in the scientific fields that our brains were hardwired at birth, but now we know we can will them to change. The brain's ability for neuroplasticity, which is its ability to adapt itself in response to things that happen in our environment, has many benefits for us. Our brains are not hard-wired like computers as we once thought, but instead, are like "Play-doh." This means our thoughts can change the structure and function of our brains. Additionally, by doing certain exercises, we can physically increase our brain's size, strength, and density. At its core, neuroplasticity is a series of miracles that are taking place in your cranium, which means we can be better athletes, learn to love the taste of kale, and can become better parents. Through conscious effort, we can treat eating disorders, prevent cancer, and realize our true essence of joy and peace. We can even teach ourselves the "skill" of happiness, and train our brains to become higher functioning. Age is no limitation to this phenomenon. Neuroplasticity has shown that our minds are designed to improve as we get older.[42]

My same friend who is a pilot, mentioned earlier, also told me that the key to flying is small corrections and not overcorrecting. Nothing major, just minor corrections. Small incremental changes always change everything in the long run. So the shift doesn't even have to be difficult. Merely changing your route to work or using your non-dominant hand to comb your hair can increase your brain power. Your brain is not in charge of you; you are in charge of your brain. Almost everything we do, all of our behaviors, thoughts, and emotions, physically change our brains in ways that underpin brain chemistry or function. Today you're going to get better, or you're going to get worse, but you're never going to be the same. Those small corrections add up. It's one day at a time. It's the small victories that lead to the larger ones; it's a gradual process. Make small corrections, and don't overcorrect. We all want instant gratification, but good things take time. Remind yourself that you can't lift a thousand pounds all at once, but you can lift one pound a thousand times. Tiny, repeated efforts will get you there, steadily.

ASSESS YOURSELF

The first step to any personal development is to admit that you can be better. You have to look in the mirror and assess you and you alone. You have to keep your finger on the pulse to see what's happening. The truth is that many of us stop at adequate. We shoot for good enough and don't always give our best. Our best isn't always best because often it's just a shell of who we are. However, I'm encouraging you to look past your limits and get better. Go higher, be more, feel deeper. Reach your potential, and when you get to the end of your life, you don't want to leave anything on the table. Reach for the eternal. Don't just be great; be historic. Go to higher and higher heights. Build new capabilities. Be internally motivated. It needs to be your intrinsic desire to be your best self. You have to want to improve if you're going to stay ahead. In my own life, I know I'm good at my strengths and getting better because I work at them every day. It's something you have to keep working at. I'm not where I need to be, and I'm not where I'm going to be. Things can always be better, even me. It's not about doing one thing well; it's about doing everything better. Don't go yo-yo back and forth; make up your mind to be better. It's about not being worried about losing or failing; this is about you getting better.

The secrets of high achievers always include brutal self-criticism − assessing yourself and reexamining and reflecting on where you are in your career at least every two years. High achievers examine themselves to see if there's a pattern of behavior that causes bad things to happen. First, take a hard look at yourself and be flexible about making changes. Take inventory of your life. What can you do today to improve? What was promised, what have you performed, and what's left to accomplish? Every three months have a summit with yourself. Do a quick audit of yourself, analyzing what's changed. Where am I? Am I going in the right direction? What am I doing now? How am I positioned? This could change how your life unfolds. Every day, ask yourself, “Am I growing or am I dying?” Always ask yourself what you can improve on. I always ask myself in the best of times and the worst of times how I can get better. I ask myself, “What can I improve?” “What do I need to change?” “What more can I do?” “How much better can I become?” If you don't do anything or you do the same thing over and over again, you stay the same.

Moreover, staying the same means going backward. Every day we get to rewrite history and change our future. So assess yourself. Your skills may not be anything out of the ordinary, but you can do miraculous things with what you've got. We all have unique abilities and talents. Too many of us don't know our own strengths until we push ourselves. I know you want so much to be good, but you have to do infinitely better to get to where you want to go. You have to keep getting better morning, noon, and night. I'll admit when I exercise, I'm not as fast, or as strong as others, but I'm still going for my personal best. I'm determined to be great for myself. I'm determined to be somebody for myself. I know I'm good, but I know I'm capable of better than good. The key to success is enhancing the capacity, competence, and skills of oneself.

INVEST IN YOURSELF

Life is all about creating skills and value and bringing those capacities to the marketplace to see what they can return for you. The truth is you must work harder on yourself than you do on your job. What you become is far more important than what you get. In any job, the question should not be, "What am I getting?" but rather, "What am I becoming?" The great axiom of life is that you can have more – if you become more. There is plenty of opportunity in the marketplace, but you must be ready for it and prepare for it. We must spend a portion of today getting ready for tomorrow, and a portion this year getting ready for next year, and so on. A large share of life is spent getting ready, getting prepared.

Consequently, you must start with personal development, self-improvement, making measurable progress. Personal growth is a push, a struggle, and a challenge. It is the struggle and the challenge to develop ourselves along with our skills that create our fate. Wall off anything that's not serving you or making you better. New habits don't come easy, but they can be developed. Now is the time to do the mental pushups and get yourself ready for your future. Your willingness to tackle challenging subjects will give you an extraordinary edge in the marketplace. Master your high skills and exceptional skills. Most people shy away from difficult things or self-improvement. But if you always back away from something that seems difficult at first, you leave yourself weak and unprepared.

Michael Johnson said, "Life is often compared to a marathon, but I think it is more like being a sprinter; long stretches of hard work punctuated by brief moments in which we are given the opportunity to do our best." Invest in yourself to get the most out of yourself. Don't repeat yourself, and don't refuse your own success. You have to invest. You get out what you put in in this world. Invest in yourself; be curious about everything. Research means to study phenomenon and to control and predict. We have to research what we can do to invest in ourselves. It's like any financial investment strategy; the best start early and go often. We live in this instant bake, quick fix, 30 minutes or less age, and we have forgotten what a slow cooked meal tastes like. Some things take time. So even though you invest in yourself, it still takes time to see the fruit of those investments. You need to have a strong foundation. We want to work on the above ground, look at the stone, look at the walls, look at the colors, look at the windows, but focus on the foundation first. The work goes down before the building goes up.

All you need is consistent, incremental improvement. Consistent, as in going early and often. It's very infrequent you see people who want to improve themselves. So set yourself apart. I challenge you to find your value and invest in yourself. Invest time – some people spend so much time with other people, they don't even know who they are. Invest time in you; spend time alone. I challenge you to spend time by yourself. Time is more valuable than money itself. Treat time like money. Don't spend it, invest it. Invest the time you have into yourself. People who don't invest time or money, won't have time or money. Every season isn't spring, and you're not going to grow if you're always in harvest season. You need to plant and till the soil; you need sunshine and rain, all preparing you for the harvest. Be content in the planting season, watering season, and pulling-up-weeds season. Remember that winter always gives way to spring. This is only day we are promised; you have to enjoy it and see each day as a gift and be grateful for what God has given you. I challenge you to get to the point where people don't even want to hang out with you anymore because you're too busy trying to make it and become the best you can be. Invest in yourself so you can be excellent, and watch people take notice. Insist on excellence in your life.

Why is it that people aren't pursuing their dreams? Why is it that people are not doing better than they could be doing? How much time do you spend working on you or working on your dream? In the last 90 days, what kind of investments have you made in you? What new skills have you acquired? According to bestselling author, Robert Greene, there are two types of time in our lives: dead time and alive time. In dead time, people are passive and waiting, while in alive time, people are learning and acting and utilizing every second.[43] I hear clients say to me all the time, "I am not who I need to be, and I have not been who I need to be. I want to be the best version of myself." They ask me what I can do to help them, and I say, "The best thing you can do is help yourself. Be informed, be prepared, be ready, et cetera." Life is hard enough, don't make it tougher than it needs to be; help yourself.

Robin Sharma said, "Investing in yourself is the best investment you will ever make. It will not only improve your life, it will improve the lives of all those around you." Plant seeds. Basic garden math states that 1% of the seeds turn into 50% of the flowers. So plant lots of seeds because you want as much latitude as possible. This goes to the heart of the 'Making of Me.' Investing in yourself is how to stay leaps and bounds ahead of the competition. It's your responsibility to invest in yourself. Spend your time improving yourself. Don't look to waste time with other people. Cultivating a successful inner life is what should be front and center. Rule yourself. It has to come from within if you're going to make it. The key is to be more selfish (at times). If you're not taking care of yourself, who is? Taking care of yourself first is not selfish at all. Self-care is not selfish. Put yourself first, your needs and your interests. Make yourself a priority. Start putting yourself first. You're responsible for your own development.

Focus on building your capacity to do more. Some is good; more is better. The safest and best investment is always in yourself. You need to update your personal operating system. Invest in yourself to increase your commitment level and hold yourself accountable. The best education you can receive is investing in yourself and reinventing yourself constantly. Every change that you are going to make starts with yourself. Investing time in yourself is time well spent. Money can vanish from life; friends too, but skill never leaves. There's a difference between an expense and an investment. I invest in myself all the time. Paying for my gym membership is an investment, learning something new is an investment, exploring the world is an investment, reading is an investment. It's time to double-down on your investments.

CENTRAL INTELLIGENCE

One of my crowning achievements was graduating from university and law school. Moreover, my achievement was not because of affirmative action. I did not sell out; I bought in. I doubled-down on my brain. The return on investment on a book is instant because it could trigger an idea, a business, motivation, et cetera. Proverbs 2:3-5 says, "If you scream for insight and call loudly for understanding, if you pursue it like you would money, and search it out as you would hidden treasure, then the Lord will be awesome to you, and you will come into possession of the knowledge of God."

The most valuable commodity is information. We live in a world of intellectual bankruptcy, in which there is no excuse for not knowing better or knowing more, especially since IQ has been commoditized. All information can be accessed immediately. So you don't need to be a genius to be successful or make a lot of money;

you just have to tie the information together. You can use intellect rather than force. Intelligence is diverse. We think about the world in all the ways we experience it: by sound, movement, touch, language. Intelligence is dynamic, and intelligence is distinct. It's about having the ability to learn and pull together disparate pieces of information on the fly. That's why it's so important to invest in your intelligence. You have to think about how we can make things better. Shaking your ass doesn't have to be your currency. You can be intelligent. Knowledge is the new currency. Knowledge is money; you always get paid for what you know.

All it takes is a little wisdom and a hint of insight to change the course of your life. Don't forgo your heart, and don't neglect your mind. You've got the hardware, and now it's just time for the software. Invest in intelligence and know-how, and apply it more actively. In sports and in life, you win from the neck up first. Wisdom and better judgment prevail at the end of the day. You have to invest, not only in things that make you money, but in ideas that make your mind rich and people who give you stability and peace. Invest your time to acquire the right intelligence and know-how. That will accelerate your career advancement.

Most people want to build their personal brand, yet don't invest in the process of developing one. Never assume that you don't need to get smarter, wiser, and more strategic about how to better manage your life. You need to always be smart and calculating. Your mind is a weapon; always keep it loaded. Your power is your mind. Everything around you someone thought of first. Look at Nehemiah in the Bible in Nehemiah 4:17, carrying a "weapon in one hand and a tool in the other." Knowledge is both a tool and a weapon.

Your greatest source of wealth is between your ears. The lottery is not going to make you rich; your mind is. You cannot transcend what you do not know. So when you know better, you do better. Change is proportional to your knowledge. The more you know, the more you change. We need an informed and engaged citizenship. Be educated, be engaged, and be committed. You can't be genuinely engaged unless you're informed. Ignorance is not a virtue. It's not cool to not know what you're talking about. You have to get smart and get smart fast. Know your stuff, know where you're going, and know how you're going to get there. It's criminal incompetence not to know. The problem with society is that we keep successfully shooting ourselves in the foot. We continue to deny our own success. It's a low watermark for the human race, being willfully ignorant. Don't sabotage your success by making a comedy of errors. Stop the cycle of self-sabotage. Indeed, ignorance is bliss because with knowledge comes responsibility.

Knowing is owning. That's why people who are successful have learned to optimize their brain. Whether its counterterrorism or making tons of money or establishing a successful business enterprise, intelligence is key. You need intelligence. People will pay tons for intelligence so always be informed. The Bible says in Proverbs 4:7, "wisdom is the principal thing; therefore get wisdom: and in all thy getting, get understanding."

If you want financial freedom it's not about working harder or smarter or longer; it's about making the shift from working for money to having your money work for you, and you can't do that by saving. You have to invest, and you have to invest in your intelligence. No one is better than you or smarter than you; they just know more. They have knowledge and skills that you can learn too. Part of education is learning that you can learn. That's why Aristotle said, "All men by nature desire to know." We learn from Edmond Dantes in *The Count of Monte Cristo,* that knowledge is priceless; freedom can be taken away.[44] Confidence and competence always win. While some skills aren't always innate, knowledge allows you to learn the skills necessary for you to escape. Learning is an imperfect process. It's an incremental process, where you learn little by little, inch by inch. First, you learn, then you remove the 'L.' Leverage what you know. So always invest. Isaiah 55:2 says, "Why do you spend your money for that which is not bread? And your labor on what does not satisfy?" Don't buy your wants and beg your needs. You're wearing what you should be investing. Invest in your intelligence.

Education

Most universities are built on the principles of the enlightenment that people possess the capacity to think and reason. These principles highlight the fact that what you don't know can get you killed. Law school for me was a street fight; it was a slugfest. I felt like a big fish in a small pond, but the pond is deep. Law school was about formalizing your knowledge and knowing what you know. It's a question of how quickly you can gather information and how quickly can you process it. I remember during orientation the dean telling us: "Don't come to us for answers, you won't get any. You have to find the answers for yourself." One of the biggest problems I see is that young people look to others for answers. Learning how to solve problems, learning how to find answers on your own is very important. Its where success comes from. There comes a time when you have to figure out the answers for yourself.

Law school taught me you have to figure out <u>how</u> things work, so you will know how things <u>will</u> work. You must question everything; you must question the answers and answer the questions. Ponder deep questions and be curious. When you read anything, always wonder what happened before page one. Law school taught me that you must grow yourself and get to know yourself. It's about making the most of yourself. You have to stretch yourself to get to know yourself. Law school wasn't just about thinking, but it teaches you how to reason. It's not enough to think; you have to reason. You can't just read text; you have to read it and say, "*Ok, now that I've read it, what do I think about it.*" You have to think critically because you don't win unless you think strategically.

Regardless of the schooling, all school is about developing your skills. Everyone has skills to get you anywhere you want to go, but you have to build them. Education is about character development because character is everything. You look at things very differently when you have knowledge. Ignorance brings arrogance; knowledge makes you humble. Knowledge is how we treat people; it's in everything we do. My education is my own, and it was a high watermark for me personally. I love learning and being extremely inquisitive. But I'm more impassioned about ameliorating myself. I'm voracious about how to improve myself. This is about making better choices concerning my life. It requires hard work and diligence. You have to study and practice every day at getting better.

Education sets the table for future success. Changes move proportionally to knowledge. You have to know more to change your environment, and education makes all the difference. An education gives you more than knowledge. An education will make you fireproof. An education gives you the power to change your life and the lives of others. An education gives you the opportunity to determine your future. Education is power. You can't waste talent or potential because you lose out on that capital when you don't invest in it. Education teaches you to take information, calculate it, put it through some kind of process, and figure out what's the next (best) thing to do. Education is a sword and a shield. The purpose of education is to turn mirrors into windows. Education builds wisdom, love, and strength.

You can't be soft in a tough world, but you can be informed and make it. The Bible even says in Hosea 4:6: "My people perish for lack of knowledge." Value learning and experience over everything else. If you want to tap the future, invest in your education. The truth is if you're not inside you're outside. If you're not part of the committees making decisions, you're on the menu. So get as much information as you can, then get involved. I cannot express enough the importance of information. Know more and protect your interests. You have to continue to read, listen, and learn conventional ways to gather information about what's happening in our world. It's not only about keeping in touch; it's about being better informed and growing as a person that other people find worthwhile. There is no knowledge won without sacrifice, and this is one of the hard-human truths.

There's a lot you don't know, and you need to be honest with yourself about what you can build upon. Don't label yourself by what you've accomplished or already learned. Instead, identify what you are learning, want to learn, and the learning process itself. If you didn't finish school, you could always go back. If you didn't go to school, you could start. If you can't afford it, google your education. If you want to apply yourself a little more, you can learn everything for a $10 library card. However, there should be no excuses. I used to think, why go to class; you have to learn it on your own anyway. But educate yourself because no one else will. Be proactive with your education. Watch what you're watching, pay attention to what you're doing. Empower yourself with a strong education, and then use that education to build a world that's worthy of your promise.

Education is the crown jewel that guarantees a degree of success. You have to go back to the workbench. You have to see your education as a continuum in which you never arrive. You just continually learn more, and you refine, refine, refine your knowledge. I am more a work in progress than I am a success. Education is more than a luxury. It is an investment for career success and growth. Education needs to nurture judgment, guide mastery of ethics and values, and support forensic analysis.

Never. Stop. Learning.

Even though your diploma is your passport to a world of possibilities, keep learning. We need to study and optimize our ability. There is a difference between learning and credentialing. Don't let education get in the way of learning. Be a lifelong learner. Much of becoming an adult is about unlearning much of what was told to you by people who didn't have it figured out themselves. Not every law, rule, or lesson is in the books; there are some unwritten rules you need to learn for yourself. It's a brave new world out there, and you can learn something new every day. You can't just go to college for four years and ride that for the next 30 years. Your studying career doesn't end after school. Knowledge is crucial, and if you are not willing to keep learning and keep growing, you will be left behind. This is an arms race. It's a knife fight out there, and you have to get smarter and smarter every day.

Keep learning and creating new neural pathways in your brain. There's always more to learn. Network and learn from others; everyone you meet knows something you don't. Your teachers aren't just the ones you had in school, your teachers are your co-workers, colleagues, neighbors, friends. Everyone can teach you something. Become rich in enlightenment. Your brain is a work in progress; from the time we were born to the day we die it continuously revises and remodels, improves or declines as a function of how we use it. Exercise your brain correctly, anyone can grow intelligence. Don't neglect your mind. Find ways to sustain your neurological health.

Stay curious, ask questions, and never stop learning. Never stop studying the competition. Keep asking questions and keep acquiring knowledge. Knowledge compounds on itself. Never be satisfied with what you know. On a daily basis, allot time to become familiar with new concepts, and understand that learning is the best way out of any trap. Through consistent learning, you can have the confidence to try lots of new things, build on things that work, and discard those that don't. Successful people ask more questions than give answers. Our egos paralyze us many times before we ask a question. It's the fear of judgment, which can become crippling. Instead of asking and gaining new knowledge, we would rather protect our image and remain mired in our lack of knowledge.

So many ordinary people seek entertainment, while extraordinary people seek education and learning. Successful people would rather be educated than entertained. Those who want to become the best at what they do never stop learning. Prioritize learning and self-education. The mindset has to be; "I can learn whatever I need to know." If you want to become the best at what you do, never stop learning. Always improve and hone your skills and knowledge. All top performers, best-selling authors, industry disruptors, entrepreneurs, and titans of industry keep learning. You need to always be innovating, tinkering, reaching, and playing to keep your mind ahead of the curve. All innovation comes from constant learning. Stay in the learning zone, read, and write.

Become an active learner. Passive learning doesn't work anymore. Gone are the days of a teacher just talking and writing on a blackboard and we just spit back what was told to us. You have to be more active. I encourage you to prefer growth in asking questions. Continually ask "What if?" as a means to improve. Always keep reaching. Keep seeking. Keep growing. Keep using your abilities to bring out the best from those around you and let them bring out the best in you. Most importantly, *educate yourself.* If you don't understand why one country is invading another, take the time to learn about the current event. Ask someone who may be intimately connected with that event and get their thoughts on the matter. We're all interconnected; being aware of the different cultures and different people can make you a more well-rounded individual. You can and you will – dare I say it, change the world! Learn something every day. Keep trying new things; keep taking risks. The onus is on you to change your life.

Forget about everything you think you know. Make yourself invaluable by learning the necessary skills you may be lacking. So many of us are focused on expecting things to happen fast, but our worth in the marketplace is based on our ability to add more value than anyone else. When you can find ways to do more for your company, your employees, your clients, than anyone else, your gifts will make room for you. The world changes on a small scale every day, so you have to keep studying and keep learning to keep up. That's why it's so important you stay informed. You don't want to be caught unaware. If you're not learning or constantly being curious and reading, you're falling behind. There is no end all be all; it's just a constant learning curve. There is no "pot of gold" at the end of the rainbow, it's just more rainbow. You have to continue and further the progress that's been made. Learn new things, gain new perspectives, get in the zone, find inspiration.

There are infinite ways to keep learning, but one of the most important is to learn advanced computer skills to give you a voice. We are in a very noisy world, where it's even harder to be heard. The ability to create content, put together websites, and share your message on social media is critical. Just learning basic coding can put you ahead of the average person. Listen to podcasts, and continuously develop new skills and techniques. Last year's methods and tricks are outdated. The only constant is change. Everything changes, and it changes quickly. At some point, you have to learn and evolve. You need to be a savant that has a thirst for knowledge and is prepared for the unexpected. Stay curious, and ask questions. Learn a language on your commute. Do whatever is necessary to learn something new. Consume knowledge like air. Education is an investment; don't let it be spoiled by stupidity. You have a responsibility to be informed. You need to be very forward-looking; it's a game of chess, not checkers. Look down the road and educate yourself on what's to come.

Be Open

Consider with me the animal kingdom; each creature resides on a species scale of generalists to specialists. Specialist creatures like the Koala bear can survive only on a minimal set of conditions: diet (eucalyptus) climate (warm) environment (trees). Generalists, on the other hand, like mice are able to survive just about anywhere.

They can withstand heat and cold, eat seeds or berries, or your breakfast cereal. Specialists thrive only when conditions are perfect. They serve a specific purpose in their ecosystem, and are adept at navigating it. Mice, on the other hand, can move spot to spot across the globe and adapt to different cultures and stay alive.

We live in an ever-changing ecosystem, and we need to be generalists. We've become a society that's data rich and meaning poor. We have specialists in science and math and history and psychology, but how valuable is that knowledge without context? It is better to know many things, to draw from an eclectic array of traditions, and accept ambiguity and contradictions than to be a so-called expert and rely on a single perspective. Take, for example, grapes versus raisins. Grapes are specialists, whereas raisins are generalists. Grapes are plump and juicy, but they don't work. Look at raisins, they'll work together in a box, they'll work in oatmeal, in cookies; you can leave them in your car because they've been through enough and they've been exposed already; all you see are the wrinkles. You can't leave grapes in the car. They only last for so long until they're no good anymore. So my point is, part of being successful is being able to be a lateral player and being useful in many situations, and you can't do that all the time as a specialist. Sometimes a knowledge that is an inch deep but a mile wide is all you need.

I'm always amazed at how smart I am not. I see kids younger than me doing amazing things, people from around the world doing incredible things. So I've learned that you need to be humble, you're not as smart as you think you are. In this world, pitches come faster, so be as humble as you possibly can. If I may offer some advice: Forget everything you think you know. Don't believe everything you think you know. Be open to new information. You don't always know what you don't know. So it's crucial you know what you don't know. Here's the thing about declaring anything about anything. Nobody knows. We're all in the dark, feeling our way around. Nothing is ever set in stone. People are afraid to say 'I don't know.' However, the truth is that we're all just learning as we go. People are fearful of what they don't know, so know what you don't know.

Get informed, get involved. Be reflective and self-aware. Work hard to master something (law, software development, sales, et cetera). Create circumstances to be successful (move to the right city, go to the right school, et cetera), Remain open to new opportunities to develop and grow. Listen, observe, be curious, ask questions, problem solve, make connections, learn from others' mistakes and successes, because forewarned is to forearmed. Travel widely and meet as many people as possible. Mark Twain said, "Travel is fatal to prejudice, bigotry, and narrow-mindedness." Remember that everybody is a teacher. They can teach you what to do, and they can teach you what not to do.

Learn from everyone but also realize it's more important to figure out what works for you. Life is filled with possibilities; don't foreclose them. Find a way to say 'yes' to things. You can't learn what you think you already know. So be open to learning something new. But above all, expose yourself to better. Most people don't want anything because they haven't been exposed to anything. Slavery is an excellent example. If you teach people to read, they'll want more.

If you give people a television, they will see that not everyone lives barefooted. If you see big homes and yachts, chances are you will want more. If you have been exposed to more, chances are you will go after more in your reality. So always be open.

Apply It

The central questions I get asked are “How do I get from here to there?” “How do people get from where they are to where they want to be?” I say, “How do you become good at anything, like sports, medicine, or law?” The answer is to study and practice. Learning is good; doing is better. Apply this knowledge, apply this practice over the length of your life. Remember that talk is cheap because having knowledge is not enough; we must apply. Likewise, being alacritous is not enough; we must do. Confucius said, "I hear, and I forget. I see, and I remember. I do, and I understand.” Knowledge requires application. People always know what to do, but they don't always do what they know. So actively engage with your education, and apply your learning every day.

PERFECT YOUR CRAFT

One of the things I love to do is attend the theatre and travel to Italy to experience the arts. The arts are about imagining beyond the bounds of the known, embracing both past and future of the human mind and spirit. Specifically, music stresses individual practice and technical excellence. Professional musicians and athletes are notorious for spending exuberant amounts of time practicing their craft or sport, but many people with their own careers don't. But if you think about it, whatever industry or profession you're in, your job is a performance of sorts, and you should be consciously practicing your job skills with the goal of improving and receiving feedback on your performance. That's the piece that is missing for many people in their work: feedback. We don't receive as much feedback as we need. It's as hard to see one's self as to look backward without turning around and looking for ways to improve. You have to be brutally honest with yourself and really look at yourself. Success and winning masks your deficiencies. When you win or when you're successful, it masks what you may need to improve on. Sometimes it's good to lose so you can improve, or fail so you can learn what needs to be worked on. So sometimes when you lose you really win, and when you win you really lose. Look for cracks in your armor so that you can get better. Make career investments that align with your passionate pursuits and ultimate career ambitions. Keep your instrument sharp and know that your skills pay the bills.

Let's say, God forbid, that you lose your job today. To find a new one, you would have to draw on your career capital, which is the sum total of your knowledge, skills, experiences, and relationships. Pay into your career capital regularly by improving your skills and adopting new ones important in your line of work. Take professional development courses, and develop a portfolio of your work. Take a look at the dedication of Bruce Lee. I saw a biography on his life, and I was inspired by his intensity and the way he pushed his body. He would generate all of his body weight into the point of impact during a punch. He made the most of his time. In one day he threw 2,000 punches and 1,000 kicks; he ran 3 miles, and biked 15 miles. However, even after his success, he pushed himself even harder. Bruce Lee found that it was necessary to adapt quickly, like water. Water is amazing because it becomes whatever it is in. Bruce Lee said, "Be water, my friend. Formless and flexible." Bruce Lee knew it was all about work, investing in his craft, and making himself useful in every situation. He said, "I'm not afraid of the person who kicks 10,000 times, I'm afraid of the person who does the same kick 10,000 times." So steadily be improving, trying new things, and perfecting your craft.

You don't get a black karate belt by being lazy or by not washing your white belt. You have to work for it and push yourself to get it. You have to compete. You have to invest in your craft. Talent you have naturally, skill you have to develop over hours and hours of work ethic. There's no easy way around it. Your talent will fail you if you're not skilled. All of us will age, and pretty looks will only take you so far. So when the rose has lost its blossom, and the star has lost its shine, that's when your mechanics need to be sound and your preparation and investments you've made come into play. In today's world, the skills you must have in business are communication, sales, marketing and branding, product and service innovation, emotional intelligence, organizing, goal setting and planning, money management, philanthropy, networking, leadership, and time management. Are you investing in your gift? In your dream? The fire comes from within, that desire to be great. We can do better and dig deeper, but we must invest and perfect.

FOCUS ON YOUR STRENGTHS

Economics tells us that in life there are no solutions, only tradeoffs. Sure it would be nice to end poverty or give free schooling, but we're going to have to give something up to do it. We all have infinite wants, but we can't always get what we want because we don't have enough time or resources. So we have to make choices and set priorities. Adam Smith said, “Self-sufficiency is inefficiency, and inefficiency is the road to poverty.” You are better off specializing in what you do best and trade (outsource)where you’re not. Find a yin to your yang. To know that you can work with it, you’ve got to know what you have.

What do you have? Can you build on it, and build with it? You need to know that you are a tour de force. You have to know your strengths and weaknesses and be true to yourself and stay within yourself. If you do that you'll be great. Only you can know what you have, and only you can use all of what you have. Use everything you have. Consider your S.W.O.T. – strengths, weaknesses, opportunities, and threats. Focus on what you do best, and outsource the rest. Take advantage of all your strengths because you’re going need all of them. Use your gifts no matter how small; don't discount the gifts you have. Competence is what you can do, those skills that only you can do. What are you good at? What should you probably never do again? Create a Ben Franklin map: Grab a sheet of paper and write the area of interest you’re solving for at the top. Next, draw a vertical line down the center labeling the left side “strengths” and the right side “challenges.” Write down as many as you can think of on both sides and when you’re finished go back through and rate the significance of each one. For example, if you found yourself having 15 strengths, then your strongest skill would be number one, and your weakest would be number 15. Do the same thing for “challenges.” Finally, weigh the magnitude for each strength against each challenge. The goal is to “push away” the obstacles comprising your challenges by pulling from your strengths. Play to your advantage.

Most life coaches will say ‘Your weakest skills set the height of your income.’ Even the Greek hero Achilles was only as strong as his heel. Most people would agree that their weakness is strong. So improve your weaknesses and build on your strengths. The key is to make your strengths productive. It's all about leverage. Take advantage of your advantages. What's your advantage? Maybe you’re tall, or you’re young, or you have some particular domain expertise. Think about what your winning edges are. Work from strengths and set high expectations.

Work on your strengths. It's so easy and much more fun to work on your strengths because you get immediate positive feedback. However, the thing you're practicing you’re already good at. You end up improving on that stuff naturally. So you need to work on what you're not good at as well. You must embrace your strengths and hire around your weaknesses. Forget working on your weaknesses; play to your strengths. Concentrate on what you do best. Invest in your strengths and use them more frequently. You are far better off capitalizing on what you do best instead of trying to offset your weakness.

You only have limited resources, so you need to maximize your potential. Recognize where you have leverage and exploit it mercilessly. Become increasingly aware of your natural strengths that allow your skill sets and capabilities to thrive, and make a commitment to invest in them. Discover your strengths because your strengths are ultimately the keys to success. When we do things we're already good at, we're very successful. Leverage your ability by going through your strengths. If you don't know how to find your strengths, do this: Watch for signs of excitement and notice what you do differently from everyone else. You don't have to be very complex in your approach, but in whatever you do, you should do well. If you go in knowing you can be successful, it's more likely to happen.

Success is an art, but it is also a science. The reason there are so few successful people is that there's no single factor for success. Let me tell you what they teach you in business school; *Absolutes don't exist; there's no one way to do anything*. There are many paths to success. There is not a linear path to success. No one really knows what contributes to success. The truth is that every person is unique and that means what works for one person won't always work for you. When it comes to listening to advice, listen to the parts that ring true for you and ignore the rest. Ultimately, you're going to take one path out of infinite possibilities, and you have to navigate it your own way. Look, everyone is a genius, you, me, everyone. But as the saying goes, “if you judge a fish by its ability to climb a tree it will go through its whole life believing it's stupid.”

All of us are great at something but growing up we figure out all the things we're not good at. As a result, we spend much of our time focusing on our weakness and not our strengths. However, people like Tiger Woods or Michael Jordan spent their time focusing on their strengths and getting better at their strengths. Focus on developing your own unique talents. Identify and strengthen your distinct set of skills, as opposed to trying to be good at things you struggle with. Never compare your weaknesses to someone else's strengths. Everyone is unique, and we all have our own special gifts. Your winning formula may be someone else's losing formula. Just because it worked for you doesn't mean it will work for someone else. So here's a simple way to find your genius; if you are doing anything that feels like hard work, you’re already doing the wrong thing. When you do what you’re best at, you can get into your flow. The goal is to live the life you love and love the life you live.

In this world, only the strong survive and typically the strong are those who focus on their strengths. T.D. Jakes offered a story about a safari tour in Africa he was on where the tour guide said to him that in every herd of lions there is an alpha male who runs the herd. The guide said that only the alpha male can reproduce, and as the younger cubs grow older they will fight the alpha male. If they lose, they cannot reproduce. Its nature’s way of certifying only the strong surviving; the weak cannot reproduce. During this same trip on a safari, the tour guide told him that lions fight during mating season, but not male with female. The males fight each other for the lioness, and the winner of the fight earns the right to reproduce with the lioness. This is nature's way of ensuring that only the strong survive. So again, you can only be strong where you have strengths. Play to your strengths and follow your passions. Determine what's your unfair advantage? What do you have that no one else does or cannot replicate? Where do you succeed where others fail? Understand your "circle of competence." It is essential to understand your strengths and weaknesses.

When deciding what to pursue, it's just as important to know what to leave out as it is to know what to focus on. You don't have to be smart everywhere, just be smart in spots, and stay around those spots. Do what you do best, and try to find people who can fill in by doing the things you are not good at. Most successful people aren't good at everything, but they became successful by honing what they excel at. Your weaknesses do not matter. You have to accept that. The only things that matter in life are your strengths. Improve them and build on them. The one thing that you have that no one else has is you: your voice, your mind, your story, your vision. Do what only you can do best. Stick to your strengths; go back to your calling card. Find what you're good at and be great at it. Multitasking is the bane of the average minded – merely doing a lot of things at once but never being great at anything. It's important to focus on your strengths and concentrate your mental energy on a single target and how you can get there; then once you've hit that target, move on to another. Live future forward.

GROWTH

There's an innate struggle between how much we should accommodate society and how much we should push past our limits. Too many of us are not living up to our potential, and we still have a lot of tread on the tire. Don't settle for average; take the limits off yourself. Mediocrity is boring. What's the point of living average? Don't dumb yourself down just to make others feel better about themselves, or to make other people feel comfortable. Don't trim your sails. There will be some people threatened by your being blessed and your growth. Move ahead anyway. Contribute to your potential. Potential always has a shelf life. Maximize your potential. This is your time to usher in your future and realize your potential. These pillars offer a path in unleashing human capability, resilience, compassion, and well-being.

Our job is to nourish and grow our own gifts. Be determined to outgrow and outperform your position. The universe evolves, stars evolve, we evolve, plants evolve; everything living evolves. Everything of God lives and grows (trees, people, plants, animals, oceans). William Shakespeare's "The Seven Ages of Man" from *As You Like It* shows just how much growth is a natural evolution, not a forced evolution. It's natural to grow and you are designed to grow, and you have to accept responsibility for the things that you do. So to keep you on track, ask yourself if you are you managing your time strategically? Are you learning new things that accelerate your growth? Are you challenging yourself enough? Do you have the right support cast? Have a personal growth plan and be specific as to how you're going to grow. Constantly evolve. Grow where the ground is fertile, and there aren't many plants there. In essence, be around other people who are like-minded and going places. Maintain success by consistently learning and adapting to your environment. Your world will get smaller and smaller as you grow in it. At some point, you have to grow up and don't make apologies for making a living for yourself. There's always a point where you have to pave your own path. A point where you have to separate the wheat from the chaff.

Growth is slow and often stunted. It's kind of like a car's stick shift; stop, go, stop, go. Life is about growing, and sometimes growth hurts. Rabbi Dr. Abraham Twerski discussed reading an article titled: "How Does a Lobster Grow?"[45] He elaborated that a lobster is a soft mushy animal that lives inside a rigid hard shell. That shell does not expand so how can the lobster grow? As the lobster grows, he feels himself under pressure because the shell becomes increasingly confining and limiting. The lobster casts off that shell and hides under a rock to protect itself from predators and grows a new shell. The lobster repeats this many times. But the stimulus that makes the lobster grow is that it feels uncomfortable. However, if the lobster had a doctor, he might be prescribed a Valium or some other painkillers and would never grow. It's a reminder that times of stress are also signals for times of growth, and if we use adversity to our advantage, we can grow from it.

Be willing to give up who you are to become who you might be. The goal is to arrest and reverse chronic problems in your life and be on a meteoric rise. There's a difference between the outward image versus the inward transformation. Seeds grow from the inside out. If an egg is broken by an outside force, life ends. If broken from within, life begins. Great things always happen from within not from the outside. When things externally aren't working out, it's time to move inside of yourself. If you go without, go within. Figure out what's going on inside to change the outside. Always ask yourself which way you should grow. Not go, but grow.

Don't be afraid to grow or end bad habits or try new things; take the initiative. You don't have to hold yourself hostage to anything you used to do or anybody you used to be. Only look back to see how far you've come. Appreciate the past but look forward to the future. Growth and comfort do not coexist. Your job is to keep growing and keep learning. Infinite growth is the target. I had a professor in college, and I swear he never graded the paper; he graded you. He graded whether you improved or not. To grow, you have to constantly learn, constantly move, constantly improve. You have to be an optimist and believe that you can be better. Every challenge, delay, setback, inconvenience, and offense is there to refine you; don't let the same things continue to hold you back.

Be thankful for the experiences that help you grow as a human being. I'm always amazed at my body because it gets sick and I know it wants stability, but what the body really needs is to grow. So be open to growth. God is the potter, and we are the clay. Nothing random happens; everything is an opportunity to be refined. Stay on the potter's wheel. We all face unpleasant and uncomfortable situations, but you can't pray away every difficulty. Stay on the potter's wheel and keep improving. The good news is you're not a finished product, stay on the potter's wheel and continue to grow and be refined.

Progress Is a Process

I'm always amazed by nature and impressed that nothing in nature blooms all year. It's a constant reminder to be patient with yourself. Seasons come and go. Self-growth is fragile, especially in your 20's. Growth is slow. The 20-year-old brain is still developing its frontal lobe, which is in charge of overriding emotion with reason. Progress is a process. Your progress is going to take time; it won't change overnight. You need to make a commitment to your development. A full commitment to growth. Take responsibility for your growth. Hold yourself accountable for your progress and your circumstance. More importantly, never pass up an opportunity to grow or redefine yourself. Focus on the quality of your growth, not the quantity of it. Life is about growth and change. The universe is always speaking to us; most of the time it's a whisper. The universe always whispers before it yells. The universe will answer us by dreams, nudges, and hints; then eventually, louder events start happening to us to get us on course. When you are no longer growing or changing, that's your whisper that you are supposed to do something else. See yourself through the prism of time, moving forward with momentum, but always evolving.

The story of America is one of hard fought, hard won progress, setbacks, achievements, et cetera. It's a story where progress was not a straight line. Don't be discouraged if you don't have any huge cinematic breakthrough – it's about making lots of tiny changes. Improvement is not about working towards a breakthrough, but rather it's about improving, healing, and fortifying yourself one day at a time. Progress is fragile, and progress is slow. You don't set out to build a wall, you just lay one brick at a time, and lay it just as perfectly as you can, and soon you have a wall. Invest a little bit over time. A jug fills drop by drop; bean by bean the bag is filled. You're not going to master your life in one day. Just master the day. Master today. Then keep doing that every day. Good things take time. Above all else, success requires time and effort. Malcolm Gladwell suggested that mastery of anything requires 10,000 hours of tireless focus.[46] One day at a time. Make progress, go forward.

Trial and Error

Thomas Edison wrote, "I never did anything worth doing by accident, nor did any of my inventions come indirectly through accident, except the phonograph. No, when I have fully decided that a result is worth getting, I go about it, and make trial after trial, until it comes." I grew up so much just by making mistakes. You're destined to fail if you don't make mistakes. If you don't fail, you're not trying. When we stop trying, we fail. Failure is neither fatal nor final. I make lots of mistakes, but I try to make mistakes in a good direction. So make lots of mistakes, just not big ones. I realized it's very difficult to make good mistakes. Trial and error is the only way to success. Most success comes from trial and error, not thinking and reasoning.

Whether you feel up against the wall of forever, whether you're skating uphill, whether the writing's on the wall, whatever the ghastly feeling, you need tenacity and a resolve to try again. Don't ever give up and don't ever take no for an answer. Don't feel inferior, washed up, or less than. We all have experienced the thrill of victory and the agony of defeat. In both cases you have to regain your composure quickly. I always believe that tomorrow is another day. Everyone gets knocked down, but it's all in how well you get back up. You will have some disappointments, but pick up the pieces and keep going. Don't give up. Try again. Sometimes your disappointments are more edifying than your successes.

Thomas Edison reminds us that successful people learn more things, try more things, and persist longer. He shows us the importance of failing fast. It's always best to start with a working set of assumptions and then subsequently test them as quick as possibly. If they're wrong, then you can pivot and adjust accordingly and be decisive with your next move. When depressed or in a funk, you have to play your way out of it. You have to work through it. You can't politic your way out of it. You can't survey your way out of it. How do you get the nutrition out of your food? You chew it. You wrestle with it. You don't eat it whole. In the same way, there's value in everything you're going through, but to get any value from it, you need to chew it, wrestle with it. That's where the nutrition lays. So whatever your trial, whatever your error, work through it.

LEARN FROM FAILURE, MISTAKES, & SETBACKS

It's essential that one knows what it's like to be disappointed. If you want to win, go and meet those who lost and learn from others' mistakes. It takes a wise person to learn from their own mistakes, but a wiser person to learn from others' mistakes. Don't make the same mistakes other people made. Make some new ones. More importantly, anybody can make a mistake, but the issue is when you compound it. You will find that successful people avoid compounding mistakes by **acting, learning, building**, and **repeating** using the following steps:

1. Figure out what you want to do (*If you want to be successful don't spend too much time planning*).
2. Take a small, smart step toward that goal (*A smart step is the action you take based on the resources you have at hand, and it never involves more than you can afford to lose*).
3. Pause after that step and see what they've learned (*It's so important to learn. Even if its criticism, just build from it. Take criticism seriously, but not personally*).
4. Build off that learning and take another step.
5. Pause after taking that step.

Whatever you do, DO NOT internalize critical comments that put you down. When you're indeed in charge of your own thoughts and feelings, no one can make you feel bad about yourself. Instead, look at the criticism objectively and rephrase it in the most neutral and unemotional language you can think of. Then ask, "Is this an area of my life that could use some development?" Don't take things personally. When people criticize you and your actions, it's not about you – it's about them. They don't know what it's like to be you and live your life. If you take things personally, you're allowing others to control your life and your happiness.

After any lousy failure of mine, I say to myself, "You have to learn from this. This will keep happening until you get smart or lucky." In effect, what I am doing isn't working, so change strategy. By the same measure, you can't focus on your mistakes or think you are less than. If you don't show you are making mistakes, you're not showing you're learning. You can't help but get better. You can't help but learn and improve either way. Whatever the endeavor, my mindset is: Heads I win, tails I learn. I've been so successful because I pay attention to my life. Every day my life is a teacher for me. In everything that happens from the traffic to checking out groceries, I try to figure out what this life is trying to teach me. Everything that happens out here (in the world) is trying to take you home to yourself. When you're home with yourself, you will have more character wins than losses.

When we face unpleasant situations in our lives, we are forced to tackle the challenge of accepting what we can't change and the pain of missing out. It is in those moments that we should reframe our predicament of regret. We should remind ourselves that feeling like you've missed out is the inevitable consequence of something good; the capacity to find worth in many ways. If you have setbacks or disappointments, use them as catalysts to strategically pivot. Try out new ideas; shed them quickly if they don't catch on, and move on to the next thing. You pivot as many times as you can, as fast as you can. This represents some of the best methodologies of those who are successful. Start something, determine it's not working, and then leverage aspects of it that are extremely powerful. That's how you become fearless about failing, and actually welcome failure. Part of that fearlessness is because you've screwed up enough times that it's all happened. You can say, 'I've been through this; I've screwed up. I've been in this barrel tumbling down the abyss, and I emerged and lived.' That's such a liberating feeling.

If you live through defeat, you're not defeated. If you are beaten but acquire wisdom, you have won. Lose yourself to improve yourself. Only when we shed all self-definition do we find who we really are. The next time you have a failure, ask, "Was I exposed or tested?" You will find that this failure didn't expose you; it tested you. You will see that it was good that you were afflicted. I'm glad many things didn't work out for me. I'm glad I didn't get certain jobs; it made me better. Forget those things which are behind you and press towards what's in front of you. God's hand is on your life. There's a difference between process and purpose. Yes, you're in this process and it sucks, but focus on the purpose of it. I don't think I've ever thanked God for my car or my clothes; I thank him for my troubles. I found strength I didn't know I had, I found resilience I didn't know I had. It was my successful failure. I didn't fail; I was rejected. There's a difference, and you have to deal with both. People who are unsuccessful bemoan what is appearing before them. If you don't fail you stop learning. Just make sure you're learning from it.

Friedrich Nietzsche said, “The mind is an impregnable fortress. And you find out about yourself through friends and enemies.” Most successful people read their negative reviews multiple times because it's about understanding how people consume you, and about respecting the market. The meritocracy of the end user is most important. When I was trying out some new diets with my nutritionist, she told me everything can't be sweet if you want to be healthy. You need some roughage, something tart, something bitter. We should look at moments of failure and mistakes as opportunities for growth and even blessings because if everything went smoothly, we would stay in one place, and never grow or stretch ourselves or question ourselves or want to be better in a certain way. But these moments force us to. It’s akin to the Chinese monk’s advice I mentioned earlier, who taught me there is a need for wholesale change and to focus on the meaning of my experiences. Ask yourself what this experience is trying to teach you. When you focus on meaning it allows you to be willing to suffer. Decide who you will be after this setback.

Blunders and gaffes are part of the learning process. You don't learn to walk by following rules. You walk by doing and by falling over. Same with life; you learn by doing. Treat every experience, especially failure, as a resource. I've never learned from success; I've always learned from failure. Mistakes are learning opportunities. If you make a mistake, you can only become better for it. Experience is always valuable, so even if things don’t turn out the way you would expect, you will walk away with experience. That experience was good for me because I learned a lot about myself.

Don't look at where you fell; look at where you slipped. Remember, stumbling is not the same as falling. A stumble might prevent a fall. When failure hits (and it will), don't stay helpless. The real test is how we react to that experience. We can either learn from it and move forward, or let it drag us down. So when you slip up, don't ignore the mistake you made; just don't wallow in it. Instead, shift your attention to what you're going to do to improve yourself in the future.

Experience is always valuable. Good and bad. Learn from each experience and keep marching towards your dream. Learning from failure is how you learned to walk, eat, talk, and drive. All greatness starts with failure because when you succeed, you're having fun, partying, living it up; but it's when you fail that you ponder and you learn, and any success comes from pondering and learning from your situation. I learned when studying chemistry in college that when you stay static, the environment will change around you, and you will become obsolete. In this world, if you become paralyzed by fear, or more specifically, the fear of failure, you will get left behind. Even changing the word failure could help. I encourage people to think of it as a decision that turned out to be wrong. But I didn't fail; I just didn't make the *BEST* decision. Pat yourself on the back for taking a risk; learn from it and move on. So if you fail, make a decision to move forward. It is better to make a decision and change it later on than to make no decision at all. There is no such thing as a wrong decision; you just make a decision, and you make it right. Make decisions the right way and you'll be fine.

In Joseph Campbell's *Hero's Journey,* a hero returns from his quest, after suffering and enduring trials, with newfound wisdom and self-knowledge required to build a better life and a new status quo in the ordinary world. The hero has changed on a cellular level. This is a period of self-discovery.[47] Wherever you are, whatever you're in, there's a lesson there, and until you learn that lesson, you're going to be staying there for a while. It's just like being in class, when you learn the lesson you get to move on, and until you learn whatever the lesson is you won't move on from it. Very rarely will you have that Road to Damascus epiphany, that flash of insight, that immediate change of heart, but on occasion you might. Whatever your failure, learn from it. How have you been changed? How are you different? How are you better? What did you learn this year that changed you? What did you suffer? What did you learn from it? How do you take something that hurt you and turn it into something that helped you? What is your ghost of Christmas past? What went wrong and what was the lesson to be learned from it? Perhaps it wasn't a life-threatening experience, but it was a life styling experience.

I have always struggled with my scoliosis, and I realized that my scoliosis was a metaphor for my life. My backbone was off and it was connected to my core. My faith was my core, and it wasn't in alignment with my life. Once I got in alignment with my faith and alignment in other areas of my life, my scoliosis resolved itself. Your specific problems are metaphors for what's wrong with you in your life. You can learn something from everything. Everything can be a teacher, and failure is no exception. Everything is a learning experience, and every story has a lesson.

So what do you have to work through and live with? Rumi said, “These pains you feel are messengers. Listen to them." Your challenges become chapters in your life. You own it, learn from it, go do what God has called you to do, and help those behind it. The greatest education is adversity. Think about what went wrong and what's going wrong; use that as a guide. The amount of time people waste dwelling on past failures rather than putting that energy into another project always amazes me. A setback is never a bad experience; it's just a learning curve. Reflect on what went wrong and what went right. Do a postmortem, per se, on the events. Figure out what the net result of that event was, and then move on. You will make mistakes, but learn from them and move on. Know that we are where we are, and we now need to decide how to proceed.

Today is all you can control. Forget about what went wrong yesterday. Learn from yesterday’s slipups, but today is what matters. It's what you do next that matters. Tomorrow is more impactful than yesterday. Failure is a cheap lesson in what's not going to make you successful. If something's not working, adjust and correct. Don't let failure stop you. Use failure as a tool to learn things you didn't know. Learn from every challenge, and you will see that failure is a success if we learn from it. All loss is gain. Display personal resilience and realize that what undermines your reputation is not making mistakes but failing to own up to and learn from them. Most people are crushed when they suffer a setback, wallow in disappointment, make excuses, and blame fate. Shrug off your failures and see them as temporary situations that teach you how to execute more effectively the next time, and there's always a next time. So fail your way to success.

It's important to remember that failure is inevitable; from the long past to the eternal future, it's unavoidable – whether making mistakes or facing rejection. How you deal with failure is the deciding factor. When failure happens, it can be heartbreaking, but when it happens, you have a choice. You can let it be your school or your funeral. You can learn from it or die from it. The Bible says in Luke 20:43 God will make your enemies footstools. It's about using failure and opposition as stepping stones to build from. Successful people are persistent through failure. Just don't let a temporary failure become a permanent one. Ben Franklin said, "Those things that hurt, instruct." Understand the cause and effect. Most people tend to focus on effects rather than the causes that created those effects. It's kind of like in poker, in which being a smart player is more important than being dealt a good hand. A wise man uses his lot to his advantage. Turn your wounds into wisdom. You will be wounded many times in your life, and you will make mistakes. Mistakes are not a problem, but not taking the opportunity to learn from them is. Identify your mistakes and learn from them fast.

The Boston Red Sox 2013 World Series championship will be remembered as evidence that you can turn around nearly anything. The team ended the previous season (2012) at the bottom of the standings, but 2013 was a new year of rallying back. The team moved forward with new resolve, and the beard-wearing Sox went on to win the division, playoffs, and ultimately, the championship. Now while their game is baseball, your game is change. Comebacks and collapses happen all of the time. In fact, in turbulent times, turnarounds are a fact of life. BlackBerry needed to be rescued from the brink of extinction. Microsoft needed a course correction even though profitable. Newspaper companies needed a momentum shift because of disruptive new technologies. These lessons work in companies, countries, communities, sports teams, and even families. The key is to spot symptoms of decline before they accumulate and then shift toward the actions that will build positive momentum. You may have a minor fall, but it will lead to a major lift. Remember, minor setback, major comeback.

I find myself frustrated by failure, but I learn by reflecting on the mistakes. A good predictor of someone's long term success is how they learn from their failures. It's not what you accomplish that matters; it's what you overcome that you remember. Adam Osborne said, “Experience is what people call their mistakes. The most valuable thing you can make is a mistake. You can't learn anything from being perfect.” I'm thankful for the good times just as much as for the bad times because it's all a journey. You learn in the bad times that inform the good times. You learn that you’re stronger, you’re wiser, you’re tougher, you’re better, and you’re more focused. There is no failure, only feedback. Human beings crave feedback. Any feedback, even negative feedback, is better than no feedback. Achievement requires continuous feedback.

So the next time someone asks you if you have any regrets, say, “I don't have any.” There are no regrets in life, just lessons learned. There is no such thing as failure; there are only situations that weren't supposed to happen THAT way. There is no pass or fail (in life). Nobody is grading you. The question moving forward is What's going to change? Yes, X happened, but how does this change? Where do we go from here? As Babe Ruth knew, "Every strike brings me closer to the next home run."

When God gave us the ten commandments, he already knew we would break them. It's expected that you fail and you fall short. However, we fall so we can learn to pick ourselves back up. The edict is to learn to pick ourselves back up. Failure gives you mental toughness and strengthens you for what the future will bring. We will make many mistakes along our personal and professional journey. If we learn from our mistakes, then life does make allowances. It's a journey, and you only learn from experience. Mistakes are the spell books of success. Study them hard and learn from them. Learn their incantations. When muscles tear they build muscles. When you are tired of rejection, revise your approach. To prevent future failures, look at what went wrong in the past. Don't give your next project an autopsy, but rather a pre-mortem to avoid a postmortem. Look at what could go wrong before it does. Plan ahead, and think on your feet. Be proactive and not reactive. You have to brush off criticism and not take it personally. Keep moving forward, and get the job done. Have a filter for opinions and criticism. Take criticism seriously, but never personally.

The truth is if you have trouble with something, you're going to start seeing more of it. So you need to have a plan and strategy. Figure out how you're going to deal with the trouble when it arises and understand how you’re going to overcome it. Get the mistakes out of the way early. What you resist persists. If you keep encountering the same problem, you must need it. If you keep asking God to remove your problem and God's not taking it away, obviously you need it. In school you are taught the lesson and then you are given the test; but, in the real world you are given the test first and then the lesson. Learn what this situation is trying to teach you. History repeats itself until we learn from it and change our paths. The truth is, when people face hard problems, they make mistakes. However, what's important is that you're learning and growing and improving and getting better and getting stronger and getting wiser. Be willing to make adjustments and improvements. If you're honest with yourself, you will see those past failures did not humiliate you, but they did humble you. Those events focused you. Failures pay more than a job, so put every experience in the bank.

Life can seem like an endless succession of failures and disappointments. However, know that if you can take it, you can make it. Failure tells you what kind of mettle you have. What do you do when your bell gets rung? When you get dumped, or passed over, or bad things happen to you, show them what you're made of. Be agile, but persistent. Don't let failure define you. Don't be defeated, depressed, and have no passion. In the end, you will be judged by your gallop, not by your stumble. Everybody makes mistakes, stumbles, and falls, but the question is whether or not you can regroup and move forward with renewed speed, conviction, and confidence. The critical belief among successful people is to view problems as a surmountable, temporary setback. Hurdles should be seen as nothing more than challenges to overcome and signals to try harder and learn from every experience. The single most defining difference between winners and losers is how they handle losing. No one can entirely avoid troubles and potential pitfalls, but the real skill is knowing how to climb out of the hole and bounce back. Disruptions, interruptions, and setbacks are everywhere, but see it as an opportunity to learn from your errors.

There are no mistakes. There aren't any, because ultimately you have a higher destiny. Oprah Winfrey tells us, “when you think in your little mind, and you're not centered, and don't recognize that you come from something greater and bigger, you won't know your real purpose.” When you don't know who you are or where you came from, you get flustered, always wanting something to be what it isn't. But remember that there is a supreme calling on your life, and it's your job to hear that, feel that, and know that. When you're not listening to the calling, you get in the wrong marriage, the wrong job, but these situations are all there to lead you to the path of who you are. There are no wrong paths. There is no such thing as failure because failure is just that thing trying to move you in the right direction. You get as much from your losses as you do from your victories. Your losses are there to wake you up, and once you understand that, you won't allow yourself to be thrown by a circumstance or some event because your life is more significant than one experience. You are not your last mistake. You are not that event that happened to you. Your biography doesn't equal your destiny. Your past is not your future. You are better than your worst moment.

When I ask people what they would you say to their younger self, they always say in one form or another, “RELAX.” Just relax.

It's going to be ok because even when you're on a detour with yourself and you're freaking out, that is the cue that you need to be moving in another direction. Don't let yourself get off your course when you're feeling off course. That's the key! How do I get back on course for my life? The way through the challenge is to get still and ask yourself what the next right move is. It's so important not to say, "Oh I have so much to do, and blah blah, woe is me." Instead, ask, "What is the next right move?" Then, from that space, what is the right move after that. It's important not to be overwhelmed by the challenge because you know your life is bigger than that one moment. You're not defined by what someone says is a failure for you. Failure is just there to point you in a different direction. All you can do is ask yourself what the next right move is?

It was when I was unemployed that I learned the ten commandments for my life:

1. **Life is 10% what happens to you and 90% how you respond.**
2. **Most people really don't care.**
3. **Family matters and is the most important thing in life.**
4. **You are responsible for your life and your own wellbeing; no one else.**
5. **You are accountable for your growth and development.**
6. **You won't always get closure, so you have to give it to yourself.**
7. **Anger and hurt only affect you, so let it go, forgive, and move on with your life.**

8. **God is still good; life is still beautiful, and still worth the living.**
9. **No matter what happens, don't lose confidence or belief in yourself.**
10. **Where you go from here is up to you.**

It is the 10th commandment above that guides my life to this day, 'where you go from here is up to you.' It's always your next move. No matter what has happened to you, what matters is what you do with it. Every weapon is a tool if you hold it the right way. Life is what you make it and we are to make our lives increase. So when setbacks come, go higher. God wants you in 1 Thessalonians 4:10 to "abound more and more," and Philippians 1:9 says, "and this is my prayer: that your love may abound more and more in knowledge and depth of insight." Both verses talk about increasing, more and more. God wants you to be profitable. Do you understand profit? I can give you a million dollars right now; it doesn't mean you have profit. If you have 1.1 million dollars' worth of debt, you're still broke. In fact you're $100,000 in the hole. Profit is what you have left after the transaction is over. It doesn't matter how much you have if you don't have anything left over. God wants you to profit from your experiences. Of all your experiences, how is it that you haven't profited from them? Nothing can sustain itself without profit. God cursed the man who buried his talents and called him an 'unprofitable servant.' The first thing God told Adam was to make a profit. God said, 'be fruitful' and 'multiply.' Ephesians 4:1 is the only time in the Bible where it tells us we should be afraid; it says, "we should be afraid lest a promise within us go unfulfilled." In other words, we should be afraid if we're not profitable. I want to be profitable. If I'm going to go through grief, let it profit me. If I'm going to go through the wilderness, let it profit me. If I have to get sick, let it profit me. If I had to cry myself to sleep, let it profit me. If I go without a job, let it profit me. I don't want to keep having experiences and not having any profit. I ought to be wiser, I ought to be smarter, I ought to be stronger, I ought to be better, I ought to be greater. Whatever it is, let it profit you.

GET BETTER

I hear people say all the time, "I'm waiting for my miracle," but the question is how are you waiting? You say you want a bigger harvest, a larger increase, but what are you doing for it? If you're going to get ahead of where you are today, there's only one way to do it: upgrade your skills. Always get better and improve yourself. You need to get better every day, every week, every month, every year. There are people waiting for you to stumble and fall so they can take your place. People will exploit your weaknesses and inexperience, so be on it. Don't confuse movement with progress because you can run in place all day long and never get anywhere. You need to see tangible progress. Even if you're on the right track, if you just sit there you're going to get run over. You have to keep moving forward and progressing every day. Life demands that you pick up the pace; otherwise, you get left behind. Progress is fragile. I want to be better than I am. I want to fix everything that's broken. I want to grow and be stimulated and be challenged, but how? If you're not getting better, you're getting worse. If you're getting weaker, don't stay weak; get stronger. Do something about it. People always say ‘someday I'll get better.’ ‘Someday things will be better.’ Listen, the future comes one day at a time. Today is the day. This is the day the Lord has made. Now is the time to make a change for your life. Someday may not come; you might not live to see one day. Today is all you're promised.

Keep your radar hot; scan for other potentially better opportunities. Always keep your options open to get better. Make everything good even better. If you want to get ahead, the only way to do it is to become better at something than you are today. What you accomplished yesterday doesn't matter much today. Don't rest on your laurels. My to-do list is always to get better. If I do that, things will take care of themselves. If you think you've arrived, you haven't. You can always improve and get better. Adequate doesn't cut it. You have to continually build on your progress, and improve. Think evolution not revolution. You don't have to completely start over with yourself, but you do have to keep improving if you want to stay ahead of the curve. If you're not improving you're falling behind. Keep up with the times and commit to a process of growth. You can't short change it; you have to take every step. So what steps are you taking to improve? Stay ahead of the curve if you want to stay ahead. You can't be happy with where you're at; you have to want to get better. You have to want to get better; there's always more that you can do, and you can always get better. My goal and focus every day is just to get better. The difference between success and failure is tiny, so marginal. In professional sports, it's always a game of inches because you win and lose by the smallest of margins. However, the up side is that simple improvements can make a crucial difference.

We live in a culture that relentlessly pursues comfort. The cost of comfort is high. Science illustrates that comfort and ease are related to disease.[48] We shouldn't always be fleeing hardships but should welcome them. Hardship brings people together. Ease is a greater threat to progress than hardship. There's a story I love about a caterpillar in a chrysalis and struggling to get out. And there's a man who comes by and feels bad for the caterpillar and cuts the chrysalis and this beautiful butterfly falls and dies and can never fly because it needs to go through the process of emergence and struggle literally. It literally has to do that in order to manifest. Work and resistance keep you alive.

Commit yourself to be better. It's not enough to be intrigued or interested; you have to be committed. You have to decide for yourself that you're going to be better. Work at the edge of your comfort zone; work tirelessly toward your goals. Keep giving to the process and keep investing in yourself. Rather than always looking ahead at the end goal, immerse yourself in the daily practice of building toward it. It takes a deliberate, conscious decision to get better to tip the balance in your favor. You have to stack the deck in your favor. If you only do what you can do, you will never be more than you are now. You have to push yourself, and you have to improve yourself and refine yourself.

Strengthen your hand. You have to look widely for anything that will give you a competitive advantage. We don't have to produce miracles, just progress. If it's not a win, at least show progress. My father and I had season tickets for the Minnesota Timberwolves and Minnesota Vikings when I was growing up. We used to love going to the games, but when the playoffs came around they were tough to watch because they kept making the same mistakes over and over again. As a fan, I don’t need them to be perfect, but show improvement. Don't keep making the same mistakes in the playoffs that you made during the season. Most of us aren't messing up; we just stay messed. Always improve on the progress that was made and the challenges that still remain. If you have high expectations, you want to see improvement every day, and then you're going to get what you expect.

The way to be safe in this world is never to be secure. Always be looking over your shoulder, keeping your head on a swivel, looking for ways to improve and checking for who's after you and yours. That's why only the paranoid succeed. Real enemies never sleep; there’s always someone who wants your place. Get in the weight room of your life because you've got to build capacity, build speed, build leverage, build lightning, and build thunder. Push yourself to be great at all times. Not good, but great because if you look behind, there's a million people who want your spot. You can't take a breath; there are people out there who want your job, want your house, want your spot, so you have to stay ahead of the game. Competitive paranoia is needed to stay on top. You have to act like you're running scared all the time and don't let up. Be continually obsessed about getting better and getting ahead.

Some people never live up to their capability. You can't waste your life and talent; potential has a shelf life. Start tipping the scale in your favor. Life is a battery of tests, so give it your best and improve where you can. Many things need to be improved; a lot of people's game needs to be stepped up. It's our duty to get the best out of ourselves. We are all in need of practice. In 5th or 6th gear, some people leak oil. Push yourself, not to the extent of self-destruction, but get the most out of you. We don't necessarily have acute problems, but rather chronic ones. You always need critique. Pay attention to things you're not doing right, and make corrections. That's how you move from good to great. It's the jump from novice to lothario. It starts and ends with me if I want to be great.

Get yourself mentally and physically prepared to be the best of yourself. Build equity and increase your capacity in everything you do. You play like you practice, so practice perfect. One thing I love doing is rock climbing. Rock climbing is all about learning movements and technique, but the problem I inevitably see is that people load on dysfunction. Whether rock climbing or weight training, it's about learning the true range and function of your muscles. Build a good foundation and practice technique. Any progress is progress. If you can be good on Monday, Tuesday, Wednesday and every other day, when the test comes, you will be good then too. It's better to be lucky than good, but you won't always be lucky, so always be good. There's no excuse for not being great. Train and be the most prepared. As a former athlete, I realize that you have to work hard to make it look easy, but that's how you stay in lockstep with your goals and advance the ball. You have to strive for perfection, strive to be better, and always be on the ascent. Nature of any kind thrives on forward progress.

Take the 1% approach. Whatever you want to get better at, do 1% more each day. 1% a day, compounded is 3800% a year of increase. Be gradual, be consistent, do more. Stop making the same mistakes over and over. If you're not the best, you're not working hard enough. Don't look at what you can get first, but think about how you can do your best. Be the very best of yourself that you can be. Don't let where you are be an excuse to stop growing. You have to get better if you want to be the best you can be. Think chess, not checkers; stay one step ahead. Every day is a new day to be our best and to exercise our exceptionalism. Strive for greatness; pursue excellence.

Nothing in life is 100% guaranteed, but show yourself capable. It's like baseball; it's percentages. It's all about increasing your odds of success and lowering the chances for failure. Worry about improving and getting better, and winning will take care of themselves. Success takes care of itself. All that matters is the ability, and that comes in many forms. I have one goal, and it's specific and transparent: to be the best I can be. Develop your skills, continually improve, and tap into your potential. Year in and year out, try to get better. You have to put pressure on yourself and ask more of yourself than anyone else to get better and be the best. Over and above, above and beyond: what do you do when you reach the top? You go over the top. You never arrive, you just always get better. Always be on the onward march upward.

Chess is an incredible game that I recommend for anyone to play. It teaches you that different phases of the game require different skills. It took me a while to realize that Chess is really three separate games: Opening Game, Middle Game, and the End Game. The opening game requires a bit of memorization and experience with common tactical and strategic themes. The middle game requires imagination and creative risk-taking. Finally, the end game involves exactitude and mathematical calculation. Imagine dating as Chess game. Many people struggle in the opening; take for example, approaching women. In the beginning, the game is literally wide open and can go in a myriad of ways, so you have to make strong, decisive moves that cover a wide variety of situations. At the same time, you need to study your own previous 'games' and as well as others' to be able to react or respond to whatever happens. The point is, Chess is a microcosm of life in which it's a competitive world for winning, so you have to get better and build capacities for different phases of your life. More importantly, you have to always stay several steps ahead.

Always ask yourself how you can improve and what you are afraid to do. That's usually the thing you should try. How we change or improve is individual specific, it's culturally specific, it could be fast, it could be slow. You're not the same, and you change over time, so you find things you get good at doing. The skills that made you successful five years ago won't necessarily be the skills you need to be successful today. Adapt and change. What got you "here" won't get you "there." What "there" is for you, I don't know. However, assuming that you wish to grow and progress, I know one thing for sure: what has worked for you up to this point will not continue to work for you. You have to invent and reinvent yourself continually. As a human being, you evolve, both out of necessity and biology. You need to keep adapting and taking on new ideas, beliefs, concepts, and identities. You have to keep moving, you have to keep progressing, you have to keep innovating. Those who refuse are the ones who get left behind. Someone who achieves great success is always improving. It doesn't matter if it's a career, project, product, or service. Continuous improvement means getting good at something, then becoming better, and then aiming to become our best at it.

Successful people are continually getting better. They understand that success approximation beats postponed perfection. Iteration in our world is everything. It's an unending process where you have to keep getting better each day. The minute you stop going is the minute you stop growing. Progress is hard, and even when you have victories you have to battle it out. However, if you stay with it, good things can happen. Take advantage of every opportunity because it will be gone before you know it. You have to make the most of your opportunities. By asking yourself how you can improve and what are you afraid to do, that's usually the thing you should try. That's a starting point but start now. Everything depends on what you decide to do at that moment. My motto is: **everything depends on this**. Whatever you're doing, everything depends on that. If your washing dishes, everything depends on that. If your driving your care, everything depends on that. Every moment of our life matters, everything we do matters, how we show up in our life matters in everything small or big. What you do this moment is the most important thing you can ever do. Everything hinges on what you do this moment. Even if you're brushing your teeth or putting on clothes, everything depends on this. Ernest Hemingway said, "Today is only one day in all the days that ever will be. But what will happen in all the other days that ever come can depend on what you do today."

Now is the time to settle for more. You can always do better; don't sell yourself short. There's a difference between getting by and getting ahead. Want better, not more. That's why I love being a Christian. It's a constant reminder that we are to die and rise again, die to our flesh and rise better, die to selfishness and rise to better. We are to continually die and rise thereafter. We are to always get up better than before. Ephesians 2:1-6 says, "but God has quickened us, made us alive with Christ; if God is risen, then so should we." We are to die and rise. Die to selfishness, die to sin and rise. So many of us stay in the 'grave' and don't get to 'grace.' Moreover, the difference between grave and grace is one letter. If you change one thing, if you do one thing differently, you will step into grace. One change can change everything.

Luke 24:5 says, "Why do you seek the living among the dead?" That's why I love Easter. It's a reminder that 'he' is not here, 'he' is risen. Jesus has gone into another dimension. I'm talking about a shift. Easter is about transcending, going higher, rising up. It's a reminder that you won't end up where you start. Where you are is not where you are staying. Black holes collapse into one singularity. Nothing ever dies, there is no end, just transformation. Every death is a rebirth. That job that ended is giving you life somewhere else. All of our human crucifixions lead to resurrection, and are not dead-end tragedies. It's an invitation to die to addictions and rise, die to temptation and rise again. Always be moving ahead, pushing yourself to go further and higher. Life is the ultimate video game; it keeps leveling up, and you need to level up with it. You have to continually compete, compete, compete so that you can get better. The video game isn't trying to kill you, it's just trying to make you better. To go beyond yourself, you must improve yourself. Your goal needs to be to just continually progress, always improve, and take the opportunity to learn and to grow. Strive to become better, not the best. Know that getting better requires consistency. Consistent action creates consistent results.

Be able to say to yourself, "I'm better than I was yesterday. I am much older, wiser, and even more experienced than I have ever been before." You don't have to compete with anyone; you just need to get better for yourself. Each day you have to prime yourself to develop yourself. The concept of developing yourself every day can really affect your success in life. When you take small steps each day to become better than you were the previous day, you compound your results, your value, and your skills. The only crowning achievement worth mentioning is being better today than you were yesterday. My goal is not to be better than anyone else, but to be better than I used to be, to improve myself daily, to use my time productively. Success is not a set-it and forget-it pursuit; you need to always be trending upward.

Some people have more of a past than a future, but don't let that be you. It's a statistical truth that most people are below average, so it takes less than you think to move into the group of top performers. Most people are lazy, they don’t eat healthy, they’re unmotivated. So it doesn't take much to be a top performer. Watching your diet, waking up an hour earlier, meditating, making small corrections can make you “above average.” It's similar to swimming. You don't have to be the fastest in the water; just faster than the guy next to you. Don't bask in your own sunlight, keep getting better. Always be in the process of perfecting yourself. Never stop working on yourself. It’s not how you start, it’s how you finish. Your life can indeed be a tale of two halves. Your life can be better going forward, it doesn't have to be what it was. Even though history runs in cycles, don’t repeat history. You don’t have to make history, but you can break history.

Perfection Doesn’t Exist

Don't set perfection as your target. Perfection doesn't exist. By our very nature, human beings are fallible. If perfection is your goal, you're always left with a nagging sense of failure that will make you want to give up or reduce your effort. Voltaire said, “Don’t let perfect be the enemy of the good.” Don’t waste time, hours, days, or months trying to put together a perfect plan. Just do something today and make progress every day. Don't let imperfection stop you from being good or doing good. When we fail to be perfect, we spend too much time lamenting what we failed to accomplish rather than learning from it what could have been done differently. People say 'practice makes perfect,' but that's not necessarily true; practice makes an improvement. Perfect doesn't exist. You can always better your best. Let go of your need for perfection. There's a difference between perfection and improvement. There is no perfect outcome; it's just a continual collective effort towards progress. The more we try to make it perfect the less perfect it becomes. All you can do is improve. Don't say, 'I should've known better than that;' just improve. It's about progress, not perfection. Good coaches will tell you that at a certain point, it's not just about wins and losses because games are zero-sum (you either win or lose), but it's about point differential. By how much are you winning, by how much are you losing, and is there improvement? It's no longer about success and failure, but degrees of success and degrees of failure. Avoid that strive for perfectionism. Healthy striving is fine since the purpose of life is to progress evolution. However, I know that progress is a more noble pursuit.

Martin Luther King Jr. said, "If you can't fly, run. If you can't run, walk, if you can't walk crawl, but whatever you do, keep moving." It does not matter how slowly you go so long as you don't stop. Do your best and ask what you can do to get better. Get better for the long term, not just the short term. All of us fight against our weaknesses, struggles, and temptations. However, keep striving. They wrote these ideals in the United States Constitution and we're never going to reach them because we're human and we will always fall short, but we must keep pursuing the perfect union our founders intended for us. We all fall short and we all sin, but we all don't fall truthfully. We all don't do the best we can do; not all of us are doing the best we can to reach our fullest potential. Even though perfection doesn't exist, there's always more you can do. I'm not saying you have to be a Paragon of Virtue, but you should work to be the best you can be. Striving for excellence is stimulating and rewarding. But remember that shooting for perfection is neurotic, and will only drive you crazy.

Be the Best (You Can Be)

The older I get, the more I realize that life has taught me just to try and be the best I can be. You have to take the hand you've been given and make the best out of it. I don't look back, and I don't even look too far ahead, I just try to do the best I can for today. Make your best your message. This life is short, so you might as well be the best you can while you're living it. That dream you have inside of you is there; you just have to let it out. You are ready and able to do beautiful things in this world, so let your insides out. Be the best you can be at everything you do because life is about attitude and when you start doing the best you can, people start watching and the universe takes notice. That's called life attraction. You attract everything you want. So always be excellent; people notice. Ralph Waldo Emerson said, "Make the most of yourself…for that is all there is to you." Success is always about traveling to the edge of yourself. You haven't even scraped the surface of your potential yet.

Confucius wrote, "To put the world in order, we must first put the nation in order; to put the nation in order, we must put the family in order; to put the family in order, we must cultivate our personal life; and to cultivate our personal life, we must first set our hearts right." For me, this means that if I want to contribute to the greater public good, I have to begin working on myself. Only by doing that can I see progress radiate out from myself to society. Each one of us has the ability to enrich our lives and grow our power. We are to strive to perfect the human condition. Make a commitment to be great. Once you accept that competition is just life's way of weeding out the weak, you will figure out that confronting challenges head-on with a can-do spirit leads to positive results. Moreover, that, in turn, leads to the conclusion that you're at your best *because* of life's challenges, not in spite of them. So, test yourself. Never settle for less than you think you can achieve. That's how you keep your professional growth and career trajectory moving up and to the right. Strive for perfection in everything you do. If you shoot for perfection, you'll never get there, but you'll achieve excellence, and that's what you want.

So do your best, play your strings, and do what you do. If you want to be good, do the work. You can be good with a little effort, or you can be really good with a bit more effort. However, you can't be great at anything unless put in an incredible amount of focused effort. Average is never good enough. I sometimes think about Jackie Robinson and the cultural impact he had and why it was so important to him that he was great and not just ok. You can't make a difference if you're just ok. It's harder to lead from a marginal position. You have to lead from the front, and the only way to be at the front is to be great. It's better to be great then to be caught somewhere in the middle (to just be good).

As an African-American, I know that by being black you have to run faster, jump higher, and do everything better. Being black, you have to be better than good. Good is a disappointment, even great is underwhelming. In order to be memorable, you have to be legendary. You have to have a desire to be great. You have to want to be on Mount Olympus, to sit with kings and titans. I can't want it for you; you have to want it for you. You need to have a relentless dedication to excellence. Excellence is complicated and context-specific, and there are no short cuts. Anything worth doing is worth overdoing. I have a friend who is a swim coach who told me, “You have to be as good out of the water as you are in the water.” As a coach, she typically will stand behind a swimmer in the water and watch how s/he looks both in and out of the water. You have to be good in both trenches.

Be so great that you cannot be ignored; that's the best advice. Constantly develop yourself and push the limits of your own skill set. The goal is to become an irreplaceable linchpin; someone who controls their own destiny by being so good they can't be ignored. Don't allow anyone to put ‘but' after your name. Don’t let people say “yeah s/he is good, but _________.” Don't give people a reason to discount you. Have a determination to achieve excellence in whatever area of life you choose to pursue. Once you discover what it will be, do it, and do it well. Douglas Malloch said, "If you can't be a highway, be a trail. If you can't be the sun, be a star, for it isn't by size that you win or fail, be the best of whatever you are." Whatever you decide to do, make it great. Be the best you can be at it. Be the best at everything you do. Be the best version of you. Make the most of it. Strive for excellence even if you are making burgers at Shake Shack. If you are excellent, everyone will want to be in your line. Whatever you do that is excellent, people notice and talk about you, and will say, “Did you see him over there?”

Bloom where you are planted; grow where life puts you down. No matter your circumstance, be all that you can be. Preserve yourself, believe in yourself, have confidence in yourself. No matter what you do, even if you’re sweeping floors or painting ceilings, do it better than anybody else in the world. No matter what it is that you do, be the best at it. My point is shine, no matter the weather. It doesn't matter if you go to the worst school; even the worst have their best. Learn to be the best you can be. As people, let's just be our best and if that's not good enough, we'll deal with the results. It's all about staying ready because you never know when you're going to get an opportunity or how it's going to come.

When we are our best selves, there's no problem we can't solve. So I'm encouraging you to live your best life; you won't regret it. Your best varies from moment to moment. For example, when I'm in the gym, some days I'm able to lift heavier weights than on other days. That's ok. Just do your best. Success is about being the best you can be. We have an obligation to ourselves. We owe it our ourselves to be the best that we can be. We owe it to ourselves to become master of our craft. While others are chillaxing, you should be practicing and perfecting. Always keep your standards high in all you do. Be tolerant with others, but strict with yourself. Don't give up on the person you're becoming. Give things your best, but never your all; that's for God.

We're all on the same journey of improving ourselves. From now on we have to be different. We need more personal development, more personal growth, more self-actualization, and more self-transcendence. Being a complete human being is the biggest and most noble goal you can aspire to have. You can rise higher, go further, and accomplish more than you know if you seek to be the best you can every day. Too many of us have been consistent in being inconsistent. My challenge for you is to be consistent. Never cease trying to be the best you can be; that's under your control. If you get too concerned with things you cannot control, it will directly adversely affect those things over which you do have control. Ultimately, we're on the same team, and the goal is to run your leg of the race, and then pass the baton off. Just keep moving the ball forward.

Success is about making an effort to be the best of which you are capable of. Some people are born on third base, some people are born outside the stadium, some people are born without a bat. One person's floor may be another's ceiling. Don't be jealous; focus on your race. The biggest failure in life is a low aim. You don't have the luxury of being average; you don't have the luxury not to do your homework. It's time you get better for yourself. You are great, and I believe we have not seen the best of you yet.

CHALLENGE YOURSELF

Look at the telemetry of a space shuttle launch according to NASA. During the ascent, the shuttle's main engines are used to throttle up to 104.5 percent of capacity. However, that didn't make too much sense to me when I watched the liftoffs. If they're at maximum, wouldn't that be 100 percent? It turns out that upgrades to the engine components over the course of the shuttle program improved performance, but NASA never changed the baseline measurements. So if a rocket scientist could accept 104.5 percent as a legitimate standard, is it possible for us to validate the athlete cliché of giving 110 percent? Because of statistical evidence, there are times when we do exceed our limits. We are capable of doing more than our limits.

We need high standards because self-esteem comes from achievement, not lack of standards and praise. Set lofty goals for yourself and achieve them. Be a goal digger. Do you want to be good or do you want to be great? Do you want to get by or do you want to get ahead? I'm asking, because some people just want to get by. But I will posit to you, stretch and reach for more. Start by achieving a level of competence. Think of the future, and set goals worth fighting for. Stop coasting, keep learning, keep growing. Ask yourself what the best use of your time is right now. Succumbing to the comforts of success is easy. You can get placed on a pedestal for so long that you forget the steps it takes to get there. But never stop working hard. Be on top of the stack, not on the bottom of the pile. Expect more of yourself. Keep pushing yourself. You have to read, you have to dig, you have to actually walk the walk.

Life doesn't get easier; you only get stronger. Jeremiah 12:5 says, “If you have raced with men on foot and they have wearied you, how will you compete with horses?” In other words, it only gets harder. Anything worth doing is hard. If it were easy, it wouldn't be worth doing. There is no shortcut in life, and there is no magic bullet. It just takes a lot of hard work. Stay hungry and humble, pin your ears back, and be hardworking. You need a strong work ethic, and you need to be extremely intuitive. You need that inner conflict; you need that tension, you need that internal drive to be perfect. Motivation comes from within, and unless you internalize your motivation, you're done. This is gut check time. That's how you attain and sustain success. Check your ego at the door, burn the candle at both ends, and GET FIT. I don't mean necessarily physically fit (although that's very important); I mean you have to challenge being tired. When I first started working out, I would get tired quickly, but the more I worked out the point at which I would get tired before, the more I would just push right past it. Most people will tire out before they wear out. Push yourself. People ask me why I work so hard, and I say ‘I'm working to get better.’ This isn't a gift; it’s something I worked for. I'm in the business of moving mountains. I want to work hard and do more.

There have been so many times I was insecure and scared, but the best thing that happened to me in those situations was no one helped me. I had to figure out that I wasn't going to be this punk kid my whole life. So the only way I could turn it around was to suffer. I started building calluses in my brain just like the calluses on my hands. In those situations, I realized that the only person who's going to turn this around is me. I began training my mind, my body, and my spirit so that when something terrible happens in my life, I don't fall apart. I'm training myself to be ready for my life. I'm preparing myself so I can handle whatever life is going to throw at me. Life is going to throw a bunch at you, and if you're not physically and mentally prepared for that, you're just going to crumble, and you will be no good to anybody. I had to push myself. So for me to become the man I wanted to become, I saw myself as the weakest person God ever created and built myself up.

I became driven from that point on. I wanted to see how far could I go. I wanted to know how hot could I burn, I wanted to push myself to the edge of myself. All anyone can ask for is an opportunity to figure out how good they can be. When you have done literally everything you can, that's the time you need to do more. That's the moment to redouble your effort. You don't know what you've got until you need it. That experience taught me not to count the cost because if you count the cost, you might not pay the price; you might not do it. So you do whatever it takes, you do as many reps as it takes, you study for as long as it takes, and you pay whatever the price. Be great at all costs.

You must have a relentless pursuit of excellence. It's all a mindset. Throw down the gauntlet and shrink your mental deadlines to work faster and with greater focus. It's akin to running a marathon. Running a marathon is much more mental than physical. Moreover, the ability to run a marathon – or accomplish anything hard – is more of a reflection of someone's mental strength than the person's actual ability. If you challenge yourself, you will get the most out of yourself. I know you are poised for greatness. Only then will you know yourself. There are no limits, only plateaus.

Many people are good at what they do. Some are even elite. However, a select few, esoteric bunch are completely unstoppable. Those who are unstoppable are in their own world, and they don't compete with anyone but themselves. They are the ones who strengthen their minds, wake up early, eat better, work harder, and push themselves to the brink and beyond every day. I challenge you to never be satisfied. Even after you achieve a goal, don't be content. Continue to climb and push yourself. We're all capable of much more than we think we are; we just have to focus on it. Stop asking yourself what the least you need to do is, and start asking yourself how much you can bear. Most people will rust out before they wear out. Challenge yourself every day to be the best you can be. Good enough isn't good enough if it can be better, better isn't good enough if it can be best. Be formidable; defy expectations. This is your time to shine. Push yourself past the point of resistance, past your breaking point. Know that if things stop being easy, you're on the right path. Don't be an underachiever.

Set the bar high for yourself. Start saying less, doing more, and committing yourself to excellence no matter the cost. Master yourself. Sometimes you don't know how strong you are until you have to be – you're capable of more than you know. You're stronger than you think. It all starts from within. It's all about what you want to accomplish, and going to get it. But you need that internal drive and motivation first. It can't be some external reward or punishment that gets you going. You need to be willing and have the courage not to be a victim. You can be a victim, but you must not allow yourself to be a victim. Shake off the fear. You have to be self-motivated. You need to be able to actuate yourself without someone else telling you what to do. Don't be motivated by money or anything external. Having nice things is, well, nice. But if you take away things external (money, fame, et cetera), you are still you, and nothing changes for who you are.

Go the Extra Mile

The 2014 phenomenon, *Whiplash,* is a movie that is driven by the detriment of two words 'Good Job.' The main character is, at best, an average drummer. However, he connects with a mentor who pushes him to expect more from himself. Towards the end of the movie, the mentor explains, "There are no two words more harmful than *good job*." The rationale provided is that approval is fleeting and does nothing but encourage complacency. To believe that you are "good enough" is to believe that you have nowhere left to go and nothing more to improve upon. So, as expected in the final scene of the movie, this average drummer becomes a master drummer. The point is that you can always get better. While "Good job" comments can make you feel good, "You can do better than that" comments may seem harsher and more challenging. However, that's what is required for you to make it to the higher levels of success you may want. Just make sure you aren't saying 'Good job' much more than you're asking, "How can I make myself better?" So push yourself to get better. Do it for yourself because you owe it to yourself to be the best you can be. Cut yourself some slack, but don't let go of the rope. Successful people always go the extra mile. They're pushing themselves to go the extra mile.

There's a story of Bruce Lee and one of his pupils running three miles together every day. One day, they were nearing the three-mile mark when Bruce said, "let's do two more." With his pupil tired he said, "I'll die if I run two more." Bruce responded, "then do it." His pupil was furious when he finished the five miles. Exhausted and angry, he confronted Bruce about the comment. Bruce explained it this way: "Quit, and you might as well be dead. If you always put limits on what you can do, physical or anything else, it'll spread over into the rest of your life. It'll spread into your work, into your morality, into your entire being. There are no limits. There are plateaus, but you must not stay there; you must go beyond them. If it kills you, it kills you. A man must constantly exceed his level."[49] So if you aren't getting a little better each day, chances are you're getting a little worse – and what kind of life is that? There's no traffic when you go the extra mile. Muhammad Ali was asked how many sit-ups he does. He said, "I don't count my sit-ups. I only start counting when it hurts because that's when it really counts." That's the truth. If you continuously compete with others, you become bitter. However, if you compete with yourself, you become better.

You have to challenge yourself and prepare yourself. I can't stress enough how important it is that we accept the challenge. No matter what the challenge is, accept it. Always choose to accept your mission. You will win, you will lose, you will succeed, you will fail, but it's all part of the process. Always challenge yourself. Maximize what you have and what you can do. Challenge yourself all the days of your life. Life requires nothing less than all of you. Life is a collection of challenges; take each challenge as an opportunity to rise higher. Pressure makes diamonds or busts pipes, but I believe you are a diamond. You are made under pressure. Each new day should bring new challenges and promises. Keep testing and pushing your limits. Respond to opportunities and embrace challenges. Don't back down from competition; challenge yourself because the more you're challenged, the more that tends to come out of you.

Life is about learning, unlearning, developing, and growing, always challenging yourself. I pride myself on pushing past my limits and seeing opportunities that other people don't see. Have the stamina to work on something until it becomes right. Have the stamina to work on yourself. It's a never-ending pursuit of improvement and excellence. I want to go above and beyond and just further. I want to be the best that I can be and keep pushing and challenging myself. It's the difference between potential energy and kinetic energy; one is being put to use. Martha Graham said, "No artist is ever pleased. There is no satisfaction whatever at any time. There is only a queer divine dissatisfaction; a blessed unrest that keeps us marching and makes us more alive than the others." Never be pleased, always strive for greater and better. It takes a passion for excellence and a desire for greatness to have the kind of success you're envisioning.

You must always go beyond what is required. Your increase in success creates an opportunity for envy. Don't worry about that. People hate successful people, get used to it. Choose to be the best you. Say, 'I'm going for it. I'm going to be the best I can be no matter what happens.' That's the choice you have to make; otherwise, don't get in the game. Don't hold back just because everyone else isn't pressing forward. Constantly be driven by the distant horizon. It's not meant to be easy; it's meant to be challenging. It's meant to push and pull you in the direction you wish to go. It's meant to test your staying power. If it were easy, there would be no Serena Williams or Michael Jordan. If it were easy, everybody would be doing it. So never give up. Keep growing, keep learning, keep moving, and I'll meet you at the workbench.

Comfort Zone

Eradicate the human tendency to relax, to feel as though you've made it. Every day you need to be stretching and reaching higher, living better, knowing more, getting closer, growing in faith, growing in grace. Stretch yourself past your limits every day. That's how stars are born. Everyone, everywhere, every day needs to be doing something to improve themselves. You should be getting your ass kicked every day. These are the most impressionable, malleable and formative stages of your professional career. Work for someone who demands excellence and pushes your limits beyond your comfort zone. Face discomfort head-on. Trust your abilities and know you will come out on top. You have to take it to the next step, go to a higher level of expression. You need to have an edge. Because only on the edge of comfortable can you be great. It has to be hard because only from hard can you get good. You have to be challenged to get the most out of you.

All of my successes took place outside of my comfort zone. Those experiences pushed me and got me out of my comfort zone. It just goes to show that when you're pushed, you push back. So rise to the occasion because success might be waiting for you around the corner. Turn your back on what's comfortable. The easy way out is always there. All you have to do is pick up your feet. In many respects, we have to get back to being scared again. People get too complacent, people get so comfortable. They need to keep their edge, keep getting smart, keep getting better. Being fearless doesn't make you strong; it makes you weak. Fear makes you alive; fear is a strength. It lets you know that a fight is present, and demands you get involved.

You can stay the same and be good or take a chance and be great. The only thing holding you back is you and your willingness to try. It’s an ethic of life that before you quit, try. But there's still the possibility of being great, and that's worth it. Like America’s founding fathers, create something new for yourselves and the next generations. We ask too much of others and ask too little of ourselves. If you want to be great, you can't just sit on your hands. You have to do something. Every step I take is the first step. Each day in every way I am pushing myself and exploring my world. Move outside your comfort zone. Test yourself - daily. When I decided on a college, I chose Pepperdine University because it was the furthest away from home, where I knew that failure couldn't be an option. But that wasn’t far enough, because I then studied abroad in Shanghai, China then Lausanne, Switzerland; London, England; and Florence, Italy. Don't be afraid to move beyond your comfort zone because the greatest part of you is the undiscovered part of you. Defy the unknown and achieve the unexpected. The sense of achievement yielded from your efforts will have a snowball effect on your self-efficacy. Remember, every day counts. If you're not growing, you're dying. You need to continually challenge yourself; define and redefine yourself.

I love exercise. It teaches me that you have the mental fortitude to create yourself. It shapes your body and sharpens your mind. Exert yourself, breathe heavily, and sweat profusely, then your mind feels the same effects and raises its pain threshold. You can't stay where you are and go where you're trying to go. Too many of us love our comfort zones. Challenge yourself to develop your talents and abilities. The brain has 100 billion neurons, which is similar to the estimated number of stars in the Milky Way galaxy. Yet we only use a fraction of our brains. We can do so much more outside our comfort zone. Get new experiences and more exposure. Every blessing I have ever received came outside of my comfort zone. To be successful, first, you have to be uncomfortable. So get used to being uncomfortable. Getting comfortable with discomfort is crucial to success. Being comfortable is the enemy. No one likes to move beyond their comfort zone, but that's really where the magic happens. It's where we can grow to learn and develop in a way that expands our horizons beyond what we thought was possible. Sometimes it's healthy to get thrown into the deep end. It's a character builder and relationship builder. Being able to see who sinks and who swims is very telling.

All opportunities for growth are beyond your comfort zone. Make leaving it a habit. Life withers away in luxury and comfort. Find your discomfort zone and then enter it. You won't always be safe and sound. Push yourself, especially when you're uncomfortable. Push yourself outside of your comfort zone. Forget safety; live where you fear to live. From a job to a relationship, we are always looking for safety. Safety is the reason behind much unhappiness. Live the life you want, in which being fearful doesn't matter; that's living.

Think about it. High school is four years because you can't stay there. College is four years because you can't stay there. Law school is three years because you can't stay there. Medical school is four years because you can't stay there. The point is every 3-4 years you should be changing, progressing, getting better, and doing whatever it takes to challenge yourself. Whatever you're doing in life, just push yourself to the limits. However, pushing yourself starts with getting out of your comfort zone. You must push through shyness, doubts, and fear. There are several ways to get out of your comfort zone: get a goal to push you, get a challenge to push you, get a deadline to push you, get others to push you, push yourself with self-discipline, get competition to push you, get a mentor to support you. Whatever it is, always push for progress. Get out there, challenge yourself, and do what you want to do even if you're afraid. Do something that scares you every day. Continually strive to improve yourself and your work. If you want an extraordinary life, you need to give up a normal one. It means doing things many people are unwilling to do. Most people will choose comfort and security over freedom. Don’t be one of them. It will be painful, it will be uncomfortable, but that's where the growth is. Never pass up an opportunity to grow.

No Limits

We all have two needs, we need certainty (everything is going to be ok) but also we need uncertainty (variety and surprise). Humans are curious about themselves; we're curious about our potential and our limits. You will face obstacles no matter what you do. There are enough obstacles in this world; don’t let yourself be one. Don’t fall victim to the carnage in this world. It’s so important not to limit yourself**.** The only limits we have are self-imposed. You just have to stay strong and decide what's important to you and what your priorities are. You have to look hard at your life and look at what you think you're capable of. What we shouldn't do is limit ourselves in any shape or form for what we believe we are capable of. That's part of the problem, we get relegated to certain fields, and we're expected to stay there. Expand your horizons; go for it. Dance, sing, act, be versatile. If someone tells you to “stay in your lane,” remember that you can create your own lane. Learning to play, paint, sing, or act means constantly being refashioned, constantly demanding risk. Don't do it just to tread water; do it to up the ante and push the limits and boundaries. Don't limit your challenges, challenge your limits because there are possibilities in you which lay dormant.

In honesty, everything is infinite. It is only us as people who takes that which may go on forever and talk about 'what's a mile from here.' Whether a mile from here or an inch from now, it's nothing but a piece of infinity. There are no limits, only the infinite universe. Don't put a limit on anything. The more you dream the further you go. Live with no limits. It doesn't matter what anyone else says to you; you are the only one who can stop you. Fear staying in place; keep moving. I believe and declare that you are well prepared for whatever is ahead of you. Remember that you're God's child; harken back to God's promises. You can do more than you think, so put yourself to the test. I was amazed at how strong I could be. How much I was capable of. It's like driving and you're testing out the gas pedal; just feather it out. Push your limits slowly; see how far you can go. You're stronger today than you were yesterday, but the only way to know how strong is to keep testing your limits. Take the shackles off. Shatter your limits. Live your life optimally. We all have limits, but almost no one reaches theirs.

Win, Win Again, and Keep Winning

I have a friend, a scout for the NBA, who says in professional sports, the first bar you have to pass is if you can compete; the second bar is if you can win. You may have passed the first bar, but can you win? You have to achieve at the highest level. Life is a competition. There is only winning and losing, and it is a competition to the death, so you have to play, work, and live to win. Win at all cost. That's why I love sports; it's the idea of being a champion. It's intoxicating. In professional sports, both sides are good, so all you can do is be more perfect. Each game is a statement game for both teams; all you can do is hope to have the better message.

In high school, during the basketball championship game I told our team one way or other we're going to be crying after this; let's make sure it's tears of joy. Winning is more than just about placing another feather in your cap. It's about competing, watching yourself rise to, and conquer the challenge. It doesn't matter if you play badly or well; what's matters is if you won. Twenty years from now people care about if you won, not how you played. Care about winning. For me, I hate losing more than I enjoy winning. The goal has to be to win, and to win at everything. The goal isn't cars, money, et cetera. It's to win. See money as an achievement. Focus on winning. It's like the old coaching saying, 'first you win, then you get good.'

CHANGE AND PROGRESS

Adapt and Adjust

When Charles Darwin went to the Galápagos Islands in 1835, he witnessed change in nature. The conventional wisdom of his time told him that things in nature were permanent and unchanging, but I believe Darwin saw better than he heard. Darwin believed his eyes. He saw change all around him. Darwin's finches were the best example of evolution which he later wrote about in *The Origin of Species*. Charles Darwin wrote, "It is not the strongest of the species that survives, nor the most intelligent that survives. It is the one that is most adaptable to change." More precisely, **adapt or die**. Darwin witnessed that the rate of your growth was in relation to how quickly you can adapt. In effect, those who can adapt are the best predictors of survival. Darwin's research is instructive and tells us that you have to make adjustments and adapt to the times. When it comes to survival, movement is life. I've traveled enough to know that those who stay in place are the ones who die, while those who are nomads and move around live. Darwin's finches illustrate that we are continually adapting to our environment. We need to adapt and face the unknown and act with certainty in uncertain situations.

Whether in business or the crucible of our life, change can be chaotic. While change is a natural occurrence, accepting it is not. To thrive in chaos and adapt to change requires the mental awareness to change one's thoughts in a moment's notice. The Navy SEALs' training involves a psychological tool used each training event called "The Only Easy Day Was Yesterday." This means that no matter how well you performed yesterday, forget about it because yesterday's over. You have to adapt to whatever challenges are placed in front of you each new day, and prove your worth over and over again. Evolve or dissolve; that's the new world order.

The biggest myth in business is that it's all about timing. Adaptability and execution are what matters, not timing. We live in a sea of change. Just look at our economy. Things change all the time. We've gone from an agricultural to an industrial to an innovative and more information based society, and there are a lot of disruptions. We have to acknowledge that technology has moved on; we have to move on too. We have to foster innovation. So in business, uncertainty is something I look for almost exclusively because I believe there's greater opportunity in uncertainty. The name of the game is to be agile and adapt. Everything is in motion and constant flux – the stars, life forms, nature, everything. We all experience change, sickness, and death; they are all around us. However, the only constant is change. Things change, and you have to learn to adapt and reinvent yourself over and over again. You're constantly changing and reforming. If there is one thing that is consistent in life, it's that change will come frequently and unpredictably. However, managing change effectively can give you a competitive advantage in business and in life. It's about being able to adapt and adjust. So don't just keep up with change, drive it.

People speak all the time about poor conditions in their life, and sadly there's not much you can do about the conditions in your life, so you just have to adjust and adapt. As Bruce Lee referenced earlier, learn to be changing and formless like water. Water can flow, or it can crash. It goes into a glass, and it becomes the glass. So be formless, always changing. The Greek philosopher, Heraclitus, lived around 500 BC in Ephesus (modern-day Turkey) and said, "No man ever steps in the same river twice, for it's not the same river and he's not the same man."[50] Even though he was born wealthy in a municipality, Heraclitus lived in the woods to contemplate the universe. Nearly 2300 years ago, he had an insight that reverberates through intellectual history that the universe is in a constant state of flux. Consider the direction of light. Light bends when it goes from one medium to another (i.e., from seeing light underwater to seeing the light out of water). This is considered the unbroken thread. We are continually changing beings, and we have an innate need to evolve and adapt to survive. Imagine you are being chased by a bear and all of sudden you can climb a tree to get away from your prey. Incredible, huh? Change does not scare those who are successful. They are continually learning and adapting their business models and themselves to fit different circumstances. So to become more successful, become more innovative and creative. To affect change in a constantly changing world, what's possible will always be a moving target.

The 1989 James Cameron film, *The Abyss*, centers around an underwater crew tasked with a dangerous rescue mission in a deep-sea trench. At the depths discussed, the pressure is so severe that the Navy invents a fictional diving suit that is filled with oxygenated water and relieves the pressure, but also requires breathing water through the lungs. In order to demonstrate how the suit works, a Navy SEAL submerges a rat into a small container of the oxygenated water. The rat thrashes frantically about thinking it’s drowning but soon is able to swallow the water and get the oxygen necessary to survive. The Navy SEAL says, "She's diggin' it." The rat's owner replies "She's doin' it; she ain't diggin' it." When I started my career a number of years ago, I was that rat. I was not too fond of it, but I was doing it; I was dealing with the change. Change, while requiring adjustment – frequently painful adjustment – will find its way back to equilibrium. Species and individuals evolve because transition and struggle are the only ways to get to someplace better. If you're not willing to change, don't expect your life to either. Change is like a wave; stand there and be crushed, but swim into it, and you'll come out the other side. Change is the name of the game. The world doesn't let you stand stagnant. The goal is to keep the blood running. Embrace change because life is change. You will change the world, and the world will change you. Be open to both. Life is a game of adjustments. Get out of your own way and purge your life of all that's stagnant. Life changes from moment to moment, and so can you. Accept what you can't change, change what you can.

Fear of Change

Frightened of change? But what can exist without it? Can any process take place without something being changed? Existence flows past us like a river. The "what" is in constant flux; the "why" has a thousand variations. Marcus Aurelius wrote, “Nothing is stable, not even what's right here.” Don't be afraid of change; understand it. The principle of life is change, and that's often frightening, as eloquently described in *Who Moved My Cheese?* We don't want to change, we don't want to grow old, but the alternative is also horrific. If there were no change we would be static, there would be no growth, and we wouldn't have life. Making changes is frightening, but shying away from it prevents growth.

The longer you wait, the harder it gets, and other people will outgrow you. There are some people who when you talk with them all they talk about are the good old times and the past. It's good and fun, but that's all they talk about. There were some old friends of mine with whom all I had in common was our history, and not our destiny. Show me how you're different, show me how have you grown since we were kids. I think about all of those makeover shows showing a before and after. Some people may have started out with you who no longer are with you. There may be some relationships you have in which there is more of a history than a future. You've grown up, while they haven't. People don't like change and don't want to be changed, especially by other people. So don't change people. People want to be inspired. Set a goal and let people figure out how to adapt. People need to see the benefit of the change. You have to give people a vision for reaching for change. Nobody ever sees the costs until they see the benefit. Developing people is a process, not an event.

In order to be changed and transformed, it takes suffering or tragedy on a primitive level. Understanding how change happens is very important. You have to have clear benefits and a clear rationale for implementing change. Let people see how it affects them. People are often afraid of something new. But maybe what you're afraid of is the very thing you should be doing. You need to have a comfort with change. If it doesn't challenge you, it won't change you. Change is a risk. Our primitive brains translate risk into danger, and historically our survival as a species was dependent on avoiding it. Whether it's a new job, new kid, new city, divorce, or lay off, all significant changes happen. However, since we can't prepare for them, what we need to do is thrive despite them.

Change is hard because fear and the status quo are the forces working against you. However, you can siphon change to benefit you. Change is always resisted. Change is dynamic, but it's a different world. We have to adjust; we have to adapt. You need to have a level of adjustment; otherwise, you become obsolete. Don't be afraid to adapt. There's nothing wrong with change as long as it's in the right direction. Change your future, not your past. So remember, things don't change; we change. Plato states this in *The Republic* famously with his *Allegory of the Cave* as the changing world around us (becoming) and an unchanging reality (being).[51] You must change yourself if you want to change your world — everything changes when you change. If you want success, you need to make successful choices. Most people are overweight, unhappy, and stuck. They stay broke, and stay stuck at jobs they hate. People stay stuck in that cycle because of their choices and their unwillingness to change. That's why I love Michael Jackson's "Man in the Mirror" song; it says, change starts with me. Too many people say they want to change and that they will change, but they keep doing the same thing. What's going to change? Nothing. We all face compounded challenges, but you must be committed to becoming someone different if anything is going to change. The people of our country can change it for the better, and I want you to know you have the capacity to change for the better. Our ability to change and adapt has been key to our existence and is flowing through our biology.

If you feel stuck, your unwillingness to change is holding you back. Look at the story of the prodigal son in Luke 15:11. The real prodigal son is the older brother who becomes disenchanted because his younger brother messed up, and now that he's back there's a party being thrown for him. The father comes out to see the disgruntled older brother and says "all I have is thine." The father is telling his older son you could've had his party whenever he wanted. Alternatively, look at Cain and Abel in Genesis 4:3. God asks both of them to offer a sacrifice. Abel has his lamb. God asks Cain, "Why has your countenance fallen?" Why are you miserable? Why are you sad? All Cain had to do was what Abel did, sacrifice. But Cain is jealous of Abel, pops off and kills Abel. It was easier for Cain to kill Abel than to kill a lamb. All Cain had to do was what Abel did to receive the same thing. It was easier for the older brother to resent his younger brother than to mature and take responsibility for his own happiness. These stories show that your refusal to change is hurting you.

Specifically, look at the story of David and Bathsheba in 2 Samuel 11. David takes Uriah's wife for himself, and Nathan, the prophet, tells David a parable of a rich man who took a farmer's only lamb, and that "thou art the man." All Uriah had was his wife, Bathsheba, and David had concubines, riches, his master Saul's house. He was king of Israel. Nathan says in 2 Samuel 12:1-9 that if that were not enough, God would have given you more and 'such and such.' The Bible says in 1 Corinthians 2:9 "eyes have not seen, ears have not heard, all that God has in store for them who love him." But with David this was about an unfair advantage. David had concubines and many wives, but he took the only thing Uriah had.

Too often we think it's the devil or the work of spirits making us miserable, but the truth is it's you. You're doing it to yourself. It's your stubbornness. You're bringing misery onto yourself. It's what you want. It's your desire. It's easier for us to stay miserable than to change. People always say 'the devil is after me,' but truthfully, most of us aren't doing enough for the devil to be after us. I don't think just trying to pay rent or pay the bills is a threat to the kingdom of darkness. The devil is not doing anything to you. Eight billion people on the planet, and he wants you? Your refusal to change is slowing you down and killing you. The Bible says in 2 Chronicles, the "eyes of the Lord go throughout the world to show himself strong." God has blessings and riches untold, and he's just waiting to give them out, but you have to change to receive them. You're waiting on God but God is waiting on you.

You Are Changing

From the moment we're made we're not finished. We're always changing and constantly being refined. Time changes everyone. Don't let anyone tell you that you can't change. That's what life is. Change. Life is full of impermanence all around us. Everything around us is changing. Our emotions change, the weather changes, we are born and eventually pass away. Right now is different from the moment before right now. The only law in the universe is that change is constant. This is important because it lets us know that our pain will pass. Our emotions will pass. Our sorrow will pass. The self is always adapting and changing. Every situation makes you reassess where you are on the evolutionary stage. In western society, we tend to believe that there is a concrete, constant self that is tucked away within ourselves. However, there is no fixed "self." All of our cells, thoughts, memories, and experiences change over time. According to Buddhism, our lives are a story we can change. Thanks to impermanence, anything is possible.

In the West, we are often taught to "find ourselves." But by rejecting this idea, we can instead create ourselves. If we are having an 'off-day,' we can realize that tomorrow will be different. Each day offers new possibilities for us to expand who we are and create ourselves. We all have our Road to Damascus moment. We have our own inflection points and points of immense change. You may be at a tangential point in your growth right now, but stay with it. Everyone will look at you strangely and say, "you've changed," like you worked hard only to stay the same. Reject that criticism. Know that when you change, the relationships around you will also be forced to change. Some people will cheer you on, but others will be steeped in jealousy and will make you feel sorry for moving forward. Don't buy into it; you're accountable for the space you hold in this world.

Everything and everyone changes all the time. Everything is transitory. Nothing is stable, not even what's right here. According to Buddhists, change is the only constant in the universe, and that means that there is no such thing as a stable self. Moreover, neuroscience says that the brain and the body are progressively flowing or continuously in action. Evan Thomson, a researcher from the University of British Colombia, confirmed that the Buddhist teaching of a continually changing self is accurate.[52] Neuroscientists coined the term 'neuroplasticity' to state that our brains are malleable and able to change. This signifies that you can change your brain in many facets, opening up your possibilities for growth. This can be incredibly liberating because you're not defined by your thoughts or your idea of who you are. The opportunities to change yourself are endless. Nothing can hold you back. Buddhist monks have said that the universe and ourselves are always in flux. By conditioning our minds, we can elevate our awareness and control. This is also why Buddhists talk about the practice of non-attachment. When we attach ourselves to something, we are desiring for it to be stable, and that goes directly against the forces of the universe.

The French poet, Charles Baudelaire, wrote over a century ago, “This life is a hospital where each patient is possessed with the desire to change his bed." A century later, today we still yearn for better relationships, bodies, houses or jobs. We desire security, health, fulfillment. We crave peace of mind, success, and happiness. Our hunger for change is nothing new, but nowadays we consider these not simply longings but a prerogative. Now more than ever, we feel entitled to make the changes that fit into our dreams and aspirations. The right to change, to be the author of one's own life is ours and ours alone. It's about freedom, autonomy, and choice. However, there is a caveat. We are so mystified as to how to go about changing that we doubt we're up to it or whether it's even possible.

A Harvard study looked at what psychologists name the "end-of-history illusion" that drew on data from more than 19,000 people ages 18 to 68. The study illustrated that the majority of people, regardless of age, believed they had changed substantially in the past, but anticipated little personal change in the future. This phenomenal blind spot, the study asserts, may be due to the fact that the cognitive processes involved in reconstructing an old story are less taxing on the mind than those necessary to build a new one.[53] In other words, we're better at changing than we are at imagining it. Overestimating the stability of today hampers the decisions we make about tomorrow.

Many of us tend to think of our bodies as changing only nominally once we reach adulthood, but in fact, we're changing all the time and constantly rebuilding ourselves. Consider our largest organ, our skin. In order to keep alive, our cells have to divide and grow. We're keenly aware of this because we see children grow. However, cells also age and die eventually. Our skin touches everything around us and is exposed to damage and is in constant need of regenerating. In fact, according to Iris Schrijver, our skin cells are replaced nearly every month or two. Moreover, we lose approximately 30,000 cells every minute throughout our lives, and the entire external surface layer is replaced once a year. Furthermore, every tissue recreates itself, but they all do it at a different rate.[54]

We are not fixed at all, and in fact, we are more like a pattern or a process. It is this transience of the body and the flow of energy and matter that interconnects us with the universe. Our bodies are never static. Our biology tells us that we're dynamic beings, and we have to be dynamic to remain alive. This is true for all living beings, not just humans. Particularly, I find sharks to be very enlightening regarding this point because sharks have to keep swimming or they die. They have to keep swimming in order to get oxygen in because of the way their gills are situated; otherwise, they suffocate. So keep swimming or die. Keep moving. Keep changing.

Change Is Good

I gave a speech recently and asked the audience, “Who wants change?” Lots of hands went up. Then I asked, “Who wants **to** change?” Fewer hands went up. The truth is that people want change, but they don't necessarily want to change. You cannot have what you are not willing to become. People want riches and abundance, but they aren't willing to become harder workers. But if you want a different result, you have to do something different. You can't change your life and not change who you are. That's how you change the world: you change your world. Winston Churchill said, “To improve is to change; to be perfect is to change often.” That’s part of why I love wine. Wine is so magical. The grapes go in one way and come out completely different. The textures, the tones, the notes of flavors, it's the work of time, and you can't do anything about it but enjoy it.

When we are no longer able to change a situation, we are then challenged to change ourselves. We have to change; otherwise, we keep fighting the same battles. Nothing changes unless you change it. At other times, sometimes you’re praying away the very thing God is trying to use to change you. God is more interested in changing you than changing your circumstances. In my own experience, we are who we are, not in spite of change, but because of it. The point is we're much better at changing than we think. It's hardwired into our biology. What neuroscience describes as plasticity (the changes that occur in our brains as our experiences unfold) is the core of who we are, from the neural, through the individual, right to the societal level. In our prefrontal cortex, one of the last parts of the brain to mature, and critical in our evolutionary advantage, is where our thoughts and actions, plans and decisions, even our personalities, are adopted. It is where what we hope for meets what we do. So, the inherent plasticity of this region and the wider neural networks underpin our brilliant ability to change.[55] So bear in mind, change – as an unfolding process, not a sovereign remedy – is who we are. By holding onto it, it gives us the best chance we have of taking on our doubts about change, our end-of-history phantoms, and any other obstacles we place between ourselves and lives we want to lead.

As a 30-year-old, I've learned that nothing stays the same, not even yourself. People have a laundry list of things they want to change. However, people don't want to change themselves entirely; they want to change parts of themselves. Be open to change notwithstanding. It doesn't matter if you're going to try a new restaurant, travel to an unknown region of the world, or do something that has always scared you; be open to change. This will allow you to grow because you are experiencing something new. Your job isn't to change deck chairs on the Titanic; it's to enact real change. Most people just play musical chairs and call that change. Implement real change, especially if your ship is sinking. Always look for ways of doing things more efficiently and more effectively. Attack change head-on. Don't wait for change to happen. Watch for it; anticipate it.

When you are not wary of change, it helps you become high functioning and self-confident. With change comes opportunity. We have to continually be ready for a world we cannot yet know. Everything is transitory. There is no point at which having arrived, we can remain. The story of history is that nothing changes and yet everything is different. Nothing is forever. Change is a given, so embrace change because the future is going to rock your world. The key to long-term success is innovation and change. One change could change everything. You can change just one thing, and it changes everything else. It's like a word, if you change one letter, it changes the word. My challenge to you is to embrace the change(s) in your life and know that sometimes from the winds of change we find our direction.

Keep Changing / Reinvent Yourself

With the constant rate of change, you have to be willing to disrupt yourself. We should be inspired by change. I don't see creation as two ends of a spectrum in which God created and then ended. It's a continuum in which God is continually creating. God is constantly working and creating in our lives. People evolve constantly, and you need to channel and focus that growth. You must be committed to becoming someone different. It's time for you to maximize your value, maximize your potential, and get what you deserve. It doesn't matter where you start; it's about where you end up. Anyone can change; we are all transformable.

Let me ask you a question, do you know why the fool is the most powerful card in the tarot? It's not because the person who draws it is a fool; rather, he's a fool because he's a clean slate and can therefore become anything. Change is transformational. Change is how you actualize yourself. During your life, you will have to invent and reinvent yourself many times. Every person reaches a point where the antiquated answers are no longer good enough for them. So innovation and change is essential when it comes to seeking your truth. Reinvent yourself when you have to; change when you need to. If all hell is breaking loose in your life, don’t allow it to tear you apart. Choose to have a positive outlook on the situation. There are a number of people who found that losing a job, losing an opportunity, meant finding something better. Reinvent yourself; do nothing the same. Where you are isn't where you're going to be because you're becoming something greater and you're going someplace higher. Lao Tzu says, "When I let go of what I am, I become what I might be.” Change yourself, change the world. It's about becoming. It's not about arriving. It's a constant forward motion, a means of evolving, a way to reach continuously toward a better self.

Most of the changes we make have a short half-life anyway. The question is how we implement lasting changes. Disrupting the status quo is essential for change. From change, we have to learn and reinvent at the same time. Stay nowhere very long. Don't do anything for too long. If you're sitting too long, stand. If you're standing too long, sit. Keep changing, keep growing, keep stretching. Consistency is crucial for change. Consistency is the cure. Ask yourself what you are getting better at. Growth is the side of the ledger you want to stay on. To stay the same is to receive the same. If you do what you've always done, you'll get what you've always gotten. In order to change your life, you have to change yourself.

This is a time for change, and I will be with you every step of the way. We're going to change the way we live. We're going to change the way we eat. We're going to change the way we exercise. We're going to change the way we react. We're going to change the way we think. I wanted to change the world, but I realized early on that if I was going to change the world, I must change myself. Things don't change; we change. Changing ourselves is more important and subsequently easier than changing the world. Stay committed to reform. You have to reinvent yourself by adapting to change and have a vision for your life. You have a right to choose the way you want to live. You can make your name in a new way. Life is your genie. Whatever you want, you can have. Just speak it and as you wish!

1N73LL1G3NC3

15 7H3

4B1L17Y

70 D4P7 70

CH4NG3

— 573PH3N H4WK1NG

ABOUT THE AUTHOR

Louis A. Boney II is an author, speaker, consultant, and entrepreneur. Born in Minnesota, Louis Boney attended Pepperdine University, Seaver College in Malibu, California and studied at Fudan University in Shanghai, China successfully graduating with a Bachelor of Arts in English and minor in Asian Studies. During his collegiate tenure, Louis had the privilege to study abroad in Florence, Italy; Lausanne, Switzerland; London, England; and Shanghai, China.

As a result of his global aptitude, in 2008, he was a Congressional Intern for the United States House of Representatives in Washington D.C. and in 2010 served as a Parliamentary Apprentice for the United Kingdom House of Commons in London, England focusing on legislative affairs.

After college, Louis attended Pepperdine University School of Law, Straus Institute in Malibu, California in 2011 subsequently earning his Masters of Dispute Resolution. Simultaneous with his legal studies, Louis served as a Mediator for the Superior Court of California, County of Los Angeles. After receiving his Masters of Dispute Resolution, Louis worked in Hong Kong, S.A.R. at the Hong Kong International Arbitration Centre in 2012. By 2013, Louis served as a Project Consultant for Sempra Energy, focusing on Diversity & Inclusion, Labor Relations, and Legal initiatives.

With a vision of a conflict management consulting firm that would bring efficiency to complex cases, he launched the Boney Group, LLC in 2014. As a champion of alternative dispute resolution processes, change management initiatives, and expanding support for individual empowerment, the Boney Group employs a unique approach with individuals and organizations. Louis' goal is to help people achieve their personal and professional goals through strategic problem solving and skills training. Louis' entrance into executive coaching is indicative of his life's work as a dispute resolution advocate: a desire to diagnose problems and provide practical solutions.

As founder and CEO of the Boney Group, LLC, Louis has worked, lobbied, and lectured in these areas; specifically, advising numerous start-ups, organizations, and governmental agencies to resolve conflicts and advocate for reconciliation processes. In 2016, he served as an Ombudsman for the California Department of Aging in Los Angeles County advocating for Long-Term Care Residents. Furthermore, his passion for conflict resolution led to his tenure as Case Administrator Contractor for the Financial Industry Regulatory Authority (FINRA) in 2018. As a leading conflict resolution advocate, Louis has proven to be an outspoken champion for both peace brokering and change management processes.

Louis Boney brings his innovation-driven approach to individuals and organizations alike. His extensive conflict management experience, international awareness, rigorous education, and inherent business sense add a level of detail and depth to his clients. He has a proven track record of turning around organizational deficiencies by raising standards and holding organizations and the people who work for them accountable for collective success. By spurring creativity and growth through revitalizing old industrial guidelines, supporting employee engagement, and strengthening key initiatives, his track-record is unrivaled. His passion for coaching and consulting has reduced both litigation and time costs through ambitious new strategies for organizations which has become modeled after widely.

In recognition of his aptitude, Louis has been celebrated with some of the most prestigious honors and awards since high school including: The National Society of High School Scholars, Who's Who Among American High School Students, CALI Excellence for the Future Award Recipient, and many others.

He currently lives in Los Angeles, California where he remains active in his community, and serves as an advisor to multiple organizations including the Pepperdine/Straus American Inn of Court for Dispute Resolution. Louis continues to support projects of great importance to him, including his alma mater. During his free time, Louis provides pro-bono dispute resolution services for clients and mentoring opportunities. Additionally, he enjoys sailing, yoga, fitness training, traveling, writing, reading, and spending time with his family.

ALSO BY THE AUTHOR:

- *COME TO PLAY: A MANUAL FOR ACHIEVING YOUR SUCCESS*
- *STAYING POWER: STRATEGIES FOR TRIUMPH OVER ADVERSITY*

CONNECT WITH LOUIS:

FOLLOW @LOUISBONEY

FACEBOOK.COM/LOUISBONEYII

LINKEDIN.COM/IN/LOUISBONEY

INSTAGRAM.COM/LOUISBONEY

FOR MORE:

WWW.LOUISBONEY.COM

NOTES

[1] Kornfield, Jack. *A Path with Heart a Guide through the Perils and Promises of Spiritual Life*. MTM, 2015.

[2] Kornfield, Jack. "No Self or True Self? - Identity and Selflessness in Buddhism." *Tricycle*, tricycle.org/magazine/no-self-or-true-self/.

[3] Kornfield, Jack. "No Self or True Self? - Identity and Selflessness in Buddhism." *Tricycle*, tricycle.org/magazine/no-self-or-true-self/.

[4] Pennington, Maura. "Sherlock Holmes: A Case For The Individual." 24 March 2012. *Forbes*. https://www.forbes.com/sites/maurapennington/2012/05/24/sherlock-holmes-a-case-for-the-individual/#2a23d6d44c03.

[5] Pennington, Maura. "Sherlock Holmes: A Case For The Individual." 24 March 2012. *Forbes*. https://www.forbes.com/sites/maurapennington/2012/05/24/sherlock-holmes-a-case-for-the-individual/#2a23d6d44c03.

[6] Beer, Jeff. "Every Human Body Contains Traces of Gold, But Only A Few Can Find It." 4 August 2016. https://www.fastcompany.com/3062434/every-human-body-contains-traces-of-gold-but-only-a-few-can-find-it.

[7] Greene, Brian. "A Physicist Explains Why Parallel Universes May Exist." *NPR*, NPR, 24 Jan. 2011, www.npr.org/2011/01/24/132932268/a-physicist-explains-why-parallel-universes-may-exist.

[8] Schrijver, Karel, and Iris Schrijver. *Living with the Stars: How the Human Body Is Connected to the Life Cycles of the Earth, the Planets, and the Stars*. Oxford University Press, 2019.

[9] Newton, Isaac, et al. *The Mathematical Principles of Natural*

Philosophy. Dawsons of Pall Mall, 1968.

[10] "Natural Selection in Populations." *Khan Academy*, Khan Academy, www.khanacademy.org/science/biology/her/heredity-and-genetics/a/natural-selection-in-populations.

[11] Sterner, Robert W. "The Conservation of Mass." *Nature News*, Nature Publishing Group, www.nature.com/scitable/knowledge/library/the-conservation-of-mass-17395478.

[12] Artson, Bradley. "The Crack is What Lets in the Light." *Huffington Post.* 12 September 2013. https://www.huffpost.com/entry/the-crack-is-what-lets-in_b_3915053.

[13] Clark, Dorie and Molinsky, Andy. "Self-Promotion for Professionals from Countries Where Bragging Is Bad." *Harvard Business Review*, 2 Nov. 2014, hbr.org/2014/03/self-promotion-for-professionals-from-countries-where-bragging-is-bad.

[14] Randolph, Laura B. "Sisterspeak" *Ebony Magazine.* Vol. 52, No. 10, page 19. August 1997.

[15] Daskal, Lolly. "Accomplish Great Things at Any Age." *Inc.* 14 July 2014. https://www.inc.com/lolly-daskal/accomplish-great-things-at-any-age.html.

[16] Reed, Rose, et al. *The Velveteen Rabbit*. Western Pub. Co., 1990.

[17] Clifford, Catherine. "Steve Jobs: These are 2 essential ingredients for success." *CNBC.* 15 November 2017. https://www.cnbc.com/2017/11/15/steve-jobs-bill-gates-how-to-be-successful.html.

[18] Goleman, Daniel. *Emotional Intelligence: Why It Can Matter More than IQ*. Bloomsbury, 2010.
[19] Csikszentmihalyi, Mihaly. *Flow: the Psychology of Optimal*

Experience. Harper Row, 2009.

[20] Griffiths, Mark D. "The Search For Happiness." *Psychology Today.* 20 July 2016. https://www.psychologytoday.com/us/blog/in-excess/201607/the-search-happiness.

[21] Harvard Health Publishing. "Strengthen Relationships for Longer, Healthier Life." *Harvard Health*, www.health.harvard.edu/healthbeat/strengthen-relationships-for-longer-healthier-life.

[22] Bratskeir, Kate. "The Habits of Supremely Happy People." *Huffington Post.* 16 September 2013. https://www.huffpost.com/entry/happiness-habits-of-exuberant-human-beings_n_3909772.

[23] Linden, David J. "Exercise, pleasure and the brain." *Psychology Today.* 21 April 2011. https://www.psychologytoday.com/us/blog/the-compass-pleasure/201104/exercise-pleasure-and-the-brain.

[24] Giacoia, Frank, et al. *Huckleberry Finn.* Acclaim Books, 1997.

[25] Brendel, David. "How Philosophy Makes You a Better Leader." *Harvard Business Review.* 19 September 2014. https://hbr.org/2014/09/how-philosophy-makes-you-a-better-leader.

[26] Griswold, Alison. "Malcolm Gladwell's Fascinating Theory On Why You Should Be a Big Fish." *Business Insider.* 15 October 2013. https://www.businessinsider.com/malcolm-gladwells-david-and-goliath-2013-10.

[27] Winfrey, Graham. "Malcolm Gladwell on the Secret to Building Self-Confidence" *Inc.* 30 October 2014. https://www.inc.com/graham-winfrey/malcolm-gladwell-on-the-trick-to-building-self-confidence.html.

[28] Wachowski, Lana and Wachowski, Lilly. "The Matrix." Village

Roadshow, 1999.

[29] Goleman, Daniel. *Emotional Intelligence: Why It Can Matter More than IQ*. Bloomsbury, 2010.

[30] Slavich, George M. and Irwin, Michael R. "From Stress to Inflammation and Major Depressive Disorder: A Social Signal Transduction Theory of Depression." *NCBI.* 13 January 2014. https://www.ncbi.nlm.nih.gov/pmc/articles/PMC4006295/.

[31] Koloc, Nathaniel. "Build a Career Worth Having." *Harvard Business Review.* 5 August 2013. https://hbr.org/2013/08/build-a-career-worth-having.

[32] Baer, Drake. "10 quotes from ancient philosophers show they figured life out 2,000 years ago." *Business Insider.* 9 May 2016. https://www.businessinsider.com/wise-quotes-from-ancient-philosophers-2016-4.

[33] Baer, Drake. "10 quotes from ancient philosophers show they figured life out 2,000 years ago." *Business Insider.* 9 May 2016. https://www.businessinsider.com/wise-quotes-from-ancient-philosophers-2016-4.

[34] Mandel, Ernest. *The Marxist Theory of Alienation*. Pathfinder Press, 1974.

[35] Kumar, Chhavi. "What we can learn from Sisyphus and his rock." *Medium.* 8 June 2017. https://blog.usejournal.com/takeaways-from-the-story-of-sisyphus-and-the-rock-81721c6e499.

[36] Tyson, Neil deGrasse. "Cosmos: A Spacetime Odyssey." 2014.

[37] Pink, Daniel H. *Drive: The Surprising Truth about What Motivates Us*. Canongate Books, 2018.

[38] Brooks, David. "How Adulthood Happens." *New York Times.* 12 June 2015. https://www.nytimes.com/2015/06/12/opinion/david-

brooks-how-adulthood-happens.html.

[39] Campbell, Joseph. *The Hero with a Thousand Faces*. New World Library, 2008.

[40] Dweck, Carol S. *Mindset: the New Psychology of Success: Summary*. Ant Hive Media, 2016.

[41] Shellenbarger, Sue. "Ways to Inflate Your IQ." *Wall Street Journal.* 29 November 2011. https://www.wsj.com/articles/SB10001424052970203935604577066293669642830.

[42] Liou, Stephanie. "Neuroplasticity." *Huntington's Outreach Project For Education, At Stanford.* 26 June 2010. https://hopes.stanford.edu/neuroplasticity/.

[43] Keefe, Paul. "Alive Time vs. Dead Time (& Boredom)." *Medium.* 7 June 2018. https://medium.com/@paulkeefe/alive-time-vs-dead-time-boredom-b44387a16f3b.

[44] Dumas, Alexandre. *The Count of Monte Cristo.* Macmillan Collector's Library, 2017.

[45] Twerski, Abraham. *How do Lobsters Grow.* Youtube. 7 April 2016. https://www.youtube.com/watch?v=dcUAIpZrwog.

[46] Baer, Drake. "Malcolm Gladwell Explains What Everyone Gets Wrong About His Famous '10,000 Hour Rule.'" *Business Insider.* 2 June 2014. https://www.businessinsider.com/malcolm-gladwell-explains-the-10000-hour-rule-2014-6.

[47] Campbell, Joseph. *The Hero with a Thousand Faces*. New World Library, 2008.

[48] Singer, Emily and Quanta. "The New Science of Disease Recovery." *The Atlantic.* 6 September 2016. https://www.theatlantic.com/health/archive/2016/09/the-new-

science-of-disease-recovery/498155/.

[49] Bradberry, Travis. "Why Attitude Is More Important Than Intelligence." *SFGATE.* 23 November 2015. https://www.sfgate.com/news/article/Why-Attitude-Is-More-Important-Than-Intelligence-6651531.php.

[50] Baer, Drake. "10 quotes from ancient philosophers show they figured life out 2,000 years ago." *Business Insider.* 9 May 2016. https://www.businessinsider.com/wise-quotes-from-ancient-philosophers-2016-4.

[51] Plato and Jowett, Benjamin. *The Republic: Plato.* The World Publishing Co., 1946.

[52] Goldhill, Olivia. "Neuroscience backs up the Buddhist belief that 'the self' isn't constant, but ever-changing." *Quartz.* 20 September 2015. https://qz.com/506229/neuroscience-backs-up-the-buddhist-belief-that-the-self-isnt-constant-but-ever-changing/.

[53] Quoidbach, Jordi; Gilbert Daniel T.; and Wilson, Timothy D. "The End of History Illusion" Vol. 339. 4 January 2013. http://midus.wisc.edu/findings/pdfs/1256.pdf.

[54] Worrall, Simon. "How 40,000 Tons of Cosmic Dust Falling to Earth Affects You and Me." *National Geographic.* 28 January 2015. https://news.nationalgeographic.com/2015/01/150128-big-bang-universe-supernova-astrophysics-health-space-ngbooktalk/.

[55] Morland, Polly. "Are We Programmed to Change?" *Nikos Marinos Consultancy.* 3 October 2016. https://www.nikosmarinos.com/are-we-programmed-to-change.html.